CHARLES II
AND THE DUKE OF
BUCKINGHAM
The Merry Monarch & the Aristocratic Rogue

DAVID C. HANRAHAN

SUTTON PUBLISHING

In memory of Michael Hanrahan
(1925 – 2004)

First published in 2006 by
Sutton Publishing Limited · Phoenix Mill
Thrupp · Stroud · Gloucestershire · GL5 2BU

British Library Cataloguing in Publication Data
A catalogue record for this book is available from the British Library.

ISBN 0-7509-3916-8

Typeset in 11/14pt Garamond.
Typesetting and origination by
Sutton Publishing Limited.
Printed and bound in England by
J.H. Haynes & Co. Ltd, Sparkford.

CONTENTS

PREFACE

A unique relationship existed between King Charles II (1630–85) and George Villiers (1628–87), 2nd Duke of Buckingham. The life and reign of King Charles II, the so-called 'Merry Monarch', was like that of no other King: Charles had to survive a civil war, the execution of his father, the rule of Oliver Cromwell and the life of a king in exile without a kingdom, before his eventual restoration to the throne in 1660. At his side from childhood, and throughout all these events, was the Duke of Buckingham.

The relationship of these two childhood friends, although close, was at times a tempestuous one. They alternated between periods of almost brotherly love to complete alienation from each other. They had a number of serious disputes and the Duke was sent to the Tower of London on a number of occasions. Yet, for all that, it was a friendship that managed to endure right to the end of their lives.

'They must be very silly, that think he can do anything out of a good intention,' wrote Samuel Pepys about Buckingham. The poet John Dryden thought no more of him when he satirised him as Zimri in *Absalom and Achitophel*:

> Stiff in opinions, always in the wrong;
> Was everything by starts and nothing long;

Yet he was also described as the 'most graceful and beautiful person that any Court in Europe ever saw'.[1]

King Charles II was a man of varied interests who enjoyed entertainment and a good laugh. It is no wonder that he found Buckingham's company stimulating. The Duke had great charm and was a renowned wit, and often amused the members of the royal court with his impersonations of other courtiers. Because of his relationship with the King, Buckingham was also an extremely influential figure in the politics of the Restoration period. He kept close ties with his cousin and mistress of Charles II, Barbara Villiers, a woman with almost unrivalled influence at court. He was suspected of having links with Colonel Thomas Blood and other Protestant Nonconformist radicals. (Blood was later convicted of being involved in a plot to destroy the reputation of the Duke of Buckingham by accusing him of sodomy.) Buckingham was also a man who held grudges and among his enemies were the Earl of Clarendon and the Duke of Ormonde. Not all his fights took the form of words, either, as he was involved in a duel in which he seriously wounded the husband of his mistress, Lady Shrewsbury. The unfortunate man died and Buckingham, who received a pardon from his friend King Charles, brought Lady Shrewsbury to live with him in the same house as his wife!

The relationship between Charles II and the Duke of Buckingham was an abiding one that managed to survive the treachery, dishonesty and political manoeuvring of the Restoration Court.

ACKNOWLEDGEMENTS

This book would not have been possible without the assistance of a great many people and institutions. I wish to thank the following: the Hardiman Library, National University of Ireland, Galway, and in particular Special Collections and Inter-Library Loans; the British Library; the Bodleian Library, Oxford; The National Portrait Gallery, London; my friends and colleagues at the Education Department, National University of Ireland, Galway; all at Sutton Publishing, in particular Christopher Feeney for his excellent editorial guidance; my agent, David O'Leary, for his great support as ever. A special word of thanks and love goes to all my family: my wife Margaret, my daughter Aisling, my son Michael, my mother Mary and my brothers and their families. Finally, this book is dedicated to the memory of my late father, Michael, whose support and encouragement are irreplaceable.

I want to note that where I have quoted from contemporary accounts, in the interest of simplicity and when it does not alter the meaning, I have modernised the form of spelling and capitalisation.

One

THE FATHERS

It was the morning of 23 August 1628 and George Villiers, 1st Duke of Buckingham, or Steenie as he was known, was in Portsmouth. He was attending to business as Lord High Admiral and Commander-in-Chief of the English forces. It was well known that the influence enjoyed by the Duke, as well as his political activities, had earned him many enemies. Despite this he had ignored recent advice to wear a protective shirt of mail under his clothes. As he made his way to breakfast that morning in the house of the Treasurer to the Army and his private secretary, Captain Mason, he paused for a moment in the passage between the hall and the parlour to speak to one of his colonels, Sir Thomas Fryer.[1] Suddenly, a man stepped forward from behind the hangings and stabbed Steenie deeply in the left side of his chest. Pulling out the knife Steenie cried 'Villain', and with great courage made a number of steps forward in an attempt to apprehend his attacker. However, the noble Duke fell against a table and in a few moments was dead. He was 37 years of age.

The 1st Duke of Buckingham had been assassinated by John Felton, a discharged naval officer. Felton, inspired by the degree of political unrest in the country, believed that by plunging his knife into Steenie's chest he was fulfilling his God-given duty. Leaving the confusion in the hallway, he made his way to the kitchens of the house. He soon gave himself up, admitted his guilt and was taken to Portsmouth gaol. He was later tried, found guilty and hanged at Tyburn, but not before he had repented of his crime, describing it as 'abhorrent'.[2]

Steenie had been a close friend not only to the King but also to the King's father, James I. Beginning his life at the royal court of James I as a lowly courtier, the tall, impressive-looking Steenie managed to climb the social ladder until he became the first non-royal duke to be created in over a century. His father had held the much lower rank of knight and sheriff in Leicestershire. Steenie's progress through the classes was rapid. He was first introduced to King James I in 1614; by 1616 he was Master of the Horse; by 1617 Earl of Buckingham; and by 1619 Lord High Admiral. He was raised to the dukedom of Buckingham in May 1623. The 1st Duke of Buckingham became one of the richest noblemen in England.

This astonishingly rapid elevation in life was due to the close relationship he enjoyed with James I. The King's interest in him was nothing short of an infatuation and seems to have been evident from their first meeting. One contemporary noted: '. . . a youth, his name is Villiers, a Northamptonshire man; he begins to be in favour with His Majesty'.[3] James is reported to have said that 'Christ has his John, and I have my George'. It was widely believed that their relationship grew into a passionate homosexual one, a rumour that did no good at all to the King's reputation.[4] When James's son ascended the throne as Charles I, Steenie continued to enjoy considerable influence over affairs of state, much of it responsible for damaging the new king's relationship with Parliament. Charles I was devastated at the news of Steenie's assassination. According to Edward Hyde, Earl of Clarendon:

[King Charles I] departed to his chamber, and threw himself upon his bed, lamenting with much passion and with abundance of tears the loss he had of an excellent servant and the horrid manner in which he had been deprived of him; and he continued in this melancholic . . . discomposure of mind many days.[5]

Such was Steenie's lack of popularity among the people, however, that the news of his assassination was greeted by widespread rejoicing. The reasons for this lack of affection were many. He had been prominent in arranging the marriage between Charles I and the French Catholic Princess Henrietta-Maria, which took place in 1625. This marriage brought with it the possibility of a Catholic succession to the throne, which greatly alarmed both the King's Protestant subjects and the Protestant-dominated Parliament. He was also blamed for a number of embarrassing military defeats such as a doomed military expedition to take the Spanish port of Cadiz in October 1625 and the defeat of an English force sent to the French port of La Rochelle in support of the Huguenots. Buckingham was described by one contemporary as 'the cause of all our miseries . . . the grievance of grievances'.[6] A short time before, even his personal astrologer had been attacked by a mob and lynched on a London street.

Yet, no matter how unpopular Steenie became, Charles I continued to stand by him. When an attempt was made to impeach the Duke in May 1626 on a range of charges including the purchase of honours, failure to guard the sea and 'mis-employing' the King's revenue, the King refuted all the charges made against his favourite, and had him successfully elected to the position of Chancellor of Cambridge University while the impeachment debates were still in progress. Charles eventually saved him by dissolving Parliament. He was then tried before the Royal Court of Star Chamber but the charges were dismissed. In 1628 Parliament once again tried to force the King to dismiss him, but without success. Later that year Steenie lay dead on a floor in Portsmouth.

Two

THE SONS

As the blood-soaked body of the 1st Duke of Buckingham lay on the floor in Portsmouth, Lady Katherine Manners, the Duke's pregnant wife, pushed though the crowd of shocked onlookers to her husband's side. Katherine was the daughter of Francis Manners, 6th Earl of Rutland. Her father's objections to her marriage had been overcome by Steenie arranging for the granting of valuable royal monopolies to her family. Such was the King's affection for Steenie that as preparations were made for her husband to be buried in Henry VII's chapel at Westminster Abbey, he promised Katherine 'he would be a father to her children, and a husband to herself'.[1] This was just as well, since Steenie had left behind massive debts to the tune of £70,000 and mortgages on many of his lands.[2] Within a few years most of these debts were paid off.[3]

Steenie's son, George Villiers, Earl of Coventry, now inherited the title of Duke of Buckingham. The new duke would, in time, become the man who has been described as 'of all the bad men in a bad time . . . perhaps the worst, without shame, honour, or decency'.[4] The 2nd Duke of Buckingham was born on 30 January 1628. He was christened at a lavish ceremony held at Wallingford House, officiated over by William Laud, Bishop of London and later Archbishop of Canterbury, his father's confessor and someone to whom Steenie had been a good patron. Standing as godfathers were none other than the King and the Earl of Suffolk. The Duchess of Richmond acted as a godmother in place of the Queen who, as a Catholic, could not take part in a Protestant ceremony.

Buckingham was only seven months old when his father was assassinated. With the murderous stroke of John Felton's dagger the influence of father over son had been denied.

In April 1629, only months after the murder of her husband, the Duchess gave birth to another baby boy, giving Buckingham a new brother, Francis, in addition to an older sister, Mary, who was by then six years old. An elder brother Charles had died in infancy in 1627.

A few months after her husband's assassination, Katherine took the monumental step of converting back to Catholicism, the religion of her birth. Her conversion to Protestantism had merely been an attempt to facilitate her marriage to Steenie. At the same time she discharged most of the late Duke's Protestant servants.[5] The religious conversion of his dear friend's widow in this way perturbed the fervently Protestant King, who was worried, in particular, about the fate of Steenie's children. He decided to have them removed from their mother and to take responsibility for them himself.

Thus it happened that the 2nd Duke of Buckingham, along with his brother Lord Francis, was brought up at court alongside the royal family. Their sister, Lady Mary, or Mall as she was known, was sent to live with the family of the Earl of Pembroke. On Christmas day 1634, at 12 years of age, Mall married the Earl's son and heir, the 17-year-old Charles, Lord Herbert of Shurland. After the wedding the young bridegroom was sent to complete his studies on the Continent, where he contracted smallpox and died. After this tragedy the young widow was also brought to the royal court for a time to live with her two brothers.

It did not take long for Mall to cast aside her role as grieving widow and become involved in the fun and games of the children at the royal court in a way that befitted her young age. In particular, she loved to climb the apple trees in Charles I's private garden. In the branches of one of these trees Charles, Prince of Wales, spotted the shape of a strange and exotic bird one day. He sent a boy called George Porter to shoot the fowl, believing that it would make a most splendid specimen. Luckily, Porter did not use his firearm too hastily as the 'specimen' in question turned out to be Mall, whose widow's veil had become entangled in the branches of the tree she had been climbing. She pelted the boy with apples before agreeing to be assisted to the ground.

When Mall heard that Charles had mistaken her for an exotic bird, she insisted that Porter carry her to the Prince in a big basket. Porter laid the basket before the Prince of Wales telling him that it was a butterfly and that he had managed to capture it alive. When Charles lifted the cover he was greeted by Mall, who jumped from the basket and gave him an affectionate hug. Thereafter, she was known to those at court as the 'butterfly'.[6] In 1636 such days of childhood fun came to an end for Mall when she was married for a second time, on this occasion to James Stuart, Duke of Lennox and Richmond, a close relative of the King.

In 1635 Buckingham's mother decided to marry the Earl of Antrim, Randal Mc Donnell. This act worsened her relations with the royal court as Mc Donnell was regarded there as a Catholic fanatic. The King's attitude towards her contact with the children hardened even more.

While King Charles I was a strong supporter of the Anglican or Episcopalian Protestant Church, Henrietta-Maria was a staunch, practising Catholic throughout her life.[7] Until the time of Steenie's death, the Queen had come very much second in her husband's affections, excluded as she was from the close association of King and favourite. Even at his coronation ceremony, when he stumbled on the steps to the throne and was assisted by Steenie, Charles took the Duke's arm and said, 'I have as much need to help you as you to assist me.'[8] (As a result of her reluctance to take part in a Protestant ceremony, Henrietta-Maria was not present at the coronation.) During the early years of their marriage they quarrelled frequently. After the Duke's assassination their relationship grew closer, with Charles now turning to his wife for the support he needed.[9]

It is significant that soon after Steenie's death the Queen conceived. Their first son, Charles James, was born and died in May 1629. The future Charles II was born one year later, on 29 May 1630, at St James's Palace. Henrietta-Maria would describe her baby as ugly, and at four months old the size of a one-year-old.[10] No wonder that in adulthood he would grow to stand six feet tall, a remarkable height at that time. Neither of his parents attained this stature: the King's growth had been stunted by rickets and the Queen was a small, slight woman. The baby also had the first signs of that dark complexion which he was to retain throughout his life. Charles was baptised, on 27 June, by Bishop Laud, just as Buckingham had been.

Other babies followed, with six out of their nine children managing to survive the early years. Mary, Princess Royal, was born in 1631, James, Duke of York, in 1633, Elizabeth in 1635, Henry, Duke of Gloucester, in 1640, and Henrietta in 1644. Neither Anne, born in 1637, nor Catherine, born in 1639, survived infancy.

Buckingham was only two years older than Charles, Prince of Wales, with whom he would now share an upbringing. From this young age Buckingham was inducted into the world of the royal court:

The bending knee, the hushed speech, the highly polished manners and graceful smoothness required for daily intercourse with majesty were thinly spread over a gruelling routine of lessons, religion, exquisitely artificial entertainments and violent exercise.[11]

The experience of being brought up at court undoubtedly influenced Buckingham's view of life. As one writer puts it, 'It was hard for Buckingham to remember that he was not truly a prince.'[12] It must also have engendered jealousy in him at times, since he was not the future king of England. How obvious it must have been to him that, although the two boys shared everything from governors to games, there was a difference between the way people reacted to a young duke and to the heir to the throne. Their little male group was completed by their brothers James, Duke of York, and Francis Villiers.

Charles, James, Buckingham and Francis spent their summers enjoying the amenities offered by a variety of royal palaces such as Greenwich, Hampton Court and Oatlands, while they wintered usually at St James's Palace.[13] All evidence suggests that the children experienced a caring and loving environment. In 1638, at the age of 8, Charles was made a Knight of the Garter and Prince of Wales. It was also time for him to be granted his own household.

The boys' education was guided by a number of people throughout these years. One of their most influential governors was William Cavendish, Earl of Newcastle, who was described by Edward Hyde as:

> . . . a very fine gentleman, active and full of courage, and most accomplished in those qualities of horsemanship, dancing and fencing . . . amorous in poetry and music, to which he indulged the greatest part of his time . . .[14]

In 1636 Newcastle had been officially appointed joint guardian of Buckingham, along with the boy's uncle, the Earl of Rutland.[15] Two years later he was appointed governor to the Prince of Wales. Although an intellectual himself, with a number of plays to his name, he did not overload his charges with intellectual study, giving at least equal attention to practical pursuits such as horsemanship, dancing, tennis and fencing. He was also the author of two authoritative works on horsemanship. In fact he would later blame the Civil War on too much education, which he believed gave the lower social classes ideas above their station.[16] Among other things, Newcastle urged the future king not to be too devout and always to be civil to women.[17] He was a faithful supporter of the Stuarts, and many years later, as King Charles II, the student would raise his old governor to the dukedom of Newcastle.

The importance of the education received by the heir to the throne for the later fortunes of his kingdom was not lost on Parliament. Members were very concerned about the people charged with educating the future king, especially as the Prince of Wales's mother was a Catholic. On a number of occasions Parliament even put forward specific proposals for the upbringing of the royal children. As part of ten proposals it put to the King in June 1641, one dealt with the children's education:

> That some persons of public trust, and well affected in religion, may be placed about the Prince; who may take care of his education, and the rest of the children; especially in matters of religion and liberty.[18]

The wording used a year later in June 1642 is noticeably firmer:

> That he or they unto whom the government and education of the King's children shall be committed, shall be approved of by both Houses of Parliament; and, in the intervals of Parliaments, by assent of the major part of the Council . . . And that all such servants as are now about them, against whom the Houses shall have any just exception, shall be removed.[19]

When Newcastle, who was disliked by many MPs for his ultra-royalist views, resigned in May 1641, he was replaced by William Seymour, Marquess of Hertford. Hertford was felt to be a more acceptable choice to Parliament, but his advanced years made him a less successful governor from the point of view of his charges. He also had very little interest in the job and only took it on because the King had asked him to. On a number of occasions Parliament expressed concern over whether the Marquess was safeguarding the security of the Prince of Wales by giving him enough 'personal attendance' and instructed him to do so.[20] Seymour was governor for less than two years, and was replaced by Thomas Howard, Earl of Berkshire. Howard, unlike Seymour, actually sought the position and held it from 1643 to 1646.

Dr Brian Duppa, Bishop of Chichester, was an academic and a firm believer in the link between the Church of England and the monarchy. He had enjoyed advancement in his career thanks to the assistance of Buckingham's late father. He was appointed tutor to the boys and said of Charles that 'The Prince . . . hastens apace out of his childhood and is likely to be a man betimes, and an excellent man if my presage deceive me not, and flattery and humouring him, the bane of Princes, do not spoil him.'[21] For his part Charles had great affection for Duppa and remained his friend until the Bishop's death.

Another of their tutors, John Earle, was described as 'A man of great piety and devotion, a most eloquent and powerful preacher; and of a conversation so pleasant and delightful . . . He was among the few excellent men who never had nor ever could have an enemy.'[22] Earle was a clergyman who had been chaplain to the Chancellor of Oxford University. In 1641 he took over from Brian Duppa as senior tutor.

Others also had an influence upon the boys, such as Richard Steward, Charles's clerk of the closet, and a number of tutors and instructors in languages and skills such as archery, fencing and dancing. The boys were extremely lucky in those chosen to guide their education. At a time when 'beating' knowledge into a pupil's head was regarded as normal teaching practice, the royal tutors were of a different calibre. They tended to be men of stature, who attempted to interest and inspire their pupils.

Throughout his life Charles was a pragmatic character, often characterised as lazy, doing as much as was necessary in any particular situation and no more. He adopted the same approach to his studies. Although, later, he would learn to speak fluent French and adequate Italian when it was necessary for communication while in exile on the Continent, he managed to learn very little Latin or Greek from his governors. He did however possess a curious mind and was always interested in matters of science. Buckingham later developed into a poet and playwright whose literary skills, quick wit and abundance of classical allusions owe something to the education of those early years. It was during these years, spent together as brothers, that the foundations of a lifetime's relationship between Charles and Buckingham were laid. That resilient quality of personality that enabled them both to meet the challenges that lay ahead came in no small way from the stability and security of their shared childhood.

Three

THE CIVIL WAR

The little group of boys brought up together at the royal court was broken up when Buckingham and his brother Francis were sent off to be educated at Trinity College, Cambridge, around the age of 12. Cambridge, of course, was the university of which their father had once been elected Chancellor. On account of their noble descent, the Villiers boys were spared the usual effort of seven years' academic study normally required in those days to complete the syllabus, but were simply awarded their degrees.[1] It was at Cambridge that Buckingham first came into the company of writers such as Abraham Cowley, Martin Clifford and John Cleveland, who undoubtedly had an influence upon the development of his own literary ambitions. Cowley, who was ten years his senior and with whom he enjoyed a lifelong friendship, went on to become a major poet of the age. He had, in fact, already built up a reputation as a talented writer when Buckingham met him, although he was still a very young man. He went on to receive generous patronage from Buckingham, who later in life bought him a farm and even paid for his funeral.[2]

On 21 March 1641 the University was honoured with a special visitor when the Prince of Wales, then almost 11 years of age, arrived on an official visit. He was awarded the honorary degree of Master of Arts by the Vice-Chancellor. Buckingham and Francis were also conferred with their Masters' degrees. When prayers were said at King's Chapel there was some criticism of the Prince for not praying into his hat as was the custom of undergraduates at the time.[3] Later, the party dined at Trinity Hall and afterwards enjoyed two plays, *The Guardian* by Cowley and *Paria* by Thomas Vincent. Throughout the day the Prince was accompanied by the Villiers boys, and it was noticed that they fraternised with him bareheaded, a fact which signified to onlookers their familiarity with the young royal. They did not know it, but these joyful years of youth were nearing their end.

Political and religious trouble had been brewing for some time in the country. Many among Charles I's Protestant subjects and Members of Parliament had been unhappy about his marriage to the Catholic Henrietta-Maria. They knew that she was devout and attended Mass every day. There was also great unrest, expecially among the Puritan Members of Parliament, over the King's religious policy of supporting the High Church style of Protestantism as promoted by William Laud, now Archbishop of Canterbury. The Puritans found Bishop Laud's beliefs too close to Catholicism. Their faith placed its major emphasis upon the 'word of God' as given to its followers through the Scriptures. They disliked, in particular, the compulsory use of the 1559 prayer book, the episcopalian nature of the Church under Laud, which elevated the status of bishops and parish clergy, and the emphasis upon sacraments. In addition, they did not like to see the use of stained glass, statues and railed-off altars in churches. Their aim was to purify the Church of England of all these developments, which they regarded as being of Catholic origin. They believed that 'Popish' feasts such as Christmas and Easter should not be celebrated, and that bishoprics should be abolished.

King Charles I was not a man who liked to be told what to do by his subjects. He had a strong belief in the right of the monarch to absolute rule under the privilege of the Royal Prerogative or the divine right of the king to rule. Among the monarch's privileges enshrined in the Royal Prerogative were the right to determine foreign policy and to prorogue or dissolve parliament. A prorogation of parliament amounted to a suspension until the monarch deemed to recall it, a dissolution brought a parliament to an end and necessitated the calling of elections, but not within any specified time limit.

In 1628 Parliament had presented Charles with a document known as the Petition of Right in response to his request for money to cover his military expenses. It was an attempt to curb the King's privileges in regard to arrests and taxation, and was thus an attempt to amend his royal authority. Charles questioned the Petition closely but eventually gave it his assent. However, in 1629, after a number of parliamentary battles, he dissolved Parliament and had several of its members thrown into gaol. Since the law did not compel him to call fresh elections within any set time frame, he went on to rule without Parliament for the next eleven years in a period known as the Eleven Years' Tyranny.

In 1637 a crisis developed when the King tried to impose changes to the Anglican liturgy and prayer book in Scotland in line with the High Church teachings of Archbishop Laud. Presbyterianism was the form taken by Puritanism north of the border, and the Presbyterians in Scotland revolted against these religious reforms. The King urgently needed funds to put together a military response. In 1638 the Scottish Presbyterians showed their determination and solidarity by signing the National Covenant under which they pledged to preserve their form of worship and Church government. Consequently, they became known as Covenanters. Finally, after eleven years, Charles I was forced to call a new parliament in order to raise funds for his military response. The Short Parliament, as it became known, was called to sit for one month in 1640. However, once again, demands were made in return for raising the necessary money. Parliament drew up a list of public grievances and demanded that Charles make peace with the Covenanters. Charles decided instead to attack the Scots without the support of his Parliament.

The crisis worsened when the Scots crossed the border into England as far as Newcastle and Durham. The King's financial situation became so difficult that by November 1640 he was to forced to call yet another parliament. This so-called Long Parliament led by John Pym impeached both Archbishop Laud and Sir Thomas Wentworth, the 1st Earl of

Strafford. Strafford was Lord Lieutenant of Ireland and a great servant to the Crown. He had moved, in his political career, from a position of opposing the Crown to eventually promoting, along with Laud, absolutism in Church and State. He became known to those who opposed him as Black Tom Tyrant. Nevertheless, it was he who had urged Charles to call the previous Short Parliament. In the present crisis Strafford offered the use of Irish troops to help crush the Scots, a plan which most MPs regarded as tantamount to a Catholic invasion. Strafford found himself accused by Parliament of subverting the fundamental laws of the kingdom.

The 10-year-old Prince Charles was required to attend Strafford's trial held in Westminster Hall. Although the trial failed to convict Strafford, the House of Commons voted through an Act of Attainder, accusing him of treason. A mob was soon out on the streets calling for his head. The King agonised but eventually gave the royal assent for Strafford's execution. The following day the Prince of Wales was sent by his father to the House of Lords with a letter requesting that Strafford be spared. It was in vain, however, and Strafford was executed on Tower Hill on 12 May 1641 before a large and eager crowd. Archbishop Laud was thrown into the Tower of London and executed some years later.

The King now had no option but to accept the Long Parliament's demands for reforms, which included more religious liberties for the Scots and the concession that in future Parliament could not be dissolved without its own consent.

To add to all these problems, trouble had also erupted in Ireland. The King's father, James I, had 'planted' Protestant settlers in Ireland. Most of these people, who had come from both Scotland and England, settled in Ulster, taking over 4 million acres of good land while the native Catholic Irish were forced to survive on much poorer holdings.[4] The population of Ireland now consisted of a potentially dangerous religious mix of these relatively new Protestant settlers, the native Irish Catholics and the 'old English' settlers who consisted of both Catholics and

Protestants. The native Irish were unhappy about the repression of their religion, an unhappiness only deepened by their fear of a Puritan-led parliament in London. Although, traditionally, the Catholic 'old English' had no love for their native Irish co-religionists, in this instance they shared their religious concerns. In 1641 these tensions led to a violent Catholic rebellion in Ireland.

In order to put down the Irish rebellion Charles I once again had to turn to his Parliament for much-needed funds. But the MPs, fearing that in the prevailing political climate any well-equipped army might be used against themselves, refused his request and instead presented him with a document entitled the Grand Remonstrance on the State of the Kingdom. In this piece, heavily influenced by John Pym, they ascribed all the present difficulties to what they termed 'the oppressions of the Popish party'.[5] They made a number of demands including that all bishops be dismissed from parliament and the King's Council, that all Crown land in Ireland be preserved, and that from then on they would control the King's choice of ministers. The King's response came after the Christmas recess when an armed force arrived at Westminster Hall to arrest Pym and four other prominent MPs. However, by the time the soldiers arrived, these leading figures had already left. The kingdom was now plunged into civil war, a development that would have serious implications for both the Prince of Wales and Buckingham.

Charles and James were with the King, their father, when he raised the standard of war at Nottingham Castle in August 1642. Their mother and their sister Mary had been sent to the Continent. The 12-year-old Charles was also present at the battle of Edgehill in October 1642. Although the battle is generally regarded as a Royalist victory, Charles found himself in danger twice that day. In an attempt to keep them safe the two brothers were put in the care of the physician Dr William Harvey. However, the doctor did not move them far enough away from the action and a cannon-ball grazed the ground right beside them. The same evening they had another close escape, only just avoiding capture.

Although only 15 years of age, Buckingham was eager to join the Royalist forces. In 1643 he and his brother Francis, who was only 14, joined Prince Rupert and Lord Gerard at Lichfield. However, when the King heard of the boys' involvement in the fight he had them sent abroad under the guardianship of the Earl of Northumberland. During this period they explored France and Italy in the company of a tutor, Dr Aglionby.[6] Meanwhile their property was sequestered by Parliament.

The King and Charles set up base at Oxford, where the Royalist cause enjoyed great support and a Parliament was established as an alternative to the one at Westminster. Although laid low for a while by a bout of measles, followed by conjunctivitis, the young Charles was present at the battle of Cropredy Bridge in June 1644 and the second battle of Newbury in October. The decision was then made that it would be prudent to split up monarch and heir. The young Charles was made nominal General of the Western Association and nominal Generalissimo of all the King's forces in England and in March 1645 left for Bristol accompanied by Sir Edward Hyde, later Earl of Clarendon. The young boy did not know it, but he would never again see his father.

The relationship between the young Prince and his keeper, Edward Hyde, was not an easy one. As one writer puts it, 'Hyde liked to guide by disapproval; Charles liked to learn by encouragement: it was never an ideal combination.'[7] Although only 36 years of age, Hyde had a wealth of administrative experience, having already served as Chancellor of the Exchequer. A lawyer by training, he had become one the King's most trusted advisers. A firm supporter of the Church of England and a man for whom moral principles were of critical importance, he consistently urged the King to stand by the constitution and thereby appeal to the conservative element in society. He immediately took a dislike to the frivolity and lack of morality that he perceived in the personality of the Prince of Wales. Hyde was particularly annoyed when Charles engaged in a possibly intimate liaison with his former nurse, Mrs Wyndham, a liaison of which the lady herself made a proud public display.[8] He was also concerned at how willing Charles was 'to lend an ear to the jests and licentious conversation of the debauched soldiers of his army'.[9]

As the war was not going well for the Royalist side, there was much debate over whether the heir to the throne should remain on English soil.[10] Therefore, in March 1646, Charles went to the Scilly Isles. By April he had sailed to Jersey, where he may have had a relationship with Marguerite Carteret, daughter of the Lieutenant-Governor: it was later rumoured that her son was in fact a royal bastard.[11] With his father now held captive by the Scots, the 16-year-old Prince sailed for France in June.

Oliver Cromwell had been nearly 40 when he experienced his religious 'rebirth' to the ideals and beliefs of Puritanism and became a fierce opponent of Catholicism. At the outbreak of the Civil War Cromwell returned home to Huntingdon to raise a volunteer force of about a hundred men. By 1643 his troop of horse numbered 2,000 and, mainly as a result of their leader's reputation in battle, had earned for themselves the name 'Ironsides'. Cromwell's proficiency in war assured his rapid rise through the military ranks until he eventually became leader of the Roundhead army. His influence would be decisive in the years ahead.

In 1643 there was a worrying development for the Royalist side when the Parliamentarians signed the Solemn League and Covenant with the Presbyterian Covenanters in Scotland, according to which, in return for the dismissal of all bishops and the Church of England becoming Presbyterian, the Covenanters agreed to support the English Parliament in the war.

When the King gave himself up to the Scots in May 1646 the so-called First Civil War came to an end. While the Scots attempted to convert him to their point of view, the Queen also urged him to agree to the establishment of an official Presbyterian Church in return for the support of a Scots army.[12]

Meanwhile, Charles arrived in Paris in June 1647 and was reunited with Buckingham. Charles went on to stay with his mother, Queen

Henrietta-Maria, at the old palace of Saint-Germain. After all he had been through it was not easy for him to come once again under the controlling influence of his mother:

> One of Henrietta Maria's failings was an inordinate possessiveness towards her children, accompanied by a conviction that she had an absolute right to control not only their movements but also their emotions and opinions.[13]

Charles was now 16, an age at which many in his position were already reigning monarchs. In addition, he had no money. The French Court had been paying his mother the small amount of 1,200 francs a day, which they now upped modestly to allow for Charles's added expenses.

The opportunity presented itself for Charles and Buckingham to continue their education. Their tutors, John Earle and Brian Duppa, were still with them. Earle read with them each day for an hour. In addition, the philosopher and scholar Thomas Hobbes was engaged to teach them mathematics. Hobbes had strong connections to the family of the Earl of Newcastle and had been tutor to the Earl's son. He was also a friend of the Queen's adviser and favourite, Henry Jermyn, Earl of St Albans. Hobbes was the famous mathematician and philosopher who would later write the masterpiece *Leviathan*. He was an advocate of restricting the power of the clergy and the Church and keeping them subordinate to political authority. Obviously, his philosophies did not make him a favourite of the Church and Bishop Burnet was critical of his influence upon the heir to the throne, saying that he 'laid before him his schemes both as to religion and politics, which made a deep and lasting impression on the King's mind . . .'.[14]

As his political views did not rest easily at the exiled court, Hobbes eventually returned to England. When *Leviathan* was published in 1651, Charles would reject Hobbes, following the advice of those around him, because of the book's 'many principles of atheism and gross impiety' and also ideas 'such as were prejudicial to the Church and reflected dangerously upon the majesty of sovereign princes'.[15] Later, when restored to the throne, he would welcome Hobbes back to his court.

Burnet, in his writings, was also very critical of the influence that Buckingham had upon the young Charles during these years.[16] Apart from reports of their idleness, there were rumours that the two young boys were engaged in all sorts of unseemly behaviour, including many dalliances with the opposite sex. However, the degree to which such encounters actually happened may well have been exaggerated.[17]

In April 1647, following a petition on his behalf, a Committee of Lords and Commons granted the annulment of the sequestration of Buckingham's property:

> In the case of the right honourable George Duke of Buckingham; upon hearing of counsel on both sides, and reading of several certificates in the said Duke's case, and long debate of the matter: It is resolved, upon the question, that it is the opinion of this Committee, that the sequestration of his estate be taken off, and discharged . . .[18]

There was a lull in the fighting and the Villiers brothers returned home to spend some time studying at Christ Church, Oxford.

In 1647, the King having failed to agree to their demands, the Scots handed him over to the English Parliament. However, while held prisoner on the Isle of Wight, he once again opened negotiations with the Scots. Agreement was finally reached, which resulted in a second outbreak of hostilities in 1648, known as the Second Civil War. It was decided that the young Prince Charles should travel to Scotland to take part in this fresh campaign. En route from France Charles was informed that a part of the English Parliamentary fleet had mutinied, and, travelling to Holland to meet up with the mutineers, he met his brother, James, who had recently escaped from Parliamentary custody. Charles promptly removed his 15-year-old brother from the self-appointed post of Admiral of the Fleet, a decision that angered James and anticipated the difficult relations they were to suffer in the years ahead.

It was during this period in Holland that Charles met Lucy Walter, and although he was only with her for only a short time, she managed to conceive a child by him. Lucy may well have represented Charles's first experience of love. She was described by the diarist John Evelyn as 'a browne, beautiful, bold, but insipid creature.'[19] She had moved to Holland from London and adopted the surname Barlow when her father was granted custody of his children following a legal battle with his wife.

In July 1648 Charles was ready and he sailed with his fleet for Scotland. By this time, however, the Scots had already invaded England, and in the absence of the Prince of Wales, were regarded by many of the English to be invaders and consequently did not receive the Royalist support they might have expected. For his part Charles and his fleet engaged in a number of skirmishes along the south coast of England.

In the same month Buckingham and his brother Francis were drawn into the Civil War once again when they fought on the side of Lord Holland at Reigate. This time events were to take a tragic turn for them. The Royalists were forced to retreat from their stand at Surbiton Common. Communications on battlefields were very poor at that time and Lord Francis found himself surrounded by the enemy. He fought bravely but died in battle at the young age of 20. A lock of hair belonging to a Mrs Kirke was found on his body 'sewed in a ribbon' next to his heart.[20] His body was laid to rest in the family vault in Henry VII's chapel at Westminster Abbey, with the following words carved upon his tomb:

The body of the illustrious Lord Francis Villiers, a most beautiful youth, the posthumous son of George, Duke of Buckingham, who in the twentieth year of his age, fighting valiantly for King Charles and his country, having nine honourable wounds, died the Seventh of July, 1648.[21]

The poem *An Elegy upon the Death of My Lord Francis Villiers* was written in his honour and is sometimes credited to the poet Andrew Marvell.[22]

Buckingham managed to escape the battlefield that day although, at one point, rather bizarrely, his helmet became caught up in the branches of a tree and he was only saved from strangulation by the quick action of a soldier named Tobias Rustat who disentangled him.[23] A few days later the Parliamentarian forces managed to catch up with the Royalists at the town of St Neots, where Lord Holland was captured. Buckingham was surrounded in the house where he had spent the night, but in his inimitable style, managed to fight his way to safety. Since Lord Holland was later executed, capture at this stage would surely have meant death for Buckingham as well. He fled to London and from there joined up with Prince Charles at sea. It was reported that Charles was very glad to see his friend and gave him a warm welcome.[24] The loss of Buckingham's brother may have given the meeting an added poignancy and made the two young men even closer.

The Parliamentarians, having failed to capture Buckingham, now offered him 'liberal terms' in return for his submission to their authority within a set time period and an undertaking never to take up arms against Parliament again.[25] However, he decided to remain loyal to Charles even though the decision led to his losing, once again, all the Villiers family property and forced him into exile.

The Second Civil War was effectively brought to an end in August when the Scottish army was defeated decisively by Cromwell at the battle of Preston. Charles and Buckingham had sailed for Holland. In December 1648 the King was moved to Windsor Castle and Prince Charles was at Breda with Buckingham, Hyde, and the Marquess of Ormonde.[26] At Christmas, Charles returned to The Hague for the festive celebrations. In England all those Parliamentarians who were reluctant to move against the King were ejected from Parliament, and the remainder, the so-called Rump Parliament, proceeded to put the King on trial. The trial of Charles I began in Westminster Hall on 20 January 1649.

Prince Charles tried in vain to halt the process by seeking diplomatic and military assistance. He sent a letter to the Council of State in England in which he agreed to accept any terms in return for his father's life. All his efforts failed, however, and the King was beheaded on 30 January 1649 on a scaffold at Whitehall. His last act had been to hand the insignia of the Garter, a jewel called the George, to Bishop Juxon, with instructions that it be given to his son with the word 'remember'.[27] The monarchy and the House of Lords were abolished, England was declared a commonwealth and Oliver Cromwell became Chairman of the Council of State.

It was early February before the news reached Holland that the King had been executed. It is said that the Prince of Wales's chaplain, Dr Stephen Goffe, simply entered into Charles's presence with the ominous words, '*Your Majesty . . .*'. By March both Charles and Buckingham found themselves 'banished as enemies and traitors, to die without mercy wherever they shall be found within the limits of this nation'.[28]

Charles I was now dead and the future for Charles and Buckingham was bleak. Their lives had changed remarkably in a very short time. They had moved from having the security of a certain future laid out before them to the insecurity of having to wander through Europe, relying upon the good nature of others for survival. They had suffered a bloody civil war, the fears naturally felt by anyone having to flee their homeland, and now, the execcution of the man who had been a father figure to both of them, King Charles I. They were also two young men free from the normal controls exerted by parents and the limits placed upon behaviour by normal court decorum. They were at liberty to taste all the entertainments the Continent had to offer.

Four

THE YEARS IN EXILE

Although in Jersey and Scotland the young Charles was now proclaimed king, most of what should have been his kingdom was no longer his to rule. His court in exile consisted of a number of influential and experienced figures such as Hyde, Ormonde, Sir Edward Nicholas and Sir Francis Cottington. One of the young Charles's major challenges would be to assert his authority over these much more experienced politicians. He was fortunate to have Buckingham at his side, whom he could trust. The Council he set up in April 1650 included a number of younger members such as Buckingham, Sir Robert Long and the Duke of Hamilton, as well as his old governor, the Marquess of Newcastle. Other figures to be found around Charles's court in exile were Sir John Berkeley, Thomas Elliot and that loyal Cavalier, Henry Wilmot, 1st Earl of Rochester.

Dislikes and disagreements ignited at this stage were to colour the rest of Buckingham's life. Those who were anxious to influence or control the young Charles soon recognised his closeness to Buckingham. The favourite's influential position had been underlined by his appointment to the Privy Council and even earlier, in the autumn of 1649, by Charles's bestowal on him of the Order of the Garter. His opponents were reminded, no doubt, of the unique influence Buckingham's father had enjoyed over the two previous kings. They were aware that Buckingham would be a potentially serious rival for anyone ambitious to influence policy. Ormonde, who had been Lord Lieutenant of Ireland, was one of those who soon became an opponent of Buckingham. Another senior figure whom the Duke learned to hate, in equal measure, was Hyde. As one writer describes it, 'Buckingham never forgave Ormonde his dignified disapproval, nor Clarendon [Hyde] his sullen hostility'.[1]

These years of exile would be difficult for both Charles and Buckingham, not least in terms of their finances. We must remember that they were both accustomed to enjoying wealth and luxury, and now, for the first time, they were cut off from the opulence of their former lives and forced to lead a relatively frugal existence. This lack of funds affected the whole of the court during their time in exile. Ormonde is said to have left Ireland with no more than £500[2] and referred to the 'want of money that makes us mad'.[3] Hyde mentions in one of his letters that Charles owed for everything he had eaten for months.[4]

The States General of the Netherlands granted Charles 1,000 guilders a day for ten days, and his brother-in-law William II, who was Stadtholder, and his sister Mary of Orange, invited him to stay with them for a time, a gesture he gratefully accepted.[5] Buckingham joined him there.

With the financial situation as difficult as it was, Buckingham was fortunate that his old steward John Trayleman had managed to smuggle sixteen chests of his family's art treasures out of England and over to Amsterdam, which the Duke began to sell off. He sold Titian's *Ecce Homo* to Archduke Leopold of Prague for over £5,000.[6] It is believed that, in all, he sold around 200 paintings in 1648.[7] At first this put him in a much better financial position than most of the others, but his penchant for spending soon began to deplete his resources.

It was said that Buckingham employed an alchemist to assist in his search for the philosopher's stone, which had always fascinated him. According to Burnet he was for some years of the belief that he was very close to success in the venture.[8] He was assisted in this project by the equally enthusiastic Charles. It is said that the two young men spent much time together 'over the retort and crucible'.[9]

It has often been claimed, although not universally agreed, that Buckingham introduced the young Prince to many vices during this time spent together in continental Europe.[10] Charles, however, was well capable of indulging in vices of his own volition, as was evidenced by the fact that Lucy Walter gave birth to his son in April 1649. The child was christened James and would later become Duke of Monmouth. For the rest of his life claims would be made that Charles had in fact married Lucy Walter, and that therefore Monmouth was Charles's legitimate son and heir to the throne of England. Lucy herself made the claim consistently throughout her life, and Charles always denied it. It can be argued that the claim lacked validity and was made only to bolster Monmouth's efforts to succeed to the throne.[11] Much later Monmouth attempted to seize the throne from his uncle, King James II, and would pay for his actions with his life.

Whatever his affection for Lucy, Charles was not faithful to her, as he continued to have relationships with a number of other women. Around 1651 Elizabeth 'Betty' Killigrew, wife to Francis Boyle, later Viscount Shannon, gave birth to another royal bastard. Charles also had an affair around 1652 with Eleanor Needham, the second wife of John, Lord Byron. Charles went on to father another son in 1657 and a daughter in 1658, with Catharine Pegge. Undoubtedly there were others.

During these years of enforced exile it seems that Buckingham could not resist the temptation of visiting his homeland. There are stories of his travelling to England in disguise on a number of occasions. It is believed that he paid for at least one visit home by using his artistic talents and staging a show for large audiences in which he played a fool and sang ballads. One story, in particular, demonstrates his audacity. As a result of the political situation, Buckingham's sister Mall, Duchess of Richmond, was being held prisoner by Parliament. One day as she was being transferred from Whitehall to Windsor the prison escort was suddenly brought to a halt by an insistent jester who said that he wished to entertain the party. Mall had no option but to listen to the performance, which consisted mostly of material offensive to herself. When the performer had finished his hilarious show he announced that he wished to present the Duchess with copies of his satirical songs. The guards agreed. But, as the joker came close to the coach to hand her the songs, Mall was surprised to see the face of her brother appearing briefly from behind his mask. Buckingham handed her some secret letters before making his exit. [12]

By 1649, with the return of the monarchy looking remote and Buckingham's store of art treasures running low, the Duke came to a momentous decision. He decided to initiate tentative approaches to the Parliament in England to discuss his return home. This decision meant that he was now, for the first time, considering the option of deserting Charles. To set this decision in motion he sought the help of a cousin, Basil Feilding, Earl of Denbigh, who had fought for the Parliamentary side in the Civil War in spite of his family's Royalist background. Buckingham asked his aunt, Basil's mother, to use her influence with her son on this matter. However, in a letter to his mother written in July 1649, Basil was not hopeful regarding the Duke's return: 'the streame runs so high against him,' he wrote, 'that the issue is much to be doubted'.[13] There the matter rested for the time being.

Notwithstanding any internal rivalries, the thoughts of most of Charles's supporters in exile were set firmly upon the recovery of his kingdom. Their first thought was to look around for support in Europe, but none was forthcoming. They then began to consider that their best way back to England was through Ireland. In preparation for this, Charles made his way to France in the summer of 1649, accompanied by Lucy Walter. By September he had gone to Jersey with Buckingham and the Duke of York.[14] But, in the end, their dreams of an Irish-based fight-back were dashed by the news of Cromwell's decisive and bloody victory in Ireland.

By the beginning of 1650 they were turning their thoughts back to Scotland as the best way of regaining the throne. This was the course of action most favoured by Buckingham. A preliminary discussion between Charles and the Scots, represented by the Earl of Lauderdale, had been held before on board ship in September 1648. Buckingham was at

Charles's side during these talks and at that time had urged him strongly to accept the terms being put forward by the Scots.

The Presbyterian leader in Scotland was Archibald Campbell, Earl of Argyll, a man with a rather chequered past. He had been a member of Charles I's Privy Council but joined the Covenanters in 1638. By 1641 he had switched his allegiance back to the King again. However, he then fought on the Parliamentarian side in the Civil War. After the execution of Charles I he repudiated Cromwell and was now negotiating with the son of Charles I over a possible restoration of the monarchy.

Argyll and his supporters insisted that in return for their assistance, Charles sign the Covenant. They wanted the Presbyterian faith established throughout England and Ireland as well as Scotland. In addition, Charles would have to follow only their form of worship within his own household, and any treaties that had been signed with the Catholics would have to be annulled. Agreeing to these terms would mean Charles turning his back on both Ormonde and Montrose.

James Graham, the Marquess of Montrose, was one of those who had originally drawn up the National Covenant in support of Presbyterianism. He later expressed doubts about it and was now Argyll's fiercest enemy. He had been commissioned by Charles to go to Scotland with an army to challenge Argyll. This was an example of Charles playing both sides. If Montrose was to enjoy military success Charles would not have to worry about negotiating with the Covenanters. But, if nothing more, he might have the effect of causing the Covenanters to soften their terms somewhat.

On a personal level, the ambitious Argyll wanted to use Charles to strengthen his own position in Scotland and extend his power into England. The 19-year-old Charles looked in all directions for advice on what he should do. Hyde, Ormonde and Edward Nicholas were against this agreement with the Scottish Covenanters, seeing it as a betrayal of their faith. Charles's mother urged him to make an agreement with the Scots but on no account to sign the Covenant. His brother-in-law,

William of Orange, advised him to commit himself fully to the Covenanters and even to worship in their manner. Newcastle and Hamilton, likewise, urged Charles to form an alliance with the Scots.

His old friend Buckingham also urged him to accept their terms, aware that this was the best and perhaps the only way to regain the throne. Unlike some other court advisers Buckingham had no objection to negotiating with the Presbyterian Convenanters. He felt no principled opposition to them. In fact, a sympathy for the cause of nonconformist religions was a theme that was to run right through his life and on a number of occasions he would argue for their right to exercise freedom of conscience and worship in their own way.

By May 1650, negotiations, led by Buckingham and Newcastle for the King, were concluded at Breda, and Charles agreed to sign up to the terms of the Scottish Covenanters. Charles sent a letter to Montrose telling him 'to forbear all future acts of hostility'. The letter was never received and Montrose's small army was routed. He was captured in April 1650 and hanged by Argyll's people a month later in Edinburgh. His head was placed upon a spike.

Charles, with an entourage including Buckingham and Henry Seymour, sailed for Scotland in a man-of-war on loan from the Dutch. In July 1650 Charles reluctantly swore the oath of the Covenant while anchored at the mouth of the River Spey and landed in Scotland the following day. Notwithstanding their opposition to clergy, the Presbyterian Covenanters had allowed Buckingham to bring his chaplain with him provided he was listed in the entourage as the Duke's private secretary.

It was around this time that Buckingham was offered a favourable deal by the English Parliament to return to his estates, but, thrilled by the prospect of the agreement with the Scots, he declined. Instead, he threw himself wholeheartedly into the relationship with Argyll and his supporters.

During their stay in Scotland both Charles and Buckingham found the Presbyterian obsession with prayer and sermonising difficult to take and only occasionally were they left alone, behind shuttered windows, to drink or play cards. Charles, in particular, found the whole process of treating with the Covenanters very difficult. They kept strict control over his actions and movements. Only Buckingham and Henry Wilmot were allowed near his court at the Palace of Falkland.[15] Such was the joyous reception that Charles had received from the people of Scotland on his arrival in the country, it caused the Covenanters to fear the growth of his power, and they ensured that he was kept away from the people after that.

Charles was not even permitted to attend the meetings of the Covenanters' Council. On top of all this, pressure was mounting for a marriage between Charles and Argyll's daughter, Lady Anne. One Colonel Silas Titus, the author of *Killing no Murder*, was sent to put the case for the match to Queen Henrietta-Maria.[16] Titus was told discreetly by Charles to return with a polite refusal!

Although Buckingham disliked the lifestyle of the Covenanters, he believed that their support was indispensable, and he became impatient with the desire that was growing in Charles to be separated from them. This led to a deterioration in the relationship between the two young men. Charles's attitude hardened even further when the Covenanters presented him with a new document to sign. This time they were looking for him to express, in writing, his shame and regret not only for his own sins but also for those of his father. They also wanted him to condemn his mother's idolatry and demonstrate his abhorrence for popery, prelacy and superstition. Under pressure from Argyll, who threatened to enter negotiations with Cromwell, Charles finally agreed to sign.

At the beginning of September 1650 Cromwell, having advanced into Scotland, had already gained a victory over the Scots at Dunbar. By now Charles was reaching his breaking point. He decided to begin treating, in secret, with a group of Royalist supporters in the Highlands of Scotland led by Middleton and Hamilton. His intermediary in these negotiations was his physician, Dr Frazer. A declaration was even drafted in which Charles denounced Argyll and the Convenanters' treatment of him. There are a number of accounts of what happened next. Hyde claims that Buckingham found this declaration among Charles's papers and informed Argyll of its contents. Henry Nash's telling of the story, in a letter to William Edgeman, claims that Charles told Buckingham and some others of his intention to treat with the Royalist group.[17] Buckingham felt that Argyll was much too powerful to make any such action sensible. After much discussion it seems that they were satisfied that they had managed to persuade Charles it would be the wrong course of action. However, one day as he was mounting his horse, he announced to Buckingham and Lord Lothian that he had decided to go ahead with his plan. His aim, he claimed, was not to betray the Convenanters but to enlist the help of the Royalists in their cause. Lothian, somewhat stunned by the comments, did not reply and it was he who went immediately to inform the Committee of what had been said. According to Nash's account, Buckingham decided his duty lay in mounting a horse and following Charles, whom he failed to catch up with. By the time he got back, the Committee had sent twenty men in pursuit of the young royal. Once found, Charles agreed to return with them if they allowed Dr Frazer and his entourage to proceed safely, which was agreed.

Charles was not alone in his feelings of frustration. Buckingham expressed similar dark feelings when he wrote to his old Governor Newcastle in December 1650:

> For my own part I am so weary of our ill fortune, and the miserable condition we are in here that I do wish for some happy occasion of losing my life honourably in the King's service.[18]

If nothing else, the recent possibility of Charles's defection did force some concessions from the Convenanters. Charles was crowned King of Scotland on New Year's day 1651 at Scone, with Argyll placing the crown upon his head. A Parliament was called and the new king was from then on allowed to preside at Council meetings.

The Royalists, on the other hand, were in no doubt about who had ruined their attempts to lure their King away from the Covenanters. At the top of their list of those to blame was Buckingham, whom they regarded as a traitor. Many of those at the exiled royal court in Holland were of the same opinion. However, it can be argued that Buckingham, as ever, was being ruthlessly practical since he knew that militarily their best option lay with Argyll and his superior forces.

As preparations were made in Scotland for the war against Cromwell, Buckingham was made General of the Eastern Association. He was also appointed Secretary of State after Long was dismissed from the position by Argyll. Since it was clear that no marriage would take place between Argyll's daughter, Anne, and Charles, Buckingham decided that he would propose to her instead.[19] The proposal did not please Charles and ultimately came to nothing.

Finally, the hour they had been waiting for arrived, and the young King Charles, with Buckingham at his side, marched an army south into England in July 1651. Once they crossed the border Buckingham began badgering Charles about removing the Scot, David Leslie, from command of the army. He argued that it was important to have an Englishman in command of English soldiers, especially if they wished to recruit extra men along the way.

When asked by Charles whom he thought should take on Leslie's command, Buckingham replied, rather predictably, 'I hope Your Majesty will confer it upon myself.' Charles merely turned away without reply. Not one to be put off so easily, the following day, as they marched towards Worcester, Buckingham brought the subject up once again. This time the conversation is reputed to have gone:

Bucks: My proposal of yesterday is so suitable that Leslie himself would willingly consent to it.

Charles: I can hardly believe you are in earnest or that you can in truth believe that you could be fit for such a charge!

Bucks: Wherein lies my unfitness?

Charles: You are too young. [Buckingham was 23]

Bucks: Harry the Fourth commanded an army and won a battle when he was younger than I.[20]

Charles brought the argument to an abrupt conclusion by informing Buckingham that there would be no General but himself. Buckingham turned away angrily from the King and went into a sulk, refusing to attend the Council, hardly speaking to Charles, and, it is said, even neglecting to change his clothes or shave. This mood lasted until they reached Worcester in August.[21]

In the end the invasion from Scotland came to nothing when Charles's forces were routed by Cromwell at the battle of Worcester in September. Argyll had withdrawn himself from the march into England, refusing to offer any assistance and going to his castle in the Highlands. To his credit, Buckingham is reported to have acted bravely during the battle, remaining at Charles's side throughout. Ormonde regarded the defeat at Worcester as a result of their collaboration with what he called the 'Presbyterian gang', a collaboration for which he held Buckingham mainly responsible.[22]

After the rout the Royalists were forced to flee to safety – Charles's escape in the disguise of a commoner has become the stuff of legend. Buckingham was one of those who chose to escape with Colonel Blague, who had extensive knowledge of the area. Blague brought him to the Blorepipe House in Staffordshire, the home of George Barlowe. Luckily, Buckingham elected to sleep in the woods that night as Colonel Blague, who slept in the house, was captured. Buckingham was forced to remain hidden in a cottage for six days until he was finally smuggled out of the area. He then went to Nottinghamshire, where he stayed with his sister Mall for a time.

By the end of October Buckingham had managed to make his way to Holland and to the court of Charles's sister, Mary of Orange. Mary had been recently bereaved: her husband, William II, had died at 24 years of age. Six days after her husband's death she had given birth to a son, also called William. Buckingham was still feeling very angry about being denied leadership of the army by Charles and he soon found himself banned from Mary's court for criticising him, saying that he 'had ill-behaved himself in the battle, and that he lay now hidden in some gentlemen's house, and was happier in his own opinion, than if he was upon the throne'.[23]

By the time Charles did make it safely to the Continent, so influenced was he by his experience with the Presbyterians in Scotland that those like Hyde, who had been against the whole enterprise, became closest to him. In addition, the escapade with the Scots had done nothing for his relationship with Buckingham. Nor were people like Hyde or Ormonde slow in blackening the Duke's name whenever they could.

Eventually Mary Stuart's anger at Buckingham's disloyal statement about her brother dissipated, and not only was he allowed to visit her at court but it was rumoured that he was making romantic overtures towards the young widow. These rumours did not please Charles or the Queen Mother, Henrietta-Maria, who was outraged at 'the wild pretence of the Duke of Buckingham'.[24] According to Hyde, Henrietta-Maria said that 'if it were possible for her daughter to entertain so base a thought, she would tear her in pieces with her own hands'.[25] In the end, Buckingham was firmly rejected by the Princess – he was 'entreated . . . to forbear making visits to her'.[26] Although it was reported that 'His grace was not pleased nor edify'd with this message', he had no choice but to comply.[27]

The Duke's general feelings of anger and frustration were only augmented by this latest royal rebuttal of his affections. In addition, Charles was in no position to give him any financial support. Perhaps it is not surprising that his thoughts now began to turn once again to opening negotiations with Parliament. Through Captain Wendy Oxford, a meeting was organised in Amsterdam between the Duke and John Lilburne, an agitator for the Levellers. The pair also met later at Calais. Up to a very short time before, Lilburne had been close to Cromwell, but was now banished as a result of his writings. When reporting the meeting of Buckingham and Lilburne at Calais, a spy described them as 'very familiar together'.[28]

Lilburne was very bitter against Cromwell and spoke of little else but getting revenge and overthrowing him. He discussed the best way for Buckingham to return to England and also the possibility of an alliance between the Levellers and the Royalists. It did Buckingham's reputation no good to be seen with Lilburne. Not only did Cromwell's people want Lilburne dead, but so too did many of the Royalists on the Continent, and they were far from pleased about his dalliance with Buckingham. Captain Wendy Oxford was sounded out on the possibility of disposing of Lilburne, but Buckingham managed to talk the Royalists out of it.[29] Captain Oxford also told the Duke that he had been approached from England with instructions that if Buckingham could give incriminating information against Lilburne, he would be rewarded with a pass into his homeland. Buckingham refused the offer.

As it happened, Lilburne decided to return to England himself in June of 1653 and was arrested. One of the accusations thrown at him was his close association with the Duke of Buckingham while in exile in Holland. During his trial he spoke freely of this association, saying, 'if ever it should lye in my power to do him any personal service, without detriment to my native country (which I am confident he would never desire of me) I judge myself bound in conscience and gratitude to travel on his errand a thousand and a thousand miles upon my feet.'[30] Lilburne claimed that he owed his life to the Duke and described Buckingham's qualities of 'reason, sobriety, civility, honour and conscience'.[31] It was said that Lilburne's honesty and character were so admired by the common people that on his acquittal of high treason the shout of joy 'was heard an English mile off'.[32] He was imprisoned in Jersey.

Buckingham thought that this was an opportune time for the successful conclusion of his negotiations with Parliament. With this in mind, he decided to return to England in July 1653. It was said, by Hyde among others, that the Duke's ambitious long-term plan was to marry Cromwell's daughter in order to ensure the return of his lands.[33] However, in reality, his reception was far from friendly and the negotiations came to nothing. He returned, once again, to the Continent.

Buckingham joined the French army as a volunteer and became involved in the war against Spain. He was present at the siege of Mouzon, where he was laid low with fever, and the siege of Arras, where he was commended for his bravery.[34] He fought with the French in the summer of 1656 when they were routed by the Spaniards at Valenciennes.[35]

With the fighting over, Buckingham reviewed his difficult financial situation. His sister had become a widow and had rejoined the court of Henrietta-Maria, and so was in no position to offer him any financial assistance. Given the difficulties, Buckingham was reported to be once again criticising Charles. According to Lord Hatton, 'his ink was not black enough to express the base and horrid language Buckingham did belch out concerning our Master'.[36] But, in reality, many of these reports were mere propaganda. While he was away at war, his enemies at court, chief among them Hyde, had been busy damaging his reputation with Charles. They reported on his approaches to the Cromwellian regime as well as his rumoured thoughts of marrying Cromwell's daughter. They even claimed that he was informing on their activities to Cromwell.[37] On one occasion he seems to have played into their hands by admitting to Ormonde that he had a pass from Cromwell, which entitled him to establish himself anywhere in England.[38]

As one would expect, such reports made Charles suspicious of his companion from childhood and led to Buckingham being kept somewhat on the periphery of the royal court. Ironically, at the same time, those close to Cromwell also warned him that Buckingham was a danger, even claiming that he planned to assassinate Cromwell, by now Lord Protector, although no evidence exists of this particular accusation.[39]

As the French were now attempting to conclude an agreement with Cromwell's England, they no longer wanted to protect the young royal. So, in July 1654, Charles was persuaded to leave Paris in return for financial aid. He went to Spa, where he met up with his sister Mary, and spent an enjoyable time before travelling on to Aachen. Later they visited Aix and Cologne. Around this time Charles began negotiations with the Spanish for assistance. They were now interested in helping him because Cromwell had begun attacking them at sea and had taken the island of Jamaica. In March 1656 Charles decided to set up headquarters at Brussels, which was then the capital of the Spanish Netherlands, and later moved to Bruges. He committed Royalist troops to aid the Spanish military effort against Cromwell, many of them Irish soldiers transferred from the French army and others newly recruited.

Since 1655 Lucy Walter had become another problem for Charles when it became known that she was having a relationship at The Hague with a married man called Thomas Howard. She was also being blackmailed by her maid, who claimed that Lucy had induced two abortions on herself. Charles found out, through a representative, that Lucy intended to kill the maid using a knitting needle.[40] Charles's man managed to dissuade her using a combination of threats and bribery. When, by 1657, Lucy's love affair with Howard had finished, she persuaded her cousin to murder him in Brussels. Howard managed to survive the attack, but was wounded.

Next Lucy began to make threats that she would publish Charles's letters to her if he didn't give her money. This, along with her poor performance as a mother, convinced Charles that his son was best removed from her. One attempt to take the child away was thwarted by her loud screams. But, in 1658, Charles's people did manage to get hold of the boy and he was removed to Paris. Soon afterwards Lucy died.

As the end of the 1650s approached, the return of Charles and Buckingham to their former glory seemed nothing but a vain hope. The proposed Irish-based military fight-back had failed to materialise, and the Scottish one had ended in failure yet again. The best efforts of the Royalists to mount an insurrection from both inside England and elsewhere had come to nothing. It was clear that they could not hope for help from the French, who had signed a treaty of friendship and commerce with England in 1655 and were engaged in a war alongside Cromwell's armies against the Spanish. The hope of a Spanish victory in that war, assisted by Charles's Royalist troops, also soon proved vain.

It is true that Charles and Buckingham were lucky to be alive following their escape from Worcester. And, perhaps, there was even some advantage to be had from the experiences they were gaining on the Continent, experiences to which they would never have been exposed otherwise. There were also moments of happiness and fun in the midst of the depression, such as when they partook of the varied entertainments available at European courts. If one Cromwellian spy is to be believed, when he described what he called the 'fornication, drunkenness and adultery' of Charles's exiled court, there was no lack of entertainment.[41]

Yet, all this was small compensation. Their situation was not an easy one. The problem of not having enough money was ever present for both of them. Their prospects were dire. Buckingham had, by now, become resigned to the fact that a restoration of the monarchy was impossible, and he was about to make a tough and momentous decision.

Five

DESERTION AND MARRIAGE

In 1657 General Thomas Fairfax was granted a large part of the Villiers' sequestered property, valued at around £5,000 a year and including York House and the Manor of Helmsley.[1] In the Civil War Fairfax had served the Parliamentary side, first as General of the Parliamentary Horse and in 1645 as Supreme Commander. Yet he was one of those who had objected to the execution of Charles I. Although he assisted Cromwell in putting down the army mutiny of 1649, in 1650 he decided on conscience against fighting the Scots, who had proclaimed Charles II as their King. After this he withdrew into private life. The Villiers' property was given to him in settlement of his arrears of pay.

Fairfax was a highly respected man with a reputation for being honourable and principled. Years later, his noble character was acknowledged by none other than Buckingham himself in his *An Epitaph upon Thomas Lord Fairfax*:

> He neither Wealth nor Places sought,
> For others, not himself he fought.
> He was content to know
> For he had found it so,
> That when he pleas'd to conquer, he was able
> And left ye spoil and plunder to ye rabble.[2]

There had been a number of occasions on which Buckingham could have made his peace with the authorities in England and returned to his estates there. He had, of course, been tempted a few times, and had even made approaches to Parliament. But the fact is, up to this point, he had remained in exile. Through these difficult years he had continued to hope that they would be successful in overthrowing Cromwell's rule and restoring the monarchy. Then, they could both have returned to the life that had been laid out for them as children, with Charles as King and Buckingham, like his father, the most powerful politician in the land.

But now he had come to the very difficult conclusion that there was no longer any advantage to be had from remaining with Charles on the Continent. The chances of a restoration of the monarchy were remote, if not impossible. His money was gone, and he had no prospects of an improvement in his situation. This is why, on hearing that Fairfax had been granted much of his property, he made the momentous decision to desert Charles and the Royalist cause. Since Lord Fairfax was a distant relative of his, and eager to turn an honourable character to his advantage, Buckingham soon presented himself on the General's doorstep in England, arriving in 1657. Luckily for Buckingham, Fairfax welcomed him with considerable affection and an understanding of his difficult situation; it is surprising that two such strikingly different characters seem to have had an instant rapport.

Mary Fairfax was the only child of General Fairfax and Lady Anne. Little Moll, as they called her, was doted upon by her parents. At the age of 12 they engaged the poet, Andrew Marvell, as her tutor. Buckingham seems almost immediately to have begun making romantic overtures towards Mary. His efforts were not without considerable success, even though she was already betrothed to Lord Chesterfield.[3] Mary may not have been beautiful and is, in fact, described as a 'little round crumpled woman', but the man once described as the 'most graceful and beautiful person that any Court in Europe ever saw' stated his feelings about her in a letter written to her mother:[4]

... it is impossible to love or honour anything more than I truly do her and to wish for anything with greater longing or impatience than I do for some means of giving both her and your ladyship undeniable proofs of it, being confident that if your ladyship knew the nature of the passion I have for her, you could not be so ill-natured (however averse to me soever she might be) as not to pity my condition or to refuse the endeavouring to further me by your favour to the enjoying of what only in this world can make me perfectly happy. That is Madame, the honour of being your Ladyship's most dutiful son . . .[5]

A note probably given to a friend of Mary's, and perhaps intended for Mary's own eyes, displays no less devotion:

The little Ribbon I received from you last night, instead of binding up my wound has made it greater. And though I have kept it ever since as near my heart as I could I can find no other effects by it, than the being much less at my ease than I was before. I have not slept one wink since I saw you, neither have I been able to think of any other thing, than how to find the means of speaking to your Dear Mistress. For I dare not without her leave presume to call her mine, though it be already out of my power, ever to call justly so, anybody else . . . for one minutes conversation with that dear Mistress of yours . . . would from as troublesome a state of mind, as ever creature was in, settle me in a condition not to envy the happiest man living.[6]

Buckingham even managed to win over Mary's aunt, Lady Vere, who arrived in York accompanied by four Presbyterian ministers to speak on the suitor's behalf.

It is impossible to believe that Buckingham was being sincere in his dealings with Mary: his motive was surely a desire to regain his property and his status in society, rather than love. Mary was merely a vehicle for his ambitions. For the moment Cromwell did not have him arrested. Amazingly, perhaps in order to 'hedge his bets' romantically, it was said that Buckingham began to pay visits to the Lord Protector's daughters.[7] He did not meet the father at this time, although a number of appointments were set up and cancelled due to other business. So impressed were the young Cromwells by him that they even consulted lawyers on his legal position in England, and were told that he seemed on solid ground.[8] How much of this is nothing more than propaganda against the Duke is hard to tell.

Events progressed rapidly: Buckingham and Lady Mary Fairfax were married on 15 September 1657 by the Presbyterian, Mr Vere Harcourt, at Bolton Percy, with Abraham Cowley acting as best man.[9] Harcourt had also presumably fallen under the spell of Buckingham's charm when he remarked that he saw God in the Duke's face![10]

It may be clear why Buckingham wanted to marry Mary, and it is also understandable that Mary fell in love with someone with as much charm and wit as the Duke, but what is not so clear is why General Fairfax and his wife agreed to the marriage. Hyde was one of those surprised at General Fairfax's apparent naivety.[11] Perhaps they had also fallen under the spell of the Buckingham charm. Others, such as Lady Conway, believed that the Fairfaxes were happy about the marriage because it was, in effect, a good match for their daughter in terms of raising her social rank.[12]

At first it seemed that the risk the Duke had taken by returning to England at this time was vindicated, as Cromwell made no move to have him arrested. However, shortly after their marriage, the newlyweds were shocked by the news that Buckingham was to be arrested after all. Cromwell was reported to be 'not pleased' with the marriage. Buckingham's father-in-law, Lord Fairfax, immediately requested an audience with his former military colleague to discuss the matter.

Brian Fairfax, Lord Fairfax's cousin, accompanied his cousin on that visit to Cromwell and later wrote about the scene. Fairfax was angry at the personal insult it was for his family that his son-in-law be arrested. Attempting to control his anger he asked Cromwell that the Duke be released as soon as possible. The Protector pointedly told him that before allying himself with enemies he should have consulted with 'his old friends'.[13] Fairfax argued on Buckingham's behalf, but when he realised that he was making no progress, turned angrily on his heel and stormed out. Watching the scene between these two headstrong men, Brian feared that his cousin would be arrested as well; luckily, this did not happen.

It took some time for the authorities to find Buckingham. Probably thanks to Fairfax's influence, he was allowed, after a short time, to serve his confinement in the luxury of York House rather than being incarcerated in a conventional prison such as the Tower of London. However, in characteristic style, Buckingham refused to remain a prisoner and began using his skills of disguise to go on trips, including one to visit his sister in Cobham. Eventually, on one of these audacious excursions, he was captured. In August 1658 Colonel Gibbon wrote to Secretary Thurloe:

I this day coming from Canterbury on the road within three miles of Sittingbourne, I met with three or four men; and finding one of them to shun me, I thereupon suspected the said person and rode up to him, examined him who he was. At the last I came to be assured he was the Duke of Buckingham, knowing him to be a person searched for, I have secured him, so as to bring him with me to my house near Rochester, where I shall detain him till I know His Highness' pleasure concerning him.[14]

This time Fairfax's pleading went unheeded and Cromwell had Buckingham thrown into the Tower of London. It was here that, fearing for his life, Buckingham heard the surprising news of Cromwell's death. His thoughts are recorded:

. . . I was then close prisoner in the Tower, with a couple of Guards lying always in my chamber and a sentinel at my door. I confess I was not a little delighted with the noise of the great guns, for I presently knew what it meant, and if Oliver had lived for three days longer I had certainly been put to death.[15]

Whether Cromwell would have had him executed or not we will never know, but in any event, under the rule of Cromwell's son Richard, the situation for Buckingham became easier. By September 1658 he was moved from the Tower of London to Windsor Castle, where he 'became a rallying point for the crew of reckless conspirators, who ever gravitated towards the Duke'.[16] On 21 February 1659 the House of Commons was petitioned for his release.[17] General Fairfax, who presented the petition, not only offered a substantial amount of money in security, but also agreed to be personally responsible for the Duke:

. . . upon the engagement of the Lord Fairfax in twenty thousand pounds, that the said Duke shall peaceably demean himself for the future; and shall not join with, or abet, or have any correspondence with, any of the enemies of the Lord Protector, and of this Commonwealth . . .[18]

Among Buckingham's supporters was Anthony Ashley Cooper, the future Lord Shaftesbury, otherwise known to history as the 'Achitophel' of Dryden's famous poem.[19] He assured the House that 'one person cannot do much harm by his liberty'.[20] Probably the most powerful aspect of Buckingham's argument was the respect in which Lord Fairfax was held by the House. On 23 February 1659 the prisoner was brought before the Bar of the House and told by the Speaker that he should have his freedom provided that 'upon his own engagement upon his honour, and of the Lord Fairfax in twenty thousand pounds, that he should not abet any the enemies of this Commonwealth, either at home or abroad'.[21]

For his part, Buckingham assured them that he was 'ready to lay down his life and fortune for their service'.[22]

So Buckingham was free once again. He went to live with his wife in her father's house at Nun Appleton. Whatever peace of mind was felt by the Duke, Lord Fairfax appears to have been anything but confident when he offered his personal responsibility for his son-in-law's future behaviour. As he himself put it, 'When I engage my estate I know what I do, but when I engage his honour, I engage what is not in my power.'[23] Fairfax, it seems, was guided by love for his daughter rather than by confidence in Buckingham.

For Charles, Buckingham's return to England represented a heavy psychological blow. The friend he had known and loved as a brother since childhood had deserted him. Buckingham had treated with the enemy, the very people responsible for the execution of the king who had been a father to both of them. The Royalists in exile heard full reports of what had happened and of the undertakings made by Buckingham to the Parliament in England.[24] Hyde, in particular, took every opportunity to attack the Duke's actions in any way he could, referring to him as a poison.[25] Charles had to face the awful truth that someone he had trusted now believed that the restoration of the monarchy was nothing but an impossible dream. But for his own sanity and in memory of his father, Charles could never give up hope that the dream would yet be realised.

Six

THE RESTORATION

Inevitably it was going to be a challenge for Richard Cromwell to step into his father's role. A recent costly war against the Dutch meant that he inherited a difficult financial situation, and arrears of pay due to the army soon began to add to the tensions. When Richard personally took direct control of the army instead of appointing an experienced officer, the crisis worsened. In order to help solve his problems, he decided to call a Parliament, but, when Parliament insisted that the army's Council of Officers should not meet in future without Richard's prior approval, the officers called for Parliament to be dissolved. Richard first attempted to dismiss the Council, but in the end dissolved Parliament instead. The army officers now had the upper hand. They recalled the Rump, which promptly dismissed Richard Cromwell.

In the power struggle that ensued between the Rump Parliament and the army, the army gained the upper hand in the person of Major-General Lambert. It was left to General George Monk to travel from Scotland to crush Lambert's rule. Knowing that both Buckingham and Fairfax were among those who had come to oppose the rule of Richard Cromwell, Monk sent a secret letter to Fairfax to enlist his help in the endeavour. The letter was carried through dangerous territory by Dr Clergis, who was unable to carry Fairfax's affirmative reply back to Monk. Brian Fairfax agreed to undertake this dangerous task.[1] Buckingham disguised the messenger as a 'young country clown' and thus enabled him to pass through Lambert's many patrols and deliver the message safely to Monk.[2]

News of Fairfax and Buckingham's support for Monk eventually filtered through to their enemies, however, and on St Stephen's night a company of soldiers arrived at Nun Appleton to arrest them. Luckily they had been forewarned and had fled, agreeing to meet up later in Knaresborough. Buckingham went to Malton, where he involved himself in gathering recruits to the cause. When they joined forces at Knaresborough, they marched on to York without a fight, the enemy refusing to engage their old leader General Fairfax. Indeed as they entered the city, cries of 'Fairfax! Fairfax!' were heard.[3] Although joined at York by Monk, Fairfax decided against travelling to London to witness the seizing of power, preferring instead to disband his troops. Buckingham could not deny himself such excitement.

Buckingham and Fairfax were agreed that the best political option now available was the return of the monarchy. Eventually, agreement was reached between Charles and Parliament for a restoration under the Declaration of Breda of 1660. The Declaration promised royal pardons for all but a few and liberty of religious practice. At last the dream had become reality and, after his long years of exile, Charles was coming home. By May Parliament had proclaimed him king. At the end of the month he arrived to a triumphant welcome:

> . . . the ways strewn with flowers, the bells ringing, the streets hung with tapestry, fountains running with wine, the mayor, aldermen and all the companies in their liveries, chains of gold, banners; lords and nobles, clad in cloth of silver, gold and velvet, the windows and balconies all set with ladies, trumpets, music and myriads of people flocking the streets . . .[4]

Even though he had only recently deserted his friend in exile, with Charles now on the throne Buckingham was feeling confident about his future. As one biographer writes, 'a vision of power such as few subjects save his own father had wielded, rose before him'.[5] He felt sure that he would regain property, money and power thanks to his upbringing and close intimacy with Charles; he believed that Charles would understand the political necessity that had forced his return to Cromwell's England. He also claimed that he had played a vital role in bringing about the restoration, not least by persuading his father-in-law, Fairfax, into giving it his support. This was a fact he would often remind Charles of in the years to come.

Buckingham must have felt somewhat dejected when Charles, on his arrival in England, greeted him with a coldness not shown to others of his acquaintance: it was obvious that Buckingham's desertion, above that of anyone else, had been keenly felt. But, resilient as ever, Buckingham soon recovered from the rejection and resolved to exert his charms on his childhood companion, confident that it would only be a matter of time before Charles would forgive him and they would be close once again.

Some even reported, perhaps with excessive optimism, that even before they had reached London Buckingham was back in the King's favour.[6] Buckingham made sure to further the rehabilitation of their relationship by making efforts to meet the King nightly at the Whitehall lodgings of his cousin, Barbara Villiers, who was Charles's mistress. Soon the rebuilding of their friendship was well under way.

In June 1660 the Duke had taken out a pardon under the Great Seal for all his past offences, which was intended to protect him from any charges that might be brought against him. The formerly substantial property of his father was soon back in his ownership. Among his houses was York House in London, which was a magnificent estate backing on to the Strand with frontage on to the Thames. It was let during most of Buckingham's ownership. In June 1664 he petitioned to rebuild the house.[7] It was eventually sold and redeveloped in the 1670s.[8] He also got possession of Chelsea House, which was sold in 1674. Wallingford House became his principal residence in London.[9] The House at Burley-on-the-Hill had been burnt down during the Civil War. New Hall had, for a time, become the property of Oliver Cromwell but it now returned to Buckingham's ownership. He later sold it to the Duke of Albemarle.

By November 1660 relations with Charles had been restored to such an extent that Buckingham was sent to Calais to escort Charles's younger sister, Princess Henrietta, to England. The result, however, was that he became infatuated with this young lady, who was known as Minette. She was betrothed to Philippe, Duc d'Orléans, her cousin and the brother of King Louis XIV of France. As the result of her spending so much of her youth in France, Minette spoke English badly and felt that her real home was France. When the time came for her to travel back there, the infatuated Buckingham obtained permission to accompany the Princess and the Queen Mother on their journey. It was said that he boarded the ship at the last moment without even a change of clothes – and the voyage did not improve from there.

Poor Minette fell seriously ill, and was in grave danger of dying. Buckingham became so distraught at the prospect that his behaviour was described as being that of a 'lunatic',[10] and he became involved in a dispute with Edward Montagu over a game of cards, which almost led to a duel. The Queen Mother became so impatient with the Duke's conduct that while Minette was recovering she ordered him to go on to Paris ahead of them.

Minette and her mother set sail as soon as they were satisfied that she did not have smallpox. When they eventually arrived at their destination Buckingham's behaviour did not improve. He and Minette continued to have conversations together in English, which infuriated her future husband. The Duc complained to his mother, Anne of Austria who, through the Queen Mother, had Charles call him back to England. The order was sent and Buckingham had no option but to depart from his beloved Minette. Observers said he did so only 'after a thousand lingering farewells and renewed protestations of love and devotion'.[11]

As things turned out, perhaps Minette would have been happier married to Buckingham than to her husband, who was reported to be 'monstrous in his vices'.[12] He turned out to be a jealous cross-dresser and claimed that his love for his wife ended two weeks after their wedding.[13]

After this débâcle in France, Buckingham returned home in time for the coronation of Charles II. It was to be a lavish occasion. The crown jewels, destroyed or lost during the Cromwellian era, were replaced at a cost of over £30,000, and Buckingham himself was rumoured to have spent an equal sum on his new clothes for the occasion.[14] An indication of Buckingham's improving relationship with Charles is the fact that he received the honour of carrying the orb in the procession before the new King.

By 1661 relations between the two young men had been repaired. Charles had appointed Buckingham to the position of Gentleman of the Bedchamber, which brought with it an annual pension of £1,000 and allowed him unrivalled access to the King. When the Lord Lieutenant of the West Riding of Yorkshire, Lord Langdale, died in August 1661, Charles named Buckingham as his successor. His arrival in Doncaster as Lord Lieutenant was celebrated with music and feasting. In York the route to his inn was lined by welcoming troopers and the bells and cannon were sounded to greet him. He made Sir John Reresby his Deputy-Lieutenant. Although Sir John liked him, he did remark that Buckingham 'could not be long serious or mind business' and that he 'behaved himself with some insolence towards His Majesty'.[15]

Buckingham's return to royal favour received another boost when in April 1662 he was made a member of the Privy Council. Among its thirty members were Hyde, now Earl of Clarendon, Ormonde, now raised to the title Duke of Ormonde in the Irish peerage, the Duke of York and Secretary of State Nicholas, who was later replaced in his post by Henry Bennet. The Privy Council was responsible to Charles, who had the power to dismiss any of them instantly. The Council members not only worked but also had the right to live at the palace of Whitehall.

Buckingham, of course, because of his close ties with Charles, had many opportunities to exert his influence that were not open to others. Such intimacy, understandably, led to jealousy, which was exacerbated by his great wealth. When, in 1660, Lord Bristol told him that his record during the years of exile did not warrant all that he had received, an argument ensued between the two men. The King confined them both to their lodgings until their desire to duel had passed.

The recent turn of events, by which Buckingham had transformed himself from treacherous deserter of the Royalist cause to reunited friend, shows clearly the value of those childhood years spent with Charles. The King could be angry with him, but could never reject him entirely.

Now that Charles had been restored to the throne, attention turned to the task of finding him a wife and ensuring the succession. After much thought and negotiation, in 1662 Charles's new bride-to-be arrived in England from Portugal. Catherine of Braganza was the daughter of the King of Portugal, and her country, interested in forming an alliance with England, had pushed hard for the match. When Charles first saw Catherine, he is reputed to have said, in a reference to her hairstyle: 'Gentlemen, you have brought me a bat.'[16] His more considered thoughts were: 'Her face was not so exact as to be called a beauty, though her eyes were excellent good, and there was nothing in her face that in the least degree can disgust one.'[17] Pepys's opinion of her was that 'though she be not very charming, yet she hath a good, modest, and innocent look, which is pleasing'.[18]

Catherine was devoutly Catholic and even brought monks with her to keep her within the confines of dogma. To assuage her strong Catholic principles two wedding ceremonies had to be held. The public affair conducted by the Archbishop of Canterbury took place after the private, Catholic one in Catherine's chamber. The dowry promised to Charles was £330,000, various commercial concessions and the trading posts of Bombay and Tangier. Ironically, Bombay was not handed over for some time and a substantial part of the money was not paid either.[19] For his part, Charles had promised 10,000 troops to assist the Portuguese in their war with Spain.

The new queen was only 23 years old and up to this point had led a sheltered and pious life. Her immersion into the world of Charles's court would be difficult. She spoke neither English nor French, and found the atmosphere and culture of the court hard to understand. Worst of all, she would soon discover that she was not to be the sole recipient of her husband's attention.

Seven

COUSIN AND LOVER

Barbara Villiers was Buckingham's first cousin once removed. Her father, William Viscount Grandison, died in the Civil War when she was just a baby and she later had a stepfather. Her desire for wealth had led her at an early age into the world of illicit sexual relationships: at 15 she became involved with Philip Stanhope, Earl of Chesterfield, a relationship she continued even after her marriage to Roger Palmer in 1659, at the age of 18. She wrote to Chesterfield as she lay in danger of death, ill with smallpox:

> . . . there is nothing besides yourself that could make me desire to live a day; and if I am never so happy as to see you more, yet the last words I will say shall be a prayer for your happiness. And so I will live and die loving you above all things . . .[1]

Once the restoration of the monarchy had begun to seem a certainty, many Royalists travelled to the Continent to express their allegiance to Charles. Roger Palmer was one of these, and was accompanied abroad by his young wife. It is no wonder that Charles noticed her, as she was regarded as one of the outstanding beauties of her time. Even Sir Peter Lely, the famous painter, said that her 'sweetness and exquisite beauty are beyond the compass of art'.[2] Images of her became a big seller. Pepys saw some in November 1666 and wanted to buy them immediately. He had to wait some weeks until they were ready, but when he finally acquired them he professed himself quite delighted, and wrote: 'a very fine picture, and like her'.[3]

By the autumn of 1660 Barbara was pregnant and in February 1661 gave birth to a daughter, Anne. Several years later Charles would acknowledge Anne as his own, although her husband claimed her at the time, and many believed that she resembled Chesterfield.

In order to reward Barbara and to make sure she had an official place at court, Charles elevated her husband to the position of Earl of Castlemaine in the Irish peerage. The award stipulated that the title would pass on only to those children of Roger Palmer's who were 'gotten on Barbara Palmer'. Palmer was well aware that this was an award for Barbara and not himself, and consequently preferred not to use the title.

At around the same time as Charles's new queen was arriving in England, Barbara was about to give birth to his child. When the news arrived that a boy had been born and was to be named Charles after his father, the King left his wife at Hampton Court, and went straight to Barbara's side. Roger Palmer was clearly showing some of his anger at being the cuckolded husband when he decided to take the child and have him baptised in the Catholic faith. This was undoubtedly an embarrassment to Charles, who reciprocated by hurriedly organising the boy's christening according to the Anglican rite at St Margaret's Church in Westminster.

Charles's next action was to place Barbara's name, along with the Duchess of Buckingham, on the list of the Queen's Ladies of the Bedchamber.[4] The Queen, who by this time knew all about Barbara, reacted angrily and removed her name from the list. The King, however, was determined not to give up his relationship with Barbara, and so relations between husband and wife grew strained over the issue. He also made matters uncomfortable by bringing Barbara with him into the Queen's presence. At first Catherine nodded a welcome to the woman accompanying her husband, but when she heard the name she burst into tears, got a nose bleed and fainted. As her attendants carried her away, Charles left with his mistress on his arm.

Charles even forced Clarendon, against his wishes, to intercede with the Queen on his behalf. When Clarendon tried to object, Charles made his position very clear by saying; 'whosoever I find to be my Lady Castlemaine's enemy in this matter, I do promise, upon my word, to be his enemy as long as I live'.

In the end, Catherine had to give in, and Barbara, who left her husband, was housed in an apartment at Hampton Court where Charles could visit her any night he pleased. Samuel Pepys wrote of their affair in 1662, saying, 'His dalliance with my Lady Castlemaine being public, every day, to his great reproach'.[5]

Barbara is usually portrayed in history as a conniving, calculating, unfeeling woman, yet there is a story in Pepys's diary for August 1662 that shows the caring side to her nature. As the crowds waited on the banks of the Thames for the arrival of the Queen the following incident occurred:

> . . . there happened a scaffold below to fall, and we feared some hurt, but there was none; but she of all the great ladies only run down among the common rabble to see what hurt was done, and did take care of a child that received some little hurt which me thought was so noble.[6]

In 1663 Barbara converted to Catholicism, which, such was Buckingham's opposition to that religion, may have led to the temporary breakdown in their relationship. She became a central figure at court wielding great influence. The meals held at her apartments became events that politicians, leading courtiers and ambassadors all wanted to attend. In the 1660s she was involved in a plot to have Nicholas, Clarendon and Ormonde removed from their positions. The group of plotters also included the Queen Mother, Henry Bennet, Sir Charles Berkeley, Lord Bristol and Henry Jermyn, Earl of St Albans, and eventually succeeded in persuading the King to remove Nicholas from his position as Secretary of State, to which Bennet was then appointed. The group also did all they could to lessen the influence of Clarendon. As a measure of their success, Clarendon himself alluded to the fact that 'Sir Henry Bennet and his friends have more credit . . .'.[7] But their plans to remove him from power went awry when Lord Bristol made premature allegations against him in Parliament in 1663 and Charles felt obliged to support his Chancellor in public.

During these years Barbara was living the high life. In addition to her apartment at Hampton Court, she had lavish apartments at Whitehall, which were refurbished by the Office of Works in 1666–7. Charles paid for everything from her gambling debts to her jewellery. The word soon spread that if one wanted a position at court, Lady Castlemaine could be a very powerful advocate on your behalf. This advocacy, of course, would necessitate a fee.

Charles was willing to defy his queen and endure all the public gossip and humiliation in order to keep Barbara, whose sexual prowess became legendary. As one writer has put it:

> There is no doubt that Barbara Villiers was a vigorous, sexy, feisty lady and an extremely accomplished high-class prostitute. She had a variety of wiles and techniques with which to please her clients and, according to all the canards written about her, an insatiable desire for her own sexual gratification.[8]

Although the Queen was unable to conceive, despite trips to the healing waters of Tunbridge Wells in 1662 and Bath in 1663, Barbara had no such problems.

Like Charles, Barbara was unfaithful, and her own romantic affairs continued throughout these years. She is believed to have begun a relationship with the actor Charles Hart in revenge for the King's affairs with Nell Gwynn and Moll Davis. Another actor, Cardell Goodman, had fallen so seriously for her that he refused to begin his performance one night until she arrived at the theatre, although the Queen was already sitting in the audience. When the message was sent backstage from the Queen for the performance to begin, he made the comment, 'Damme, I care not if the playhouse be filled with queens from top to bottom. I will not tread the stage until my duchess comes.'[9] Luckily, just then Barbara arrived and the play could begin. Barbara appointed him Gentleman of the Horse and paid him a good allowance to dance attendance upon her.[10] Amazingly, much later, in 1681, Goodman would be accused of planning to poison Barbara and the King's two sons, the Duke of Grafton and the Duke of Northumberland. A man called Alexander Amadei made the accusation that Goodman had tried to persuade him to carry out the deed. Goodman was charged, tried and found guilty of the crime. When he could not pay the fine of £1,000 he was imprisoned in the Marshalsea. Two months later he was freed again under his Majesty's command, Barbara no doubt having used her influence on his behalf.[11]

Another of Barbara's lovers Jacob Hall, the rope dancer, was a performer of 'rare feats of activity and agility of body'. He was capable of 'somersaults and flip-flops, flying over thirty rapiers and over several men's heads, and also flying through several hoops'.[12] William Wycherley, renowned as one of the finest playwrights of the period, also had an affair with Barbara. He even dedicated the printed version of one of his plays to *'Her Grace the Duchess of Cleavland'*. When Charles heard of this affair he became jealous. Finding out from a maid that the couple were together one night at the house of Mrs Knight, the singer, he hastened there early in the morning only to find Wycherley leaving and Barbara still in bed. When he inquired of Barbara her reason for being there, he was told she was performing her devotions for Lent. Charles's retort was, 'Very likely, and that was your confessor I met on the stairs'.[13] It was even rumoured that Buckingham 'openly shared her favours with Charles'.[14]

Barbara was renowned for her temper, and to have an affair with her could be a dangerous enterprise, as the civil servant John Ellis discovered. When he began to boast of his sexual conquest of her she took offence and had him attacked by a gang of thugs and castrated. Pope writes of the event in his *Advice against Adultery or Sober Advice from Horace*:

> What pushed poor Ellis on th'imperial whore?
> 'Twas but to be where Charles had been before.
> The fatal steel unjustly was apply'd,
> When not his lust offended, but his pride:
> Too hard a penance for defeated sin,
> Himself shut out, and Jacob Hall let in.

Towards the end of the 1660s the ostentation of Barbara's glamorous lifestyle and the rumours of her power over the King were beginning to cause a public outcry. In 1668 there were protests and riots against the red-light districts of London, and Barbara, in a way, became the focus of many people's dissatisfaction. In addition, her physical attractiveness was beginning to decline. She had fallen out of favour with her cousin, Buckingham, and both he and Bennet, now Lord Arlington, began to think that it was time she was supplanted in Charles's affections.

Eight

THE NONCONFORMISTS

Under the restored monarchy the Anglican Church once again became the established church. Those from the Protestant Nonconformist community, such as the Puritans, the Baptists and the Quakers, now found themselves being put under extreme pressure to conform to Anglican rites. Under what became known as the Clarendon Code, a number of laws were passed, curtailing the rights of Nonconformists. In August 1662 the Act of Uniformity required all ministers of religion to testify their acceptance of the Book of Common Prayer and renounce the Solemn League and Covenant or be deprived of their ministry. As a result of this piece of legislation thousands of Nonconformist ministers lost their livings in the so-called Great Ejection.

Charles's personal inclination was at variance with Clarendon's in that he would have preferred toleration of the Nonconformists so long as they were peaceful. He even promised one group of Ulster ministers 'protection for their separate religious meetings if they could not accept the episcopalian Church'.[1] He tried, in vain, to introduce a Declaration of Indulgence according to which certain people would have been exempted from the full effects of the Act of Uniformity.

Charles's instincts were right. The heavy-handed approach to Nonconformity had the inevitable result of driving the community towards sedition, insurgency and violence. Pepys, too, had predicted the unrest when he wrote in his diary: '[The Act] will make mad work among the Presbyterian ministers. People of all sides are very much discontented.'[2] In 1661 a Nonconformist group known as the Fifth Monarchists, led by Thomas Venner, had already disrupted London for three days by mounting an insurrection. Although fourteen of their heads were later placed on London Bridge as an example, their action set the scene for Nonconformist discontent in the years to follow.

Buckingham, like Charles, always favoured a policy of toleration towards Nonconformists, as his links with people such as William Penn and Colonel Thomas Blood demonstrated.[3] The Presbyterians in Scotland had believed in his tolerance when they allowed him to remain in Charles's company in the early 1650s.[4] At various times in his life he fought in Parliament for liberty of conscience in matters of religion. But he too was soon feeling the effects of the religious dissatisfaction first hand in Yorkshire. Charles wrote to him in July 1662 to tell him that 'factious meetings' were taking place in Leeds and Wakefield, where people were coming 'from all parts, with dislike to the present Government'. Charles instructed him to 'prevent mischief . . . to suppress all tumultuary and disorderly meetings in those parts, to secure peace, and keep exorbitant people within the bounds of obedience'.[5] In 1663 the first rumours began of what became known as the Rising of Farnley Wood. Rymer and Oates, former Parliamentary officers, were considering, perhaps only vaguely at first, the possibility of a revolt against the new king. They discussed this possibility with two of their former comrades from the Cromwellian years, Colonel Smithson and Colonel Greathead. However, these two colleagues decided to pass on their intelligence to the High Sheriff of Yorkshire, Sir Thomas Gower, who requested that they lead their old friends on further with the design.

Eventually it became known that the plotters had assembled at Farnley Wood, near Pontefract, but as their numbers were small, it was decided that any possible revolt at that time would prove ineffectual, and they dispersed. Although the rising amounted to nothing, such alarm was caused by the assembly that Buckingham, as Lord Lieutenant, was hastily recalled to Yorkshire.

In October 1663 Buckingham wrote to Charles informing him of the situation and telling him that his intelligence indicated that the rebels were about to rise up:[6] 'I do not only believe they have really a designe, but that they are still resolved to make some attempt'.[7] On foot of this he informed the King of his military preparations and requested a commission to raise a regiment of horse.[8] The King ordered Henry Bennet, Secretary of State, to reply to the Duke's letter and to refuse this request.[9]

On 17 October Bennet wrote again telling the Duke that 'His Majesty bids me encourage you to be very severe with the beginners, and to be confident that you shall be avowed therein', and on the 20th of the same month to '. . . cause strict examination to be made of all persons whom you know or suspect to be guilty or contributing to the intended rising that they may be punished by such ordinary or extraordinary course of law as His Majesty shall appoint and they shall appear to have deserved: the originals of which examinations, Your Grace may please to be sent hither by an express, or copies of them, if they come by the ordinary post.'[10]

A number of people were arrested and interrogated. However, when details of these 'examinations' arrived in London, as requested, Bennet was not satisfied with them. He complained that they 'related only to what they (the conspirators) said to one another, without being able to give accompt of the bottom and source of this design'.[11] He ordered that a number of these men be brought to London for further questioning. One prisoner, Mr Walter, had made an agreement with Buckingham that in return for a full pardon he would turn King's evidence. It was agreed that he would be examined by none other than Charles himself. But Bennet expressed the desire that he be 'more ingenious and more particular than he had been'.[12] The result of all this was that about twenty of the plotters were eventually executed.

The plots, suspected plots, suspicions and fears continued, with information crossing from all parts of the country regarding the alleged activities of the Nonconformists. In November 1663 there were even rumours that a group including Lieutenant-Colonel Mason was planning to assassinate Buckingham.[13]

Information sent to Buckingham from John Dickson on 7 March 1664 is typical of the type of material being received about the activities of Nonconformists:

> They begin to revive in the West of England, and have thoughts of setting the city on fire. This is Quakers' intelligence, which came from the city into Yorkshire . . . The time will probably be the opening of Parliament, or beginning of the term, when people resort to the city; if the Anabaptists and Fifth-Monarchy men are cared for, all will be prevented, the other sects being but few.[14]

Radical Nonconformity was to prove a problem throughout Charles's reign. Hardcore groups unwilling to accept the limitations being placed upon their religious freedoms were constantly engaged in plotting to overthrow the government. The fear of such groups reached levels of hysteria at times, with much of the information circulated being of an entirely spurious nature. The weakness of the Radicals was their inability to unite into one focused group, which not only made them ineffective militarily but also very difficult to negotiate with.

Despite his efforts to put down insurrection in Yorkshire, Buckingham continued to urge Charles to allow the Nonconformists religious toleration. In fact, his own desire for toleration was often regarded as support of Nonconformist radicalism, and he was frequently suspected of actively encouraging their actions. There is no denying that he had close links with people from the radical community, people such as John Wildman, the ex-Leveller, who was a known radical and whom the Duke employed as his legal adviser and trustee; and Thomas Blood, one of the most infamous rebels of the era. In this way, the actual and potential unrest in the North Riding had been good for him. It had allowed him to portray himself as anti-radical. This is why many believed that, for his own ends, he had capitalised on what was, in reality, no more than a minor failed plot and deliberately made it look like something much more serious. As for Charles, the fact that he refused Buckingham the commission to raise a horse regiment may indicate that he was aware that the Duke was exaggerating the danger.

Charles's own favoured approach to the problem of Nonconformity was one of conciliation in return for political obedience. He tried on a number of occasions to grant the Nonconformists freedom of worship under his Declarations of Indulgence. However, this policy ultimately proved politically impossible to implement, and under pressure from Parliament, he was never permitted to give it a fair testing – in fact, he was forced, instead, to go against his own instincts and introduce repressive legislation such as the Act of Uniformity.

Nine

THE MERRY COURT OF ROMANCE
AND LEISURE

The court of the Merry Monarch has became renowned for its exuberance, informal gaiety and sexual promiscuity. The tone of the court was, in many ways, a backlash against the years of deprivation suffered by Charles and his supporters in exile. Charles led the way himself, which did not please a traditionalist like Clarendon, who said of the King that 'the same affections continue still, the same laziness and unconcernedness in business, and a proportionable abatement of reputation'.[1]

Apart from Charles's more serious illicit relationships with women such as Barbara, there were also many frivolous dalliances throughout the years. There was a fling with Winifred Wells, who became a maid of honour to the Queen in 1662 and about whom Buckingham wrote a bawdy poem in French.[2] It was said that Winifred had actually given birth to a baby while dancing at court. Among many others were Jane Roberts, the daughter of a clergyman, the singer Mrs Knight and Mary Killigrew.[3]

Buckingham and Charles both fell in love with the beauty Frances Stuart, or *'La Belle Stuart'* as she was known. Buckingham's initial actions in befriending Frances may have been an attempt to ingratiate himself with Charles, but he soon fell in love with her himself. Frances was a renowned beauty at court and it was well known that the King had become infatuated with her. She was a Scotswoman who had been forced into exile with her family during the Civil War, and had been educated in France. She was sent over to Charles's court by his sister, Minette, to be maid of honour to the Queen. Minette described her as 'the prettiest girl in the world, and one of the best fitted of any I know to adorn your Court'.[4] The fact that Henrietta emphasised Frances's great beauty lends credence to the conjecture that she may have been part of a plan to lure Charles away from the bounty that was Barbara.

Pepys, a great admirer of Barbara's beauty, also remarked on Frances, writing, 'the greatest beauty I ever saw, I think, in my life; and, if ever woman can, do exceed my Lady Castlemaine, at least in this dress'. He also predicted Charles's change in affections: 'nor do I wonder if the King changes, which I verily believe is the reason of his coldness to my Lady Castlemaine'.[5]

Frances became very fond of Buckingham and in particular enjoyed his sense of humour – so much so that if he failed to arrive at her apartment on any particular evening, she would send for him.[6] Buckingham entertained her with his stories and songs, while her childish desire for amusement found pleasure in the high card-castles he built for her. He also entertained all present with his funny imitations of Clarendon or Arlington or some other unfortunate victim. However, when the Duke decided to declare his love for Frances, she felt compelled to reject him 'with so severe a repulse that he abandoned, at once, all his designs upon her'.[7] This brought their friendship to an abrupt end.

Nor did relations between Charles and Frances run smoothly. Frances rebuffed all his enticements to physical intimacy, which, as is often the way, only served to deepen his desire for her even more. Barbara, ever devious, decided that rather than denounce her new young rival, she would help to lure her into a sexual encounter with Charles. Perhaps she believed that no matter how beautiful she was, Frances could not hope to compete with her in experience or performance, and that Charles may well find the whole episode something of an anticlimax. Barbara may also have been keen to distract the King so that she could enjoy romantic relations with her latest conquest, Henry Jermyn, nephew of the Earl of St Albans. Whatever the motive, she brought Frances to her apartment where Charles could flirt and cavort freely with the young girl.

Pepys writes of a bizarre mock wedding ceremony organised by Barbara in which she played the groom and Frances the bride: 'Married they were, with ring and all other ceremonies of church service . . . but, in the close, it is said that my Lady Castlemaine . . . rose, and the king came and took her place.'[8] He was aware of the reason for the play-acting: 'it was in order to the King's coming to Stuart, as is believed generally'.[9] Barbara brought Frances to sleep in her bed and Charles arrived to join them there. But still, Frances refused to relent. As none of these ploys worked and the resistance was only making Charles desire Frances more ardently, Barbara grew impatient and banned her from coming to her apartment any more.

Towards the end of 1663 Pepys heard that Buckingham, the Duchess of Buckingham, Edward Montagu and Arlington had decided to work together in order to contrive to get Frances to submit to the King's desires.[10] Buckingham and the Duchess had organised a dinner for the royal couple at Wallingford House in July 1663 to which Frances was invited, but not Barbara. The plan came to nothing, however, because after the dinner Charles went straight to Barbara's lodgings, where he spent the night.[11] A ball was then arranged in order to bring Frances and Charles together, but when the Queen arrived at three o'clock in the morning, tipped off by none other than Barbara, the King went home with his wife.[12]

Once, in Frances's presence, the French Ambassador asked whether he might see the legs that Charles had once declared to be the most beautiful in the world. The ambassador may have been suitably impressed when she exposed them to the knee, but the Duke of York, who was also present, commented he thought them too slender.[13] For all the interest paid to her by Buckingham and Charles, Frances managed to keep her virtue intact. Although Pepys did see her and the King kissing openly in palace corridors, Charles, like Buckingham, never managed to physically consummate his love for her. Aided and abetted by the Queen Mother, her own mother and others, Frances may well have been attempting to play a more important political game than simply becoming a well-provided-for mistress of either Buckingham or the King. Pepys certainly seems to have thought so when he wrote: 'she proves a cunning slut, and is advised . . . by the queen mother and by her mother'.[14] Frances's real aim may have been to encourage Charles to divorce Catherine and to become queen herself.

Indeed, if that was the plan, the Queen's sudden and very serious illness in October 1663 seemed to make the chance of Frances becoming queen a distinct possibility. In a letter sent to Buckingham that October, Henry Bennet tells Buckingham that 'The Queen's fever continues, but she rested last night without cordials.'[15] But his wife's sufferings during this period of illness only drew Charles closer to her, especially since her concerns during what could have been her final days of life were only for his happiness; she urged him to marry someone, after her death, who could make him happier and could give him an heir. Eventually, however, the Queen made a full recovery and yet Charles's affection for Frances continued, as the poetry he wrote for her demonstrates, and as does the fact that he used her image as the profile of Britannia on a gold medal in 1666 and on coins in 1672.[16]

When Barbara heard rumours that Frances was 'seeing' another Charles Stuart, the Duke of Richmond and Lennox, a hard-drinking man who had already buried two wives, she bribed the Keeper of the King's Closet or Privy Stairs to let her know the next time that Richmond paid Frances a visit. When he did so, she made sure that Charles went to Frances's room to find the couple in a compromising situation. Under a torrent of abuse from the King, Richmond backed away coyly. Although Charles was furious he still didn't want to lose Frances. He got Clarendon to check out Richmond's financial situation and offered to promote Frances to the rank of duchess, and went so far as to discuss with Archbishop Sheldon the possibility of divorcing the Queen.[17]

It was all to no avail: as Frances had made up her mind. At the end of March 1667 she crept away from Whitehall and married the Duke of Richmond. When Charles found out he was so upset that he vowed never to see her again. He even resisted Minette's pleading of her case, writing to her:

> I do assure you that I am very much troubled that I cannot in everything give you that satisfaction I could wish, especially in this business of the Duchess of Richmond wherein you may think me ill natured, but if you consider how hard a thing it is to swallow an injury done by a person I had so much tenderness for, you will know my good nature enough to believe that I could not be so severe if I had not great provocation . . .[18]

In 1668 Frances became ill with smallpox. Pepys remarked that 'She is . . . mighty full of the smallpox, by which all do conclude that she will be wholly spoiled'. On hearing this news, Charles relented and went to see her. The visit brought about a reconciliation between the two after a period of twelve months apart. He wrote to Minette of the visit:

> . . . I was at the Duchess of Richmond's who, you know, I have not seen this twelve months . . . She is not much marked by the small pox, and I must confess this last affliction made me pardon all that is past, and can not hinder myself from wishing her very well . . .[19]

Frances was made a Lady of the Queen's Bedchamber in 1668, and along with the Duchess of Buckingham became one of the Queen's most trusted friends. At Charles's bidding, her husband was posted as ambassador to Denmark in 1672, but he continued his heavy drinking and died the same year. The potential problem for Frances of her late husband's debts was avoided by the King's granting her an annual pension. She never married again and remained close to Charles until his death. Charles never fully forgave Clarendon, however, whom he felt had not done enough to assist him in preventing Frances's marriage. The affair played a part in souring their relationship, much to Clarendon's disadvantage later on.

Nell Gwynn was another of Charles's mistresses who enjoyed good relations with Buckingham. Charles had first been attracted to her when he saw her performing with the King's Company when she was 18 years old, and she was probably introduced to him by Buckingham.[20] Nell came from very humble origins, being brought up in 'a brothel, to fill strong waters to the gentlemen'.[21] She later worked selling oranges and other favours to the audience of the Theatre Royal, until eventually making it on to the stage. The 'bold merry slut', as Pepys called her, was known to refer to Charles as Charles the Third, coming third in line for her after the actor Charles Hart and Charles, Lord Buckhurst.

Buckingham admired Nell's abilities to woo the crowd on stage. He refers to this quality in the epilogue to his own play, *The Chances*, when he writes of the times when playwrights believed that the applause she was receiving was for themselves:

> Some of his fellows, who have writ before,
> When Nell has danc'd her jig, steal to the door,
> Hear the pit clap and conceit of that
> Swell, and believe themselves the Lord knows what.

Nell became a good friend of Buckingham and often, when the Duke was having difficulties with Charles, acted as an intermediary between them. However, on one occasion, when Buckingham became too familiar with her in Charles's presence, Nell boxed his ears. It is possible that Buckingham too enjoyed intimate sexual relations with her.[22] Nell gave birth to Charles's son, christened Charles, in 1670. Like another of

Charles's mistresses, Moll Davis, Nell was a common woman whose status was raised by her royal association. She was given a house initially in Lincoln's Inn Fields and later in Pall Mall, while Moll also had a house near Pall Mall. But, unlike someone of Barbara's social rank, they were denied rooms at Whitehall, and noble titles.

Apart from the romantic love and sexual activity at court, there was also much entertainment and fun to be had. Buckingham enjoyed a closeness to the King experienced by very few others. He was a leading figure among the humorous and often outrageous characters who frequented Charles's court. Arlington once wrote to Ormonde: 'I was going into the country to pass my Christmas at my Lord Crofts', and 'when I tell you that the Duke of Bucks and George Porter were there you will not doubt but we passed it merrily.'[23] James, Duke of York, would later attribute Charles's fondness for Buckingham to the Duke's conversation and humour.[24] Along with Buckingham the court abounded in literary figures, politicians and wits, men such as John Wilmot, Charles Sedley, Charles Sackville, George Etherege and William Wycherly.

With the presence of all these characters it is no wonder that there are many riotous stories about the happenings at court during these years. There is the tale, for instance, of Lady Muskerry who loved to dance, and who arrived at one of the Queen's parties intending to do so.[25] But she was pregnant, and seemed to be carrying the child more to one side than the other. To rectify this her friends placed a cushion inside her dress to 'balance her up' as she danced. Unfortunately, and somewhat predictably, the cushion soon fell out. It was then picked up by Buckingham who ran around the room holding the cushion carefully in his arms, imitating the crying sounds of a baby and searching for a nurse to care for the new child.

One of Buckingham's closest friends among the wits at court was the poet John Wilmot, 2nd Earl of Rochester and son of Henry Wilmot, who had been one of Charles's closest advisers. Rochester had first arrived at court in 1664 at the age of 17, and soon gained a reputation as a notorious rogue. The Count de Grammont recorded many of his pranks and Burnet tells us that Rochester himself admitted that at one period in his life he was never sober.[26] It is no surprise that Buckingham liked him. He writes to him in a letter dated 19 August 1674: 'I do assure your Lordship that I heartily love you, and shall do so till the last minute of my life.'[27]

There is a story told by St Evrémond which, if there is any truth in it, must go down as one of Buckingham and Rochester's more evil escapades.[28] The episode may have more to do with the reputations of these two aristocratic rogues than with any actual events, but it does say something about their standing in the popular imagination. The account holds that it all happened during one of Buckingham's periods of estrangement from court, when, for some reason, probably just for the novelty of it, he and Rochester decided to become landlords of an inn, the Green Mare, on the Newmarket Road. As the husbands drank their nightly fill of alcohol at the inn Buckingham and Rochester spent their time trying to seduce the wives.

They became intrigued by one particular man, a Puritan, who came every night on his own leaving his wife at home in the care of his elderly sister. One particular night, while Buckingham plied the man with more drink than usual, Rochester dressed himself up as a woman and paid a visit to the man's home. When the man's old sister answered the door, Rochester told her that he had been sent from the inn with a bottle for her pleasure. Rochester then feigned illness and let the unfortunate women help him to a bed. He soon had the sister unconscious with the aid of opiates and alcohol, and began to engage the wife, Phyllis, in conversation. It wasn't long before, under the influence of alcohol, Phyllis was openly criticising her husband for keeping her locked up at home all the time and for being too old to satisfy her sexual needs. Rochester then revealed to her that he was in fact a man in disguise. They made love before taking the man's savings and heading for the inn. On the way they were forced to lie down in a field to avoid the husband whom they saw returning home – they took this opportunity to make love once again. According to the highly dubious details of this story, on reaching the inn it was Buckingham's turn to go to bed with the woman. Soon, however, Buckingham and Rochester tired of their adventure and sent the woman to London to find a new husband. The unfortunate husband, meanwhile, finding his wife and his life's savings gone, hanged himself.

When choosing employees it seems that Buckingham looked for character traits that made him feel comfortable, since many of his servants were as troublesome as himself. In 1662 his porter, Thomas Fauster, was reported to have said that he hoped soon to trample in bishops' and king's blood, and said he could raise 2,000 or 3,000 men in that account.[29] In 1663 his servants 'fought a set battle in his courtyard' in which many of them were hurt and his porter, it was believed, would not survive.[30] One of his pages eloped 'with a rich young lady of quality'.

In fact, the Duke's life could easily have ended at the hands of one of his servants. In 1663 his steward's valet, Abraham Goodman, planned to kill him as he slept. The story is recounted by Monsieur de Comminges:

. . . carrying a sword, he left his room, to the astonishment of another fellow who slept with him. The latter enquired where he was going and what he meant to do with the weapon. He answered, that he had heard a cry of 'thief,' and that he was following the direction of the noise. He continued his journey to the Duke's chamber thinking to find him in bed, but failing to do so, he passed on to the Duchess's apartment. At the door was a servitor, who seeing him with a naked sword in his hand, was coward enough to save his own life by flight, leaving his master in danger. With the blade still in his hand he entered. The four attendants, of whom one only was armed, instantly ran away. The Duke, who was talking with his wife by the chimney-corner, rose and asked him what he sought in such a state. He replied, 'It is thou that I seek! It is thou I will have!' At these words, the Duke seized a knife from the table and was fortunate enough to disarm him. The man was clearly raving mad, and as the Duke tried to reach the door and call a servant, the unhappy wretch essayed once more to lay hold of his master and stab him with a knife he had in his pocket. In this he would undoubtedly have been successful, had not a scream from the Duchess warned her husband in the nick of time of his fresh danger. [31]

Comminges uses this story to warn of the dangers of living in England:

From this, Monsieur, you can judge of what England is. When I reflect that this land produces neither wolves nor venomous beasts, I am not surprised. The inhabitants are far more wicked and more dangerous than these vermin, and if one had to guard against every possible ill that might befall, it were better to leave the country forthwith.[32]

Abraham Goodman found himself committed to the Tower after this attack on his master. He wrote the following apologetic words to the Duke from the dungeon of the Tower on 4 April 1663:

It is my hard hap to be held a prisoner by Your Grace's command for attempting to murder Your Grace, which I call God to witness for me that I had not such intent in me neither by the persuasion of any other person. But, only what I did was to inform Your Grace I was hated by your servants for being so strict of my charge committed to me, and if through ignorance I have offended Your Grace, I hope Your Grace will forgive me.[33]

But Goodman was neither forgiven nor released. In fact, after spending a number of years in prison, he was hanged on a charge of plotting the King's death from there. Not all Buckingham's employees were engaged in such scurrilous pursuits, however. In 1672 there was a report of one of his servants winning a foot race in Newmarket against a man from Cheshire.[34]

Apart from their concern with affairs of state and the pursuit of enjoyment, Buckingham and Charles also found time to indulge in a number of other interests. They had always shared a fascination with the exciting new world of science. Charles had a special room at Whitehall where he kept all his maps, clocks and models and in his bedroom alone he had seven clocks.[35] His desire for 'a lunar globe, with the hills, eminences and cavities of the moon's surfaces as well as the degree of whiteness solidly moulded' is recorded.[36] His interest in the drawing up of star charts in order to help with navigation at sea led to his setting up the Observatory at Greenwich and appointing John Flamsteed as the first Astronomical Observator.[37]

Buckingham, with a number of others, set up the Society for the Improvement of Natural Knowledge among whose members were people such as John Dryden, John Evelyn and Abraham Cowley. When the Royal Society was established in 1660 to promote scientific research, both Charles and Buckingham were involved, Charles as sponsor (he was named as 'Founder'), while Buckingham became one of its first members. There is even a story that Buckingham once presented the Society with a piece of unicorn's horn, which was duly tested,[38] but since the test consisted of making a circle with powder made from a crushed piece of the horn, and placing a spider in the centre of the circle to see if it could escape, it is no wonder that the results were inconclusive. Buckingham also built a laboratory in which he conducted all kinds of scientific experiments, including, it was said, attempts to discover the philosopher's stone.

Buckingham's interest in science turned into a practical pursuit when he became involved in the manufacture of glass. He set up one glass-works just to the north of the Spring Garden in Vauxhall, and another at Greenwich, employing a chemist at a cost of £20,000, who is said to have developed a new method of making flint glass; in 1663 Buckingham had his patent renewed for 'making crystal looking glasses, coach glasses, etc.'[39] He also brought in a company of Venetian craftsmen. In September 1676 John Evelyn visited one of Buckingham's factories where he witnessed the manufacture of 'huge vases of metall as cleare, ponderous, and thicke as crystal; also looking-glasses far larger and better than any that come from Venice'.[40]

The glass produced was used in all manner of items, including spectacles, lenses and mirrors. Buckingham even managed to get Parliament to prohibit the importation of these items from abroad. According to the Venetian Ambassador, Buckingham's glassworks were severely affecting the glass trade in Venice.[41] Despite these protestations, in April 1666 a warrant was issued to the Commissioners of Ordinance to deliver to him '50 bags of saltpetre, to prevent interruption and cost in the glass works lately set up at his expense'.[42]

One assumes that Buckingham's experience of manufacturing was considered when he was appointed a member of a committee set up to report on the petition of George Herriot. Herriot requested a patent for fourteen years to practise the art of cold pressing cloth, a practice he had seen in Holland. The petition was granted, as the committee felt it would 'be an encouragement to other ingenious inventions'.[43]

Both Buckingham and Charles shared a great interest in the theatre. Charles's mother had been a lover of the stage and had enjoyed taking an active part in performances held at court. It was an interest he had maintained during his years of exile, paying particular attention to the work of the French playwrights. Meanwhile, in contrast, from 1642 stage plays in England had been essentially banned under the Puritans. No wonder then that once Charles assumed the throne, he was keen to lend his support to the development of public theatre in England.

Two men were significant in this redevelopment of the English theatre. William Davenant, who had stood almost alone in gaining permission to stage performances during the Cromwellian years, now stepped forward to offer his skills to the Restoration stage. He established a troupe in Lincoln's Inn Fields under the patronage of the

Duke of York. Another troupe, called the King's Men, was established by Thomas Killigrew and performed at the Theatre Royal.

In addition to the revival of works by masters such as Shakespeare and Jonson, new material was needed for the Restoration stage. Buckingham himself began to write. His first enterprise in the theatre consisted of an adaptation of a play by John Fletcher called *The Chances*. Fletcher had originally written the play around 1617, adapting it from Cervantes' novella, *La Señora Cornelia*. The play deals with the intended elopement of the Duke of Ferrara with the sister of the Governor, Constantia, and the 'chances' or coincidences that thwart their love. Buckingham added two new acts, developed the plot and altered, removed and created some new characters. By doing so he managed to increase the level of farce and comedy.

The production, staged in London in January 1667, was a big success. Samuel Pepys's mistress, Mrs Knipp, played a role in the play, along with Charles Hart. Pepys went to see the performance and enjoyed it:

> To the King's house, to see *The Chances*. A good play I find it, and the actors most good in it; and pretty to hear Knipp sing in the play very properly, 'all night I weep'; and sang it admirably. The whole play pleases me well; and most of all, the sight of many fine ladies . . .[44]

In 1672 Dryden also praised Buckingham's work, saying that one of the characters, Don John, was now 'maintained with much more vigour in the fourth and fifth acts than it was by Fletcher in the three former'.[45]

Another art much enjoyed by Buckingham and Charles was music. Charles was influential in having music introduced to the English theatre and for the introduction of the violin into English church music, a development that did not please traditionalists. His years in exile had given him a particular love of French instrumental music, and he was not averse to singing a part in an Italian opera from time to time. Charles enjoyed close relations with the composer Henry Purcell, who wrote a number of pieces in his honour. Buckingham played the violin, composed music and even maintained his own string quartet.

The fact that Charles and Buckingham had Newcastle, an expert on horses, as their governor in childhood meant that they both shared an interest in equestrian activities and became owners and breeders of fine horses. Charles is recognised as the person who made Newmarket a famous horse-racing venue. His favourite and rather unusual way of watching a race was to wait half-way around the course on horseback, and then finish the race beside the runners. At other times he actually took part in the race. Newcastle said of him: 'No man makes a horse go better than I have seen some go under his Majesty'.[46] Buckingham and the King enjoyed many memorable race meetings together. The Duke bred and owned many winning racehorses himself and is believed to have been the founder of the first fox-hunting group in England.[47]

The relationship between Buckingham and Charles was founded on a shared upbringing, companionship during their years of exile and the fact that they both regarded King Charles I as a father figure. But these were not the only reasons for their closeness. Charles's brother, James, Duke of York, also shared these experiences but never enjoyed the same closeness to the King as Buckingham did. Charles and James were too different in character for their relationship to be close. Buckingham and Charles were friends because they felt comfortable together – they were alike in many ways, sharing the same interests, laughing at the same jokes. Charles always found Buckingham's sense of humour and his ability to imitate people greatly amusing. At a gathering the Duke could always be relied upon to entertain people by telling a funny story, doing an imitation or playing the violin. He did not possess the stuffiness or sense of moral righteousness of someone like the Chancellor, Clarendon, a quality which Charles found so distasteful. Charles preferred those in his company to be lively, interesting, entertaining and fun, which is why he liked having Buckingham around. This meant that he could never remain estranged from him for long, and no matter what the Duke did, Charles always welcomed him back to court.

Ten

THE SECOND DUTCH WAR

The Second Dutch War was primarily a conflict about world trade. The Dutch were enjoying a dominance in trade which the English wanted to bring to an end by taking over the Dutch trade routes. Hostilities had been simmering for some time. Under a treaty of 1662 Dutch ships were obliged to salute the British flag first, which caused resentment since in most cases they did not receive a salute in return. There was a desire for war among the people and Parliament of England. James, Duke of York, who was Lord High Admiral, was very eager for war and he was supported in this desire by a group of like-minded young men. They imagined that a victory would be quickly secured. Charles, on the other hand, would have preferred to avoid war and settle matters by diplomacy instead. He wrote to his sister Minette in September 1664: 'except myself I believe there is scarce an Englishman that does not desire passionately a war with them.'[1] Samuel Pepys, as Clerk of the Acts of the Navy, knowing the state of readiness of the navy, was also worried about the prospect of war: 'all the news now is what will become of the Dutch business, whether war or peace. We all seem to desire it, as thinking ourselves to have advantages at present over them; but for my part I dread it.'[2]

Preceded by tensions and minor incidents, the war eventually broke out in 1665. Buckingham was anxious to be involved from the beginning and requested the command of a ship: this request was turned down by the Duke of York, who was no admirer of his – in fact, married to Clarendon's daughter, Anne Hyde, he was perhaps encouraged by his father-in-law to thwart Buckingham's desires. The Earl of Peterborough reports seeing Buckingham around this time and says that he was 'not in the esteem a great man should be'.[3] Buckingham was indeed extremely disgruntled by the treatment he had received, but he was still determined to take part in the war. He declared that he would go instead as a volunteer on board a flagship.

Buckingham then demanded that he be involved in all councils of war as he was, after all, a member of the Privy Council. This request too was refused by James. On hearing of this rejection Buckingham angrily left the fleet and rushed to Charles to state his grievance. James had guessed that this would be the Duke's next move, and knowing the influence that Buckingham was able to exert on Charles, decided to pre-empt him. He sent Harry Killigrew to the King with letters, making sure he arrived before Buckingham.[4] In fact, Killigrew got there six hours ahead of him, which meant that by the time Buckingham arrived Charles was prepared and had already been briefed about the controversy. He informed Buckingham that these matters were the responsibility of the Lord High Admiral and that he would not interfere.

Frustrated, Buckingham knew that he was defeated and decided to return to the fleet and 'thrust himself as volunteer on the Earl of Sandwich's ship, to the dislike of everyone'.[5] No one was in any doubt about his feelings on how he had been treated. The Earl of Peterborough reported in April that his 'fickleness gives great scandal'.[6]

In June 1666 Buckingham saw action in a battle made famous by Dryden's poem *Annus Mirabilis*. George Monk, now the Duke of Albemarle, decided to engage the numerically superior Dutch on sighting the enemy off the North Foreland. Buckingham noticed that as Albemarle rallied the sailors, he had slipped a loaded pistol into his pocket – Buckingham was convinced that he was determined to destroy the ship and die rather than surrender. For his part, Buckingham says that he and some others had agreed that they would throw the Admiral overboard if it came to that![7] Luckily this mutinous course of action was averted, firstly by the arrival of reinforcements in the form of Prince Rupert, and secondly by the fog, which caused the fleets to separate.

While Buckingham was away from his post of Lord Lieutenant in York, William Coventry became concerned about the militia in the West Riding reporting that they were 'very unsettled' and stating that they needed officers. He was loath to interfere while Buckingham was away, being aware that the Duke would be 'ready to take offence if anything be done in his sphere', but all the same recognising that 'ceremonies must not be stuck at'.

Perhaps by this time Buckingham had had enough of sea warfare for a while, because although the fleet put to sea once again on 25 June, we find that he had returned to York.[8] As soon as he arrived home he got busy making preparations for a possible invading army: 'the Duke of Buckingham has issued warrants to the chief constables to watch the beacons, and on their firing, every man between 16 and 60 is to appear at the rendezvous for the hundred, with his best arms, to be directed by the deputy lieutenants'.[9] A few months later he was praised by one writer for the preparation of his men: 'The Duke of Buckingham's prudent management has made all sorts of persons in the city and country show the greatest readiness to serve'.[10]

Even during these months of war Buckingham did not neglect his social life. In August 1665 Buckingham and the Duchess met the King in Leicester.[11] In December of the same year Arlington wrote telling the King that Buckingham was 'in warm country dances' with the King's son, the Duke of Monmouth.[12] In July of the following year he and the Duchess dined at the house of the Governor of Hull accompanied by 'the earls of Shrewsbury and Cardigan, Lord Brudenell, their ladies and other persons of quality'.[13]

Things were not going well for England. In 1665, the country had been ravaged by the plague, which caused more than 70,000 deaths in London. In January 1666 both France and Denmark threw in their lot with the Dutch and declared war on England. In the summer of the same year the English lost a major battle against the Dutch. In September the Great Fire of London brought more destruction and loss of life. As soon as news of the fire reached Yorkshire, Buckingham went to Charles. Before he left, he sent a letter to his Deputy-Lieutenants informing them of the news and giving them their orders. It is clear from this letter that he believed the fire to be the work of arsonists and the possible first move in a more widespread attack:

Gentlemen, – A servant of my own is sent to me from London to let me know, that in all probability before I could receive the letter the whole city of London within the walls would be in ashes. This messenger told me that before he came away, he saw all Cheapside and Pauls Church on fire. Thames Street and all that part of the Town had been burnt before. Since that, another man is come from London that assures me Holborne is also set on fire, and that about threescore French and Dutch are taken, that were firing of houses; besides this week, the posts are stopped, which must either proceed from the burning of the Post Office, or from some insurrection in those parts, it being almost impossible that a thing of this nature could be effected without a further design. I am going myself immediately to His Majesty, as my duty obliges me, in the meantime I have sent this to let you know the state of our affairs, and in case you receive no letters from London at the time that you ought to receive them, by the post on Saturday night next, that you immediately summon all the Militia under my command to be in arms with all the speed imaginable, and to keep them together till further order from me or from His Majesty. If I find upon my way to London, or when I am there, reason to alter this order, I shall dispatch one immediately to you about it, in the meantime I desire you to acquaint the Lords and Deputy Lieutenants of the East and North Riding of Yorkshire with what orders I have sent you, and I do not doubt but they will follow your example, – I am, Gentlemen, Your most affectionate friend and servant,

Buckingham.

Since the writing of this letter a Gentleman is come from London that assures me almost all the Strand is burnt, and that a great many Anabaptists have been taken setting houses on fire, as well as French and Dutch.[14]

In June 1667 the country suffered the ignominy of having the Dutch Admiral, de Ruyter, sail his ships up the Medway, where he inflicted severe damage on the English fleet and patrolled the mouth of the river for a number of weeks. Three ships were burned: the *Royal Oak*, the *Loyal London* and the *Royal James*. The English flagship, the *Royal Charles*, was abandoned by its crew and towed back to the Netherlands by the enemy. All of this, of course, spread panic throughout the city and was very damaging to national pride.

The costly Second Dutch War was officially brought to an end by the signing of the Treaty of Breda in July 1667. The war had been a failure from the English point of view, and in the inevitable course of events, someone would have to shoulder the responsibility. Ultimately, the blame would fall upon Clarendon, even though he was one of those who had opposed the war.

For Buckingham, the King's refusal to appoint him to a position of responsibility reminded him of the way he had been treated back in 1651 when he had wanted to command the forces against Cromwell's army and had been similarly rejected. Once again he felt angry and frustrated, and would become a main critic in Parliament of the way in which the war had been handled. The fact that Charles had rejected his friend twice in similar circumstances indicates that, as much as he liked him, he doubted his suitability for command. This period marked a low point in their relationship, but worse was to come.

Eleven

THE HEYDON AFFAIR

Towards the end of the 1660s relations between Buckingham and Charles were disintegrating. Buckingham was understandably disgruntled about the way he had been treated by Charles and James during the Dutch War and was, in general terms, frustrated that he had not reached the high levels of political success that might have been expected. After all, his father had risen from being a lowly courtier to become Lord High Admiral and had been, after the King, arguably the most powerful man in the land.

In the autumn of 1666 Buckingham became one of the government's harshest critics in Parliament. He actively supported the Irish Cattle Bill, which was introduced with the intention of putting a ban on the importation of Irish cattle into England. English landlords had protested for some time about Irish cattle flooding on to the market and affecting both prices and rents. Clarendon, Ormonde and Charles were all opposed to the bill. Buckingham supported it both because it was popular and because he viewed it as an opportunity to make things difficult for Ormonde, such would be its economic effects on Ireland. Charles, who did not want to lose the revenue that resulted from the trade, was very annoyed by Buckingham's passionate support for the bill.

Arlington had warned Ormonde in a letter written in September 1666 that 'By all the observation we can make, from discourses in the country, the Members of Parliament are likely to come up fully bent to press his Majesty to a total prohibition of importing Irish Cattle.'[1] Similar news was coming from Lord Coventry who said: 'There is no doubt that the Irish Cattle Bill will have a speedy passage in the House of Commons, and, as the writer believes, no hard one in the Lord's House also. If resisted by the King, it would be the greatest dissatisfaction to the Parliament that can be imagined. Is sorry to tell his Grace such ill news; but undoubtedly this is the truth'.[2] They were right. The bill passed through the lower house with a firm majority. It was a defeat for Charles.

In the beginning of October Buckingham again showed his new eagerness for parliamentary work when he was given leave by the House of Lords to draw up a bill that would make death the punishment for anyone caught cheating or abusing 'in the revenue'. The bill came to nothing but it did draw attention to the Duke, especially among those who were opposed to the government. Sir Thomas Clifford wrote that he was 'hard at it . . . having nothing else in his head'.[3]

Buckingham continued to show great interest in the Irish Cattle Bill as it was debated in the House of Lords, attending almost every day of the session. Matters grew heated during a committee stage in Parliament when Buckingham made the remark that whoever was against it had either 'an Irish interest or an Irish understanding'. Ormonde's son, Lord Ossory, took this as a personal slight to his family and a reflection 'upon the whole Irish nation'. As a result, he challenged Buckingham to a duel at Chelsea Fields.

Accounts of what happened next differ. According to one version, Ossory arrived at Chelsea Fields at the appointed time and waited in vain for three hours for the arrival of his opponent. Buckingham, it seems, had no intention of allowing Ossory to satisfy his honour by running him through with a sword, and had instead gone straight to Charles, informing him of the incident. Guards were sent to Chelsea Fields with a royal warrant to arrest Lord Ossory, who was held for a time but eventually released.

The following morning Buckingham made a speech to the House of Lords wherein he informed the members of Ossory's challenge to him.

He stated that he had waited for Ossory to arrive at the agreed place until he was ordered to leave by a gentleman who had been sent by the King. Ossory, for his part, informed the house that his challenge had not been made because of Buckingham's comments in the House but 'concerning other matters out of the House'.[4]

Arlington, Ossory's brother-in-law and an enemy of Buckingham's, made an account of the proceedings in a letter to Ormonde. He said that Buckingham had spoken:

> very ineffectually, speaking much and often upon the subject matter, but often digressing from it, by endeavouring to show it was not his fault that they had not met; this obliged my lord of Ossory to make a narrative to the House of what passed in the whole quarrel, and my lord of Buckingham pressing the House to ask him what had been the subject of his quarrel, said it was some sharp railleries and unhandsome reflections the Duke had made upon his relations, and called me for a witness, how often he had resented them, and resolved to fight him. I said it was most true, and that I had ever interposed to moderate him therein, having till this occasion been ever an humble servant to the Duke of Buckingham, and for proof of this, humbly besought His Royal Highness to declare whether many weeks ago, I told him I feared much a quarrel betwixt my lord of Ossory and the Duke of Buckingham, upon the occasion aforesaid; His Royal Highness frankly avowed it, and in the whole matter concerned himself, as far as fittingly he could, much for my lord of Ossory.[5]

In the end, the Lords decided that Ossory should be confined to the Tower of London for his actions and that Buckingham should be committed to the custody of the Gentleman Usher of the Black Rod.[6] A few days later both parties made their apologies to the House and were released. Buckingham said that 'the displeasure of this honourable House has been a greater trouble to him than any thing could have befallen him in this business' and that 'he cannot be at ease till their Lordships have restored him to their favour'.[7] Obviously the bitterness had not passed as a few days later Ossory found himself having to apologise once again for comments made to Buckingham and to Lord Ashley.[8] Eventually, after some wrangling, the Irish Cattle Bill passed.

Buckingham, eager to do any damage he could to Clarendon's reputation, found another issue to support in December 1666. The Duke threw his weight behind a call in the Lords for an inquiry into the issuing by the Lord Chancellor of a patent for the Canary Company. This led him into another altercation. While both Houses were crowded in joint session in the Painted Chamber on 19 December to debate the issue, Buckingham managed to give offence to the Marquess of Dorchester by resting his elbow on him.[9] When the Marquess rebuked him by saying that 'he ought not to crowd him so much, for he was as good a man as he', Buckingham replied in kind. The two men began to struggle violently, with Buckingham pulling off the Marquess' wig, and the Marquess tugging out a handful of the Duke's hair. Clarendon, no doubt pleased to have an opportunity of criticising the Duke, was of the opinion that 'it was a greater misdemeanour than had ever happened in that place and upon such an occasion'.[10] He was indignant about the matter, saying that Buckingham's 'Offence was of so high a Nature, that this House hath taken little Time to consider of it, being a great offence to the king Himself, and an Affront to this House, bringing a Reproach upon their Lordships in the Face of the kingdom'.[11]

Both culprits found themselves incarcerated in the Tower of London for their outrageous behaviour. On 22 December statements were read to the House from both parties in which they expressed their regret for what had occurred.[12] They agreed to be reconciled with each other and after a few days were released on the grounds that they 'forbear any further proceedings and provocations concerning this business'.[13] Supporters of Lord Ossory felt that this latest incident showed everyone just how troublesome Buckingham was. As Lord Anglesey said: 'The Duke of Buckingham, upon a quarrel with the Marquess of Dorchester, hath been again in prison, which makes my Lord of Ossory pass for the more peaceable man.'[14] In the end the petition regarding the Canary Company was defeated.

Buckingham may have regained his freedom on 22 December 1666 but by Christmas day he was back in trouble. He broke protocol by arriving at Whitehall without first entreating the King's forgiveness for his recent actions, with the result that he found himself banished from the royal court. It seems that he did not take this latest controversy too seriously: as one correspondent of the Duke of Ormonde puts it, 'he seems not much concerned, knowing the infinite good nature in His Majesty to pardon such offences'.[15]

In another attempt to smear the Lord Chancellor, Buckingham supported a petition against a friend of Clarendon's, Lord Mordaunt, for having victimised and intimidated a man called William Taylor and his family. As a result of this Lord Mordaunt was impeached, but in the absence of evidence, once again the action came to nothing.

By the end of January 1667 Buckingham's banishment from court had been lifted, but he made no attempt to return, going instead to Althorp when Parliament was prorogued in February. Charles, however, was still incensed at Buckingham's behaviour, and the Duke would soon begin to feel the effects of this displeasure. Inevitably, there were many who felt annoyed that Buckingham, because of his special relationship with Charles, enjoyed an influence far in excess of that warranted by his behaviour or his political position and some were therefore glad to capitalise on his estrangement from the King. An obvious way to damage him would be to use the widespread perception that Buckingham was involved with, and even supportive of, the Nonconformist radicals.

In 1667 an employee of Buckingham named Braythwaite went to the King bearing just this kind of incriminating information. Braythwaite reported to the King that the Duke of Buckingham was colluding in secret with men 'of very desperate intentions'[16] whom he met 'at unreasonable hours and in obscure places'.

It is ironic that it should have been Braythwaite who tried to implicate the Duke in some kind of political conspiracy, since only four years earlier, as one of the Duke's estate managers, Braythwaite had been shielded from arrest by his master. In 1663, as a former Cromwellian who had been close to the Lord Protector, Braythwaite found himself in danger of being arrested on suspicion of plotting against the King. To prevent the arrest of his man, Buckingham had intervened on Braythwaite's behalf and reached an agreement with Charles – a pattern that would be repeated a number of years later with that other former Cromwellian, Thomas Blood.[17] Like Blood, Braythwaite was allowed to remain free on condition that he begin to work on the King's behalf as an informer. How much credence can be given to his accusation against Buckingham we do not know, as there is a strong possibility that Braythwaite had been bribed to make it.

There are a number of suspects for such underhand activities. Buckingham's old enemies, Clarendon and Ormonde, would have been happy to find a way to damage him. Even his own cousin Barbara felt some animosity towards him.[18] But it was Henry Bennet, Earl of Arlington, who had by now emerged as the most serious enemy. As Secretary of State, and in effect head of the intelligence service, Arlington was in a good position to gather evidence against the Duke.

The next attack on Buckingham centred around Dr John Heydon, an astrologer and member of the religious sect known as the Rosicrucian Circle. Heydon's association with Buckingham went back to 1664 when he was imprisoned for debt and the Duke, once again using his influence in high places, secured his release.[19] About a month before Buckingham was attacked by the servant Goodman, Heydon had told Buckingham in one of his astrological predictions that 'his fortune was to die as unfortunately as his father, or at least [it] would be attempted'.[20]

Heydon had a rather patchy history of getting into trouble. During the Cromwellian years Cromwell's son Richard paid him a visit in disguise to hear his predictions and was advised that the Lord Protector would be hanged. Not only was this incorrect, but the predicted date for the Lord Protector's death was out by four years – an error that led to his being imprisoned for sixteen months.[21] Heydon is described by one writer as 'one of no religion, parts or honesty, a very imposter who pretends himself to be the Secretary of Nature . . . he is a lewd fellow and no astrologer to any purpose; out of other men's writings he picks up some statements, and prints them for his own'.[22]

Heydon also had a reputation for being involved in plots against the King.[23] A government spy, William Leving, wrote a very unlikely account that when Buckingham had been incarcerated in the Tower of London for the altercation with Lord Dorchester in Parliament, Heydon, on the Duke's instructions, planned to break him free with the help of disgruntled and unpaid seamen.[24] In the end Buckingham was released before such a plot could take effect.[25]

In 1667 Heydon was arrested for conspiracy and found himself embroiled in an attack upon Buckingham. Buckingham's great interest in astrology meant that he was a frequent visitor to Heydon's lodgings at Tower Hill. During a search among Heydon's papers Arlington claimed to have found a horoscope of the King's life, which had been cast on the instructions of the Duke of Buckingham.[26] In an age when people had great belief in such things, casting a horoscope of the King's life in this way amounted to high treason. William Leving also made a statement declaring that Buckingham had been involved in assisting the Radicals.[27] Charles, already unsettled by the intelligence from Braythwaite, ordered Buckingham's immediate arrest:

Warrant to John Barcroft, serjeant-at-arms, to repair to Owthorpe, [Althorp] Co. Northampton, or elsewhere, and to seize the Duke of Buckingham and convey him in close custody to the Tower, for treason.[28]

Serjeant Bearcroft's orders to arrest the Duke of Buckingham were to prove no easy endeavour. He passed the Duke's wife and her entourage on the road as she returned from a house of Lord Cardigan's, at this point only six miles from his destination of the Duke's house at Althorp, where Buckingham was residing that day. Once Mary realised what was happening she rushed ahead to Althorp with the news, so that on Bearcroft's arrival at six o'clock he found the servants most unhelpful and the porter even refused to unlock the gate. Even Mr Fairfax, who came out to see him, offered no assistance and told him 'to show more respect to the House of the Lord Duke of Buckingham and his Duchess'.[29]

Deciding not to force the issue at this stage, Bearcroft opted to spend the night at Stamford. Next morning he arrived at the Duke's house at eight o'clock accompanied by four justices of the peace. This time he was admitted, but Bearcroft noticed that the servants had 'soards in there belts and the livery men staves in there hands'. When he demanded to see the Duke all the weapons were suddenly uncovered – but the Duke did not appear. He neither found Buckingham nor any incriminating documents that day. It is not surprising that Serjeant Bearcroft heard on his way home that the Duke had been seen travelling openly in a coach and six through St Albans the previous night.

When the King heard of this escape he threatened 'all severity to those who would harbour or conceal him'.[30] Buckingham was removed from the Privy Council and the Lord Lieutenancy of the West Riding of Yorkshire, the latter position being awarded to Lord Burlington,[31] while Rochester was appointed Gentleman of the Bedchamber.[32] Meanwhile, the fugitive was forced on to the run and Lords Lieutenant throughout the country were told to be on the lookout for him. Reresby says that he stayed for a while at Sir Henry Bellais's in Yorkshire.[33] There was a rumour reported in March 1667 that he was 'at Sir George Villiers' house in Leicestershire'.[34] At the same time, Pepys heard that he had fled to France.[35] In April it was reported that he was seen 'riding towards Yarmouth with one man'.[36] He was even arrested at one point during a riot in London, but as his captors didn't recognise him, they let him go again.[37]

The likelihood that Buckingham was being framed by Arlington is attested to by the comments of Mrs Damport, who on examination made a disturbing statement about the activities of a man called Middleton. She claimed that 'Middleton did confese that he had received £100 from my Lord Arlington to bear witness against the Duke for having the King's nativity cast by Heydon, and to testify he heard the Duke speak treason against the King and the Government.'[38] Mrs Damport also claimed that a man whom she called 'Fryr' was paid £60 for his evidence and that both were promised £500 each when it was all over. Her daughter had even been told by Middleton that there was no truth in the accusation and that he only did it for the money.

The not very reliable Heydon was also adamant about the Duke's innocence. In March 1667 he wrote:

My Lord Duke is wronged, and with my life I will let the world know it . . . for when his Majesty hears the truth, the Duke will be restored to more favour than ever, and his enemies ashamed of their actions. I am undeservedly a close prisoner, tortured in the dungeon to speak their desires against him, but death shall close up the scene, before I will be forced to damn my soul for a witness to their wicked design, My last words shall be the Duke is innocent, for I know nothing against him.[39]

Charles thus found himself petitioned by requests for leniency from Buckingham's supporters. Even the Duchess of Buckingham made a trip to London to plead with the King on her husband's behalf.[40] It seems that the public also had a great deal of sympathy for the Duke. In March 1667 Arlington's secretary was told 'that his chief offence is his activity against Papists, and in behalf of nonconformists, which makes him popular with some'.[41] It was reported to him in April 1667 that 'people think his crime small or none at all'.[42] But Charles refused to be moved. He even publicly claimed that since the Duke and his followers had not supported him in his efforts to bring the enemy to submission in the Dutch War, they had been responsible for the lengthy duration of the conflict.[43]

Ormonde and Clarendon continued to do all they could to intensify the King's feelings against Buckingham. Clarendon actively encouraged Charles to have Buckingham arrested, and while the Duke was on the run he refused a request from him for an interview to resolve the issue. Ormonde, on the other hand, returned to the issue of the inheritance of the Buckingham estates. He wrote to Clarendon at the time making the point that if the Duke's offence 'prove capital', Buckingham's niece, the wife of his son, Lord Arran, was innocent of any crime and shouldn't lose out on her inheritance.[44]

Despite the best efforts of the authorities, all attempts to arrest the rogue Duke failed. He spent his time sleeping by day and moving by night. By the end of June his circumstances began to improve. Better relations with his cousin Barbara meant that she was using her influence with the King on his behalf once again. Also, one of the witness who had brought the main accusation against him was dying and the other had retracted his evidence.[45] At the end of June, Buckingham decided that it was time to write personally to Charles:

May it please your Majesty –
Though I could not but be afraid of your Majesty's anger, yet I dare trust your Kindness, and now I understand that your Majesty thinks your honour is concerned with my surrender, I will have no longer consideration of myself, since that comes in question, but as soon as I am in a posture fit to appear before Your Majesty I shall come and throw myself at your feet to be disposed of as Your Majesty shall think fit, being with great humility, may it please Your Majesty – Your Majesty's most dutiful and most obedient subject and servant – Buckingham.[46]

In June 1667 Buckingham presented himself to Secretary William Morrice and was sent to the Tower of London.[47] He even made the excuse that he had not handed himself in earlier because the proclamation had not had a time limit on it.[48] As one would expect, he transformed his journey to the Tower into something of a theatrical production, making sure that he was accompanied by a group of friends. On the way he dined at The Sun tavern in Bishopsgate, where, when a considerable crowd gathered hoping to see him, he gladly showed himself on the balcony. According to Pepys he had sent word to the Tower saying that he would come as soon as he had dined.[49]

The Select Commission set up to examine his case included Arlington, William Morrice, William Coventry and Clifford. Buckingham defended himself defiantly, firmly denying the charge of treason and telling them that although he was acquainted with Dr Heydon he 'took him to be so silly a fellow that . . . [he] would not think it fit to trust him with a tallow candle'.[50] He said that any letters addressed to him from Heydon were nothing more than begging letters, and as for any written by him to the doctor he claimed:

I have heard that I wrote a letter to him, and that your Lordship has it, but if I were to die this minute, and were to be forgiven my sins upon condition of speaking truth in this matter, I should swear that I never did write to him, and I am so confident of this, that I will lay your Lordship £100, if you please, I never did.[51]

He had, he claimed, only dealt with Heydon in connection with distillations for his chemical interests. In fact he thought the man 'cracked in his brain and fit only to be laughed at'.[52] Arlington asked him why, in light of these claims of innocence, 'did not Your Grace render yourself sooner to the King's Proclamation?' Buckingham's answer was that before he gave himself up he had wanted to find out 'what was in the bottom of these designs'.[53]

The Duke was brought before the King in Council. It soon emerged that the only stumbling block to his freedom was the letter in Crown possession adjudged to have been written by him to Dr Heydon – it was the King himself who had identified the letter as being in Buckingham's own hand. On being shown the letter, Buckingham denied it was his and claimed that the handwriting was in fact that of his sister, the Duchess of Richmond. The King now seemed to be less certain of the identity of the writer, and, as Clarendon puts it, 'Having looked upon it he said he had been mistaken and confessed it was the Duchess's hand.' The result was that Buckingham was cleared of all charges. Pepys wrote on 12 July 1667:

> The Duke of Buckingham was before the Council the other day, and there did carry it very submissively and pleasingly to the King; but to my lord Arlington, who did prosecute the business, he was most bitter and sharp, and very slighting.

Presumably the truth was that the King had tired of the matter, his anger had passed and he was ready to brush the whole episode under the carpet. In any event, he was aware that it had only made the Duke more popular. He was now a hero and had also become a leader for the anti-government members in Parliament. The attempt to destroy him had backfired and he emerged from the Heydon affair stronger than ever. By 14 July a warrant was issued to set Buckingham free. By 1 November he was reappointed Lord Lieutenant of the West Riding of Yorkshire.[54] Soon afterwards, William Leving, one of the relatively insignificant people who had given evidence against the Duke, was found dead, probably from poisoning.[55] No one was tried for his murder, but Buckingham was certainly one of those with a motive.

Twelve

THE FALL OF CLARENDON

Buckingham had long believed that while Clarendon and Ormonde were in positions of power, his chances of political progress would be severely retarded. His treatment during the Heydon affair had not disavowed him of that opinion, and he became a focal point for all those who held grudges against either of them. One of Buckingham's favourite amusements, and that of the court, was to imitate Clarendon's rather pompous deportment by marching around the room using a fire-shovel and a pair of bellows representing the symbolic mace and purse of the Chancellor. It was an act performed frequently, and with great hilarity, in the presence of the King.

When the breakdown in relations between Buckingham and Barbara Villiers was mended around 1667, they were united in their desire to do anything they could to bring about Clarendon's downfall. Barbara's hatred for both Clarendon and Ormonde was equal to his own. Her rooms became the place where Clarendon's enemies met to plot his end. Following the Heydon affair, Buckingham, with Barbara's help, began meeting regularly with Charles once again, and although the King was rather cold at first, relations between them gradually improved. One writer has stated the disputed opinion that 'from a hunted fugitive, Buckingham rapidly developed into the Sovereign's chief friend and adviser'.[1] Whatever the degree of influence now enjoyed by the Duke over the King, he was determined to use that influence against his enemies.

Charles had been keen to resolve the matter of Dr Heydon quickly but Clarendon was adamant that the Duke should be prosecuted. Barbara had reprimanded Charles firmly on the matter saying, 'You are a fool! And if you were not a fool you would not suffer your business to be carried on by fools – and cause your best subjects and those best able to serve you to be imprisoned.'[2] In the end, the clearing of Buckingham's name in the Heydon affair only served to further undermine Clarendon's position.

Yet at one stage there was a chance of a *rapprochement* between Buckingham and Clarendon, when Buckingham approached Clarendon for help in having Arlington impeached, who, he said, was 'an enemy to both of them'.[3] But Clarendon refused, saying that Arlington had done nothing 'but was according to the obligation and duty of his office'.[4] On the other hand, Arlington agreed to support Buckingham against Clarendon, telling him that the recent prosecution had been 'made by the information and advice of the Chancellor'.[5]

In the end, the removal of Clarendon was made easier by the fact that, by now, the Chancellor seemed very out of date, the common people had grown to dislike him and Charles was tired of his schoolmasterly attitude towards him and his personal life. Neither had the King forgotten Clarendon's role in his loss of Frances Stuart to the Duke of Richmond.[6] In addition, he was forced to shoulder the blame for the country's poor performance in the Dutch War of 1665–7, although in fact he was one of the few who had opposed the war from the beginning. Finally, the Chancellor's enemies made ground and Charles became convinced that it was time for a change.

It was Arlington and William Coventry, not Buckingham, who publicly fronted the attack on the Chancellor as a mob smashed the windows in his house.[7] In the summer of 1667 his wife died, which left the unfortunate man distraught, and he was also forced to surrender the seals of office. Even pleading on his behalf by the Duke of York and the Archbishop of Canterbury was to no avail. Similarly ineffectual was his own two-hour audience with the King.

In contrast, Buckingham was now back at Charles's side and more influential than ever. Charles's pragmatic nature told him that because of

Buckingham's popularity both with the public and within Parliament it would be wise to appease him. It was said that 'the King bid . . . him ask what he pleased and he would grant it'.[8] According to Reresby, 'The King consulted him chiefly in all matters of moment; foreign ministers applied themselves to him, before they were admitted to have audience of the King'.[9] But although it is true that Buckingham had seen one of his desires satisfied with the removal of Clarendon, historians disagree as to the actual extent to which his own political power was increased by the event. While it has been claimed that 'the power that the Chancellor had wielded now for the most part devolved on Buckingham . . . he was practically the Prime Minister of the new administration', others disagree with this view.[10]

It is interesting to note that in a letter written on 5 March 1668 Charles reassures his sister Henrietta with the comment that 'my Lord of Buckingham does not govern affairs here'.[11] However, there is no doubt that the collective influence of the political clique known as the 'CABAL', which included Clifford, Arlington, Buckingham, Ashley and Lauderdale, was undoubtedly increased in the absence of the Earl of Clarendon – although before long its members would line up in two camps, one behind Buckingham, the other behind Arlington.

Clarendon may have lost his wife and his office, but Buckingham and the others were not content to leave it there.[12] Matters grew worse for the former Chancellor when he found himself facing impeachment by Parliament, charged with a list of seventeen articles including cruelty in office, disclosing state secrets, intending to introduce military government in England, insolence to the King and mismanaging the war. Buckingham was one of the main orchestrators of the impeachment proceedings and chaired a number of the conferences on the issue.

In the end, Clarendon's life was saved only by the support of the House of Lords, which refused to condemn him on the grounds that no particular instance of treason had been specified against him. Buckingham and twenty-seven other peers protested against this decision.[13] With great reluctance, and at the King's request, Clarendon was forced into voluntary exile in France, where he died in 1674. It is clear that the Earl knew he had been injured by his enemies when he referred to 'the power and malice of those who have sworn my destruction'.[14]

At last, Buckingham had seen the fall of one of his great rivals, and life was now good for the Duke. Clarendon's demise had added to his popularity. He was back at the seat of power, enjoying a level of influence that would not have seemed possible just a few months earlier.

Thirteen

MOSES' SERPENT

Buckingham was never as sexually promiscuous as Charles. Although there is little evidence of his partaking in casual sexual encounters, one writer has argued that 'he would have been looked upon as a freak if he had not kept a mistress or occasionally visited the brothels in Moorfields, Lewkenor's Lane, or Dog and Bitch yard'.[1] Grammont speaks of his having a Portuguese mistress for a year in about 1662.[2]

He did however have one serious extra-marital relationship in his life. By the end of the 1660s, rumours of his marital infidelity had been rife for some time, but with the emergence of his new-found political power he seems to have done less than ever to hide the fact. His mistress was Anna Maria Brudenell, Countess of Shrewsbury, the daughter of Lord Cardigan. He had sincere and deep feelings for Lady Shrewsbury, and she was to have a profound effect upon his life. Her grandfather had sent her father to France at the outbreak of the Civil War and so she had been born and brought up in France, where she had received an impeccable convent education. Growing up into a beautiful woman with light-brown hair and dark eyes, her marriage to the widower, Francis Talbot, the 11th Earl of Shrewsbury, on 10 January 1659 when she was 17, was the culmination of the political and financial negotiations typical of the age. The Earl was a 36-year-old widower whose first wife had died childless. The new countess gave birth to their first son in 1660 and a second in 1665.

By the time she began her relationship with Buckingham, Lady Shrewsbury had already gained a dubious reputation and her husband had suffered on account of her infidelities. The Count de Grammont said of her, 'I would take a wager she might have a man killed for her every day, and she would only hold her head the higher for it'.[3] One pair of suitors had caused a particularly undignified scandal. Thomas Howard, a brother of the Earl of Carlisle, invited the countess to the Spring Gardens in Charing Cross. Also interested in Lady Shrewsbury at the same time was the infamous Henry Jermyn, nephew of the Earl of St Albans, who had a reputation for success in love, and has been described as 'formidable in amours'.[4] Among those reputedly attracted to him were the King's sister, Mary of Orange, and Clarendon's daughter. As already noted, one of his lovers was Barbara Villiers. He heard about the planned meeting between Lady Shrewsbury and Howard at the Spring Gardens and decided to turn up as well. He not only gate-crashed the occasion but also ridiculed the piper that Howard had brought along to entertain the lady. So incensed was Howard that the following day he challenged Jermyn to a duel. Although seconds had been agreed upon, a few days later there was no sign of the duel actually taking place. Then, as they finished a game of tennis at St James's Park, Jermyn and his second, Giles Rawlins, were challenged by Howard and Colonel Dillon. A fight ensued which left Rawlins dead and Jermyn 'with very little signs of life'.[5] Fearing the wrath of the law, Howard and Dillon sailed for France. Three months later they returned to stand trial and were acquitted. Howard went on to marry Buckingham's sister Mall. Jermyn survived and was later banished from court for six months for his relationship with Barbara Villiers.

The affair between Buckingham and Lady Shrewsbury may have already been going on when the Duke decided to lay on a lavish month-long entertainment for Lord and Lady Shrewsbury and her parents Lord and Lady Cardigan in July 1666.[6] Deciding that Fairfax House was not large enough for the festivities, he hired Lord Irwin's house. According to Reresby, 'The days were spent in visits and play and all sorts of diversion that the place could afford, and the nights in dancing, sometimes till day the next morning, only the two Earls, not being men for these sports, went to bed something early.'[7]

Although Buckingham's wife may have known nothing of the affair at this point, it was certainly known to others. Lady Shrewsbury's brother, Lord Brudenell, told Reresby that he had seen two people who he thought to be his sister and the Duke in what he described as 'a kind posture'.[8] He also told of a row that had developed between his sister and Lord Shrewsbury's friends regarding the illicit relationship she was having with Buckingham.

After his release from the Tower of London in 1667 the Duke's passion for Lady Shrewsbury seems to have grown even more ardent. He once described love as being 'Like Moses' serpent it devours all the rest' and this seems to describe his feelings for her. [9] There is little doubt that he genuinely loved Lady Shrewsbury, but her influence upon him was harmful, both personally and for his reputation. As one writer puts it, 'During the first months of his intimacy with this lady – from October, 1666, to July, 1667 – he was involved in public brawls and challenges with five different people and was three times sent to the Tower for insufferable rowdiness and general belligerency.'[10]

During this period his temper and his penchant for disagreements almost got him into trouble once again when, as the wine flowed during dinner one evening, he engaged in a heated row with Lord Falconbridge. Arrangements for a duel were made and tragedy was only prevented at the last moment by the parties reaching an amicable solution.[11]

By the summer of 1667 Buckingham's public disgrace over the affair with Lady Shrewsbury was to reach a new low. Harry Killigrew, who up to now had spent many enjoyable hours at the Duke's table betraying the libidinous secrets of Lady Shrewsbury, felt betrayed and was infuriated by Buckingham's relationship with her. Buckingham's theft of her from under Killigrew's nose was to bring their friendship to an end. The jilted lover soon began to attack the lady's reputation with the most evocative and bawdy after-dinner tales he could come up with.

Anna Maria complained to her husband and kinsmen about what was happening, but everyone was afraid to challenge Killigrew, who was a notorious duellist. Also at this time Killigrew made the mistake of slandering Barbara, saying that she was 'a little lecherous girl when she was young'. Barbara's angry outburst resulted in his banishment from court, and the Duke of York was ordered to dismiss him as Groom of the Bedchamber.

In July of 1667 the rivalry between Buckingham and Killigrew spilt over into violent hostility. Buckingham took both his wife and Lady Shrewsbury to the Duke's Theatre. As they sat in their box, Killigrew's jealousy got the better of him and he began to harangue them loudly. The Duke asked him to control himself. Killigrew then ran to the pit where he saw Lord Vaughan and asked him to carry a challenge to Buckingham, which he refused. Soon afterwards Killigrew hit Buckingham twice over the head with his sword still in its sheath. The theatre was thrown into chaos. The angry Buckingham chased Killigrew as he ran 'over the boxes and forms',[12] and when he finally caught him, according to Pepys, he 'did soundly beat Harry Killigrew, and take away his sword and made a fool of, till the fellow prayed him to spare his life'. Pepys found no fault with the Duke's actions: 'in this business the Duke of Buckingham did carry himself very innocently and well'.[13] Killigrew's injuries from this altercation were so serious that the Lords of the Council gave him permission to return home from the Tower to treat his wounds; when his date for judgment arrived on 9 August, however, he failed to appear, having fled abroad instead.

Killigrew's flight – to Paris it was believed – became a subject of correspondence between Charles and Minette. Charles wrote to his sister on 17 October 1667 saying:

For Harry Killigrew, you may see him as you please, and though I cannot commend my lady Shrewsbury's conduct in many things, yet Mr Killigrew's carriage towards her has been worse than I will repeat, and for his demele with my lord of Buckingham, he ought not to brag of, for it was in all sorts most abominable. I am glad the poor wretch has got a means of subsistence, but have one caution of him, that you believe not one word he says of us here, for he is a most notorious liar.[14]

Lady Shrewsbury's well-known temper was ignited by all this attention and one contemporary observed that 'my lady Shrewsbury with only one Chambermaid, took to her heels and they say is gone either into a monastery, or to kill Harry Killigrew herself, since none of her relations will undertake it, but her lord has sent to Dover and Rye to stop her if possible'.[15]

The result of this sordid publicity was that Lady Shrewsbury's husband, either as a result of wounded pride or goading from his family (who had been more interested in the political demise of Buckingham than dynastic honour), could no longer ignore the affair between Buckingham and his wife and in January 1668 challenged Buckingham to a duel. It was agreed that the seconds chosen by both protagonists were to take an active part in the duel, which meant that it was to be a dangerous fight of three against three, in the French style. Buckingham chose as his seconds Mr Jenkins and Sir Robert Holmes, while supporting the Earl of Shrewsbury were Mr Bernard Howard, brother to the Duke of Norfolk, and Sir John Talbot. Talbot was an ally of Arlington's and an enemy of Buckingham. Although the Earl himself was no fighting man, all the seconds involved were able swordsmen.

When Charles became aware of the intended duel he instructed the Duke of Albemarle to make sure it didn't take place. However, a misunderstanding occurred, leading to Albemarle's waiting for more information from the King on the exact location, while Charles thought that he had already dealt with the situation. In the confusion the duel was allowed to proceed.

On the chosen day all parties met at a close in Barn Elms. Once the struggle ensued Mr Jenkins was quickly killed by Mr Howard. Sir John

Talbot and Sir Robert Holmes squared up to each other and both inflicted injuries on the other. The duel ended with Buckingham running his sword through the Earl of Shrewsbury's 'right breast and coming out at the shoulder'.[16] Buckingham, also slightly wounded, retired to a house of his nearby, while Shrewsbury was carried by Talbot and Howard to a coach, which took him to Arundel House. A physician was sent for to tend to him. Initial reports indicated that he was seriously wounded, but would recover. It was reported that his spitting up of blood was a hopeful sign.

As news of the event spread throughout the country, outlandish rumours began to circulate. One stated that Lady Shrewsbury had observed the whole event in disguise. She was reputed to have run to her beloved Buckingham afterwards to congratulate him while holding the blood-stained shirt of her husband in her hand. It was also claimed that she had two pistols hidden about her, which she intended to use to kill both herself and her husband if the duel had gone against her lover.[17] Such reports may well have been nothing more than malicious rumour. Indeed, in 1674, when defending himself in the House of Lords, Buckingham was adamant that Lady Shrewsbury was in a French monastery at the time of the infamous duel. It is interesting to note that his claim was not challenged by anyone listening at the time.

All those who had taken part knew that Jenkins's death meant they were in a dangerous situation. The law stated that if one party to a duel was killed then all involved were deemed to be guilty. Howard went to France, Talbot went into hiding, hoping that his friend Arlington would protect him, and Shrewsbury was too sick to be arrested.

Buckingham had a far more secure plan. On 27 January 1668 he was granted a pardon from the King for 'all treason, misprision of treason, felony, &c., especially concerning the killing of Wm. Jenkins, and assaults on Francis Earl of Shrewsbury, or Sir John Talbot, whether or not they have died or shall die of the same'.[18] Within a few days all the others involved had received similar pardons.[19] One of Charles's reasons for granting the pardon was that he needed Buckingham in Parliament on 6 February to support the granting, as he had promised, of the funds required by the King. Before his Privy Council he gave his reason for issuing a general pardon as 'the eminent service heretofore done' by those pardoned.

For Buckingham it was life as usual. On 2 February he appeared at court. Four days later he attended the newly convened Parliament, and according to Pepys, attended the first performance of George Etherege's new play *She Would if She Could* at the Duke's Theatre along with Lord Buckhurst, Charles Sedley and the playwright himself.

With hindsight, Buckingham was wise to have obtained a pardon because around two months later, on 16 March, the Countess's husband died. Although the surgeons who performed the post mortem on his body found that his wound from the duel had already healed up at the time of his death and was consequently not the cause, there was much public discontent at the royal pardon granted to Buckingham in advance – so much so that Charles felt the need to make the assurance that 'on no pretence whatsoever any pardon shall hereafter be granted to any person whatsoever for killing of any man in any duel . . . but that the course of law shall wholly take place in all such cases'.[20]

The High Bailiff of Westminster, John Bennett, was one of those to voice his disapproval of the pardon to the King. He was annoyed because if the Duke of Buckingham's estates had been forfeited, as may well have happened but for the King's pardon, he would have stood to gain possession of a considerable amount of property in Westminster. Now that he had been deprived of this privilege, he wanted the King to recommend that he gain 'some reasonable compensation' from the Duke. He petitioned similarly in the cases of Howard, Talbot and Holmes, all of whom, he says, his Majesty was inclined to 'pardon . . . before conviction'.[21] Of course, his petitions fell on deaf ears.

None of this latest scandal deterred Buckingham from engaging in even more provocative behaviour. Now that the Earl of Shrewsbury was dead, Buckingham brought the grieving widow to live in his house alongside his wife. Pepys relates the story that when Mary complained about this situation, her husband told her that there was a coach available to take her to her father's house if she so wished.[22]

Buckingham and Lady Shrewsbury carried on their affair openly, even acting as host and hostess together. Edmund Waller, the poet, enjoyed one of their evenings of entertainment, saying, 'The Duke of Buckingham and the Lady Shrewsbury came hither last night at this time and carried me to the usual place for supper, from whence I returned home at four o'clock this morning, having been earnestly entreated to sup with them again tonight, but such hours cannot always be kept.'[23]

Buckingham's popularity with Charles was unaffected by his latest controversy. One letter writer commented in February 1668 that 'The Duke of Buckingham is the great favourite'.[24] Many people used him as an intermediary to further their business with the King.[25] In the summer of 1668 he added to his roles by buying the prestigious title of Master of the Horse from the Duke of Albemarle,[26] which gave him responsibility for the management of the royal stables, and allowed him to sell stable positions and other rights.

Those who recognised Buckingham as a supporter of Protestant Nonconformity greatly feared his influence and continued to criticise him accordingly. Viscount Conway wrote that 'The great interest now driven on in the kingdom is by the Duke of Buckingham, who heads the fanatics; the King complies with him out of fear; the Commons are swayed by him as a favourite and a premier minister; he thinks to arrive to be another Oliver, and the fanatics expect a day of redemption under him'.[27] Their fears were confirmed when on the opening of Parliament in February 1668 Buckingham attempted to bring an end to the persecution being suffered by the Protestant Nonconformist community by proposing a Toleration Act. He had Charles's support for this move. The Duke was not the only one who thought that the time was right and that the Anglicans might be ready to accept such a measure. Pepys expressed a similar belief a short time earlier:

> The Nonconformists are mighty high, and their meetings frequented and connived at; and they do expect to have their day now soon; for my Lord of Buckingham is a declared friend to them, and even to the Quakers, who had very good words the other day from the King himself.[28]

Charles played the first hand of the game when he used his opening speech to hint at a possible toleration. But, in the end, the optimism of Buckingham and his supporters was proved misplaced and the measure was rejected.

Fourteen

UNFINISHED BUSINESS: ORMONDE AND COVENTRY

With the political demise of Clarendon achieved, Buckingham and his allies could now focus their political vindictiveness squarely upon a number of other people. One major target was the Duke of Ormonde, Lord Lieutenant of Ireland. James Butler, 1st Duke of Ormonde, came from an Irish family of Anglo-Norman descent and had an unblemished reputation as a life-long supporter of the Stuart monarchs. He had commanded Charles I's army in Ireland during the Civil War and had loyally followed the King's son into exile. After the Restoration Charles had raised him to the Dukedom of Ormonde in the Irish peerage and created him Lord High Steward of England.

Along with Clarendon, Ormonde had long been a focus of Buckingham's hatred. For his part, Ormonde, in a letter to his son, described Buckingham as a 'vile man'.[1] Unsurprisingly, Buckingham was alarmed when his sister Mall betrothed her daughter to Richard, Earl of Arran, a son of Ormonde. To make matters worse, Ormonde sent Buckingham a note requesting that the Villiers' estates be settled on his son Richard's new wife since after seven years of marriage Buckingham's own marriage had not brought forth any children.

Buckingham probably held designs on acquiring the titles of Lord Lieutenant of Ireland and Steward of the Household for himself, but there were two major obstacles in his way. Firstly, there was no doubt that Charles held Ormonde in high esteem, and secondly, it would be difficult to establish any wrongdoing on Ormonde's part to use against him.[2]

On the other hand, Ormonde's great friend and supporter, Clarendon, had disappeared from the political scene, and, just as in the case of Clarendon's removal from power, Barbara was once again willing to do what she could to assist. Additionally, she bore Ormonde a personal grudge since he had stymied her attempts to get possession of the Phoenix Park and House in Dublin – Ormonde had taken possession of the property for himself and subsequent Lords Lieutenant. Barbara was outraged and the next time she met him 'fell upon him with a torrent of abusive language . . . and told him . . . that she hoped to see him hanged'.[3] Ormonde repled calmly that 'he was not in so much haste to put an end to her days, for all he wished with regard to her was, that he might live to see her old'.[4]

In 1666 Buckingham's enthusiastic support for the Irish Cattle Bill had brought the ill-feeling between Buckingham and the Ormondes to the surface. Ormonde and his sons opposed the bill arguing that Ireland needed every financial support it could get. This had led to the proposed duel between Buckingham and Ossory, and their subsequent incarceration.

By 1667 supporters of Buckingham such as Sir Robert Howard and Lord Anglesea were working on articles of impeachment that could be brought against the Duke of Ormonde. It seems that Howard, whose appointment as Commissioner for administering the Act of Explanation was blocked, harboured a grudge against Ormonde for this. At first Ormonde was not unduly concerned about the accusations being made against him, stating that he could not be accused by 'more inconsiderable fellows or more detested knaves'.[5] Roger Boyle, the Earl of Orrery and one-time friend of Ormonde, also became involved in the plot, making accusations of financial impropriety in the administration of Ireland. It seems that he had been promised the Deputy-Lieutenancy of Ireland by Buckingham in return for his assistance.[6]

In August 1668 Buckingham played a major role in persuading Parliament to appoint a committee, of which he was made a member, to examine Ormonde's administration of Ireland.[7] By now the seriousness of the situation was dawning on Ormonde and in 1668 he decided that it was important enough for him to travel to England, leaving his son, Ossory, in his place in Ireland. Incredibly, when he arrived in England, Buckingham had the audacity to pay him a ceremonial visit, assuring him that he wished him no harm.[8]

In February 1669 Ormonde was told by his chaplain, Dr Sheridan, that rumours had been circulating at a party the previous evening to the effect that Charles had at last been persuaded to remove Ormonde from the Lord Lieutenancy of Ireland.[9] The rumours proved correct. When making the announcement, however, the King was careful not to criticise his loyal servant, but on the contrary 'declared, how well he was satisfied with the duke of Ormond's thirty years' service to his father and himself . . .'.[10] Pepys noted in his diary that the event showed 'the power of Buckingham and the poor spirit of the King'.[11] It has also been pointed out that Charles may have wanted Ormonde out of the way because he was planning clandestine negotiations with the French regarding his conversion to Catholicism.[12] He admitted in correspondence to his sister that he did not trust the Duke any less, but that there were 'other considerations' too long for a letter.[13]

It was said that Buckingham expected to be appointed Lord Lieutenant of Ireland in Ormonde's place and had even begun to offer posts to people as gifts.[14] Unexpectedly, however, Charles awarded the Lord Lieutenancy of Ireland to the unpopular Lord Robartes, a man described as 'morose, overbearing, and impracticable'.[15] The King had made a conscious decision 'not to give the post to any of those who had openly aimed at it, and had shewed themselves most active and busy in attacking the Duke of Ormond'.[16] Just some seven months after his appointment Lord Berkeley of Stratton replaced Robartes as Lord Lieutenant of Ireland. Again, however, Buckingham seems to have been close to the decision-making process, with Charles assuring him that neither Ormonde nor his son Ossory would be appointed. As one letter written in cipher at the time says, 'Mr. Church [the King] is resolved to recall Mr. Blewett [Robertes], but has engaged himself to Mr. Gorgis [Buckingham] that neither Mr. Carrig [Ormonde] nor Mr. Buller [Ossory] shall succeed.'[17]

As for Ormonde, on 26 August 1669 he had the honour of being unanimously elected Chancellor of the University of Oxford. Buckingham was still keen to have him removed from the Stewardship of the Household, and so attacked him whenever he could. But this time the King was unmoved. As we shall see later, it is possible that Buckingham was planning to resort to a much more permanent solution to the problem of the Duke of Ormonde, using the services of Colonel Thomas Blood.[18]

Buckingham also found time to play a significant role in the political demise of Sir William Coventry. Coventry had worked under the Duke of York at the Admiralty and in 1667 was made Joint Commissioner of the Treasury. Pepys knew that Buckingham had taken a dislike to him when he wrote in October 1668, rather prophetically as it turned out, that Buckingham 'will ruin Coventry, if he can'.[19] Although Coventry had assisted in the destruction of Clarendon, he may have been singled out by Buckingham because in his role as Joint Commissioner of the Treasury he had been on the Select Commission appointed to examine the Duke when he was incarcerated in the Tower of London as a result of the Heydon affair.[20] He was also a firm ally of the Duke of York, which did not endear him to Buckingham, and he had refused to assist in the impeachment of Ormonde.

The circumstances of Coventry's fall from grace are farcical. Buckingham wrote a play, in collaboration with Sir Robert Howard, in which Coventry's character was lampooned. *The Country Gentleman* was a comedy based on the theme of courtship and marriage,[21] and one of the characters in the play, Sir Cautious Trouble-all, would have been instantly recognisable to everyone at court when he explained that he conducted his business sitting in a hole in the centre of a round table. This table enabled him to turn from bundle of paper to bundle of paper, each one arranged around him in an orderly manner. Everyone at Whitehall knew that Coventry had invented such a table and that he was extremely proud of it. On 4 July 1668, he had shown it to Pepys, who wrote, 'Up, and to see Sir W. Coventry . . . He showed me his closet, with his round table, for him to sit in the middle, very convenient.'[22]

The play was due to be performed at the King's House in February 1669. Coventry, however, got wind of it and complained to the King about the attack on his character. Charles demanded to see a copy of the play, but when it arrived the scene offensive to Coventry had been removed and the King could find no fault with it. Coventry felt affronted and angry, so he challenged Buckingham to a duel. When Charles was informed of this, Coventry was removed from office and imprisoned briefly in the Tower of London in March 1669.[23] When Pepys visited him there he spoke of what had happened and his anger is quite palpable:

He [Coventry] told me the matter of the play that was intended for his abuse, wherein they foolishly and sillily bring in two tables like that which he hath made, with a round hole in the middle, in his closet, to turn himself in; and he is to be in one of them as master, and Sir J. Duncomb in the other, as his man or imitator; and their discourse in those tables, about the disposing of their books and papers, very foolish. But that that he is offended with is his being made so contemptible, as that any should dare to make a gentleman a subject for the mirth of the world; and that therefore he had told Tom Killigrew that he should tell his actors, whoever they were, that did offer at anything like representing him, that he would not complain to my Lord Chamberlain, which was too weak, nor get him beaten, as Sir Charles Sedley is said to have done, but that he would cause his nose to be cut . . .[24]

Others, too, were angered by Coventry's imprisonment. Barbara went to the King to object strongly on Coventry's behalf, and James was also 'incensed' according to Pepys.[25] The King, it seems, did not share their concern about the way events had turned out. Writing to Henrietta he said, 'The truth of it is he has been a troublesome man . . . and I am well rid of him.'[26] Such a statement could lead one to speculate as to whether Charles had been involved from the beginning. Had he encouraged his friend Buckingham to lampoon Coventry, perhaps anticipating how Coventry would react? As with the removal of Ormonde, Coventry's absence may have been convenient for Charles's plans for an alliance with the French and his possible religious conversion.

Although he remained in Parliament until its dissolution in 1679, Coventry's disillusionment was such that he never took high office again.[27] Buckingham was elated over his success. Pepys wrote that 'the Duke of Buckingham will be so flushed, that he will not stop at anything'.[28] In the end the play was suppressed without a single performance.

Buckingham continued to be involved actively in other business. For example, it was he, in March 1669, who conveyed Charles's wish to Sir John Denham, the Surveyor-General, that Christopher Wren be appointed as his deputy.[29] Wren was appointed, thereby launching a career that would contribute handsomely to the city of London. Buckingham also became heavily involved in two of the biggest constitutional debates of Charles's reign. Firstly there was the case of Skinner versus the East India Company. Thomas Skinner, a merchant, had purchased the island of Barella in Sumatra from the king of Djambi during the Interregnum. In 1659, when Skinner irked the powerful East India Company by daring to trade in the East Indies, the Company responded by seizing his goods and even his island. Although he demanded damages of £17,000, the Company offered him only £1,500.[30] After a number of failed attempts at arbitration, Charles referred the dispute to the House of Lords in 1667. Although the prorogation of Parliament in February meant that no progress was made on the issue, Skinner ensured the matter was revived in the new session. The East India Company for their part claimed that the Lords had no right to adjudicate in the case since it was not an appeal. In March 1668 the Lords awarded Skinner £5,000 in damages.

The Company's next move was to turn to the Commons, once again making the argument that the Lords had had no right to adjudicate in such a case. In addition, as a number of MPs were also members of the East India Company, the Company claimed that the award amounted to an infringement of their parliamentary privilege. When the Commons came down on the side of the East India Company, a bicameral dispute erupted.

Buckingham and his supporters had a hand in both sides of this dispute. The Duke openly supported Skinner's cause and the rights and privileges of the House of Lords to adjudicate in such matters, and he chaired a number of important committee meetings on the issue.[31] But it was an associate of Buckingham's, Sir John Vaughan, who drafted the Company's petition to the House of Commons, which was vigorously supported by others from Buckingham's faction, such as Sir Robert Howard, Sir Richard Temple, Sir John Maynard and William Prynne. Buckingham was playing a political game. One possible motive may have been that the Conventicle Act of 1664 was about to expire and he wanted to distract the peers from renewing it. He may also have been attempting to encourage Charles to dissolve Parliament, in the expectation that the newly elected Parliament would be more amenable to Protestant Dissenters.

In 1668 Buckingham addressed the House of Commons on the issue:

We [the House of Lords] acknowledge it is [in] our interest to defend the right of the Commons; for, should we suffer them to be opprest, it would not be long before it might come to be our own case:

And I humbly conceive it will also appear to be the interest of the Commons, to uphold the priviledge of the Lords; that so we may be in a condition to stand by and support them . . .

. . . The power of judicature does naturally descend, and not ascend; That is, no inferiour court can have any power, which is not derived to it from some power above it . . .

. . . the highest court in which the king can possibly sit, that is, his Supreme Court of Lords in Parliament, has in it all his judicial power, and consequently no bounds: I mean no bounds of jurisdiction; for the highest court is to govern according to the laws, as well as the lowest . . .

. . . this whole case, as well as many others, could not be tried properly in any place but at our Bar . . .[32]

In October 1669 Charles aimed to bring the issue to a close by persuading Buckingham and the Duke of York to sponsor a bill abolishing the original decision made by the Lords; the bill was rejected by all but two peers. The dispute rumbled on until finally, in 1670, Charles lost his patience and ordered both houses to 'expunge all traces of it from their respective Journals'.[33]

Another parliamentary storm erupted soon afterwards over the Roos divorce case. Lord Roos, heir to the Earldom of Rutland, had already attained a separation from his wife in the religious courts; he now wanted a civil divorce and the right to remarry. His took his case to the House of Lords, where he introduced a private bill that would entitle him to do so. Charles, actively encouraged by Buckingham,[34] took a personal interest in the Roos divorce bill of 1670. Ironically, in 1666 Buckingham, who was a relative of Lord Roos, had attempted to claim the title Baron of Roos for himself.[35] The King attended the debates and canvassed on behalf of Lord Roos. Many took Charles's interest in the case as evidence that he viewed it as a potential precedent for his own divorce from his childless Queen. He is said to have described the daily debates as being 'as good as a play'.[36]

It was well known that Buckingham wanted Charles to divorce the Queen, and was therefore a vociferous supporter of the bill. The Duke of York and his supporters, on the other hand, actively opposed the bill, fearing its repercussions on the question of the succession to the throne. In the end the Bill passed, much to the delight of Buckingham.[37] It created a precedent of gaining a divorce by Act of Parliament, which Charles, or any other person of privilege, could use. However, this was a course of action that Charles would never attempt to follow.

By 1670 the popularity Buckingham had enjoyed when he was perceived as a spokesman for all those dissatisfied with the government's performance, particularly in the Dutch War, had ebbed away. His advocacy of toleration for Nonconformists had also made him very unpopular among many in Parliament. But Charles now had a new task for him – in the world of foreign affairs.

Fifteen

THE TREATY WITHIN A TREATY

Towards the end of the 1660s Charles became interested in forging a treaty with the French against the Dutch. Although a member of the Triple Alliance with the Dutch and the Swedes, he was keen to avenge the terribly humiliating events of the last war against the Dutch. Louis XIV of France was also keen to go to war with the Dutch, and for this he needed the support of Charles's navy.

Buckingham's sentiments regarding the political affairs of Europe also lay very much in favour of an alliance with the French against the Dutch. He was a particular admirer of King Louis XIV of France and may also have been influenced by the fact that Clarendon was in France and could be prevented from returning to England most easily by Louis. Arlington, on the other hand, had always favoured an alliance with the Dutch, a fact which put him and Buckingham very much on opposing sides.

Under orders to begin negotiations with the French, Buckingham sent his Catholic friend, Sir Ellis Leighton, to Paris to open talks. Buckingham had first become friendly with Leighton while in exile on the Continent. By all accounts Leighton was a kindred spirit: Pepys described him as 'a mad freaking fellow', and Hyde said he was a 'vicious atheist'. He was a good choice as negotiator though, being, like Buckingham himself, a wonderful conversationalist and entertainer. Their friendship was to last until Leighton's death in 1682. Arlington's representative in the negotiations was his secretary, Sir Joseph Williamson, while Louis' man at Whitehall, Colbert de Choisy, began to make inquiries as to what sums of money should be made available to Buckingham and Arlington to make the negotiations run smoothly.

In reality, a double game was being played. Many years earlier Buckingham had betrayed Charles by deserting him in exile and returning to live in Cromwell's England. Now it was Buckingham's turn to be betrayed. Although he was convinced that he was a main player in these important negotiations with the French, the truth was that he was being used by Charles and Louis as they privately held negotiations between themselves. These secret negotiations revolved around the possibility of Charles's conversion to Catholicism, which Buckingham would have resolutely opposed. The main players in facilitating these secret negotiations with the French were the queen mother until her death in 1669, and Charles's sister, Minette. Both were devout Catholics who dearly wanted to see an alliance between England and Catholic France.

Although the Duke of York, Arlington, Lord Arundell and Sir Thomas Clifford all knew about the King's wish to convert to Catholicism, Charles was keenly aware that Buckingham would have to be kept in ignorance of his intentions – it was imperative that the Duke continue the sham negotiations in complete ignorance. Fortunately, he was an ideal choice for such a role, as no one would believe that someone so devoted to Protestantism would take part in any 'Papist' negotiations. Charles therefore advised his sister:

It will be good that you write sometimes to Buckingham in general terms that he may not suspect that there is farther negotiations than what he knows of, but pray have a care you do not say anything to him which may make him think that I have employed anybody to Louis, which he is to know nothing of, because by the messenger he may suspect that there is something of Catholic interest in the case, which is a matter he must not be acquainted with. Therefore, you must have a great care not to say the least thing that may make him suspect any thing of it.[1]

There were rumours, however, and Buckingham's sister, Mall, while waiting on the Queen Mother, began to suspect something was afoot. She wrote to her brother warning him of negotiations she had heard were taking place without his knowledge between the King, Minette and Louis.

Minette, on the other hand, for whom Buckingham had such affection, was quick to reassure him that there was nothing going on. She appealed to his ego, telling him that Louis had told her that he would give up the whole affair if the Duke of Buckingham were to change his mind about it.[2] So it was that Buckingham remained ignorant of Charles's radical plan to convert to Catholicism. As one writer has put it:

> while the Duke remained persuaded he was forwarding a treaty to secure for England the mastery of the seas, the Spanish-American Colonies, with Minorca, Ostend, and half a dozen Dutch ports, and for himself the command of the English contingent in Flanders, Charles was, in reality, bargaining for French troops and French gold, for the sole purpose of coercing the civil and religious liberties of his subjects.[3]

The secret negotiations reached their conclusion when, in May 1670, Minette paid an important visit home to England and left soon afterwards with the signatures of Arlington, Clifford, Arundel and Sir Richard Bellings on the secret Treaty of Dover.[4] This document facilitated a combined war by England and France against the Dutch Republic, outlining troop numbers and the like. The all-important clause two of the document, dealing with the King's religious conversion, read:

> The King of England, being convinced of the truth of the Catholic Religion is resolved to declare it, and to reconcile himself with the Church of Rome as soon as the state of his country's affairs permit . . .

Therefore, under this clause, Charles had agreed, in return for two million French crowns, to convert to Catholicism at the first opportunity.

Of course, as he worked on the 'public' or 'official' treaty, Buckingham still knew nothing of this secret agreement.

Ironically, when Minette died shortly after returning to France, Buckingham was deeply saddened by her death and strongly suspected that she had been a victim of assassination. In fact, as she lay dying, the poor woman had come to a similar opinion herself. Buckingham was so angry that according to one French source he even wanted war declared.[5] The angry mob that surrounded the French Embassy in London presumably agreed with him. Although foul play was suspected at first, this was eventually ruled out by the post mortem, which found that she had died from a 'choleric disorder'.[6] Appreciating how strong Buckingham's feelings were, Charles sent for him to tell him the news as soon as the post mortem results arrived.

In time, Buckingham's anger waned and he returned to France in the summer of 1670 to continue negotiations for what was in reality a sham treaty. He did not go empty-handed: £2,000 was allocated to pay for his equipage and £3,210 for his general expenses. In addition, he was treated royally by the French, who housed him in great comfort in Minette's old apartments at St Germain, while the French army was paraded before him in St Sebastien, a mock sea battle was performed for him in the canal at Versailles and a number of balls were given in his honour – all of which was, of course, in the interests of furthering Charles's and Louis' subterfuge.[7] Louis was satisfied with the way he was manipulating Buckingham. He wrote to Colbert in August 1670: 'I have managed the Ambassador.'[8]

Arlington, who had already put his name to the secret treaty, must have been amused to receive the following letters from Buckingham:

15 August, 1670

My Lord, – If I had had the good fortune to bring my Lord Falconbridge's secretary with me, he would have entertained your Lordship with a whole sheet of paper full of the particulars of my reception here; for I have had more honours given me than ever were given to any subject. You will receive within two or three days a proposition from this Court, concerning making war upon Holland only, which you may enlarge as you please.

Monsieur de Lionne showed me the model of it last night and I shall see the particulars before they are sent. In the meantime having not yet your cipher I shall only tell you in general that nothing but our being mealy mouthed can hinder us from finding our accounts in this matter; for you may almost ask what you please. I have written more at large in cipher to my Lord Ashley, and when you have discoursed together, if you think my stay here will be of use to His Majesty let me know it, if not I will come away.[9]

17th August, 1670

My Lord, – I have nothing to add to what I wrote last but that I am every day convinced of the happy conjuncture we have at present in our hands of any conditions from this court, that we can in reason demand.

The King of France is so mightily taken with the discourses I make to him of his greatness by land, that he talks to me twenty times a day; all the Courtiers here wonder at it and I am very glad of it and am very much yours, etc.[10]

As negotiations were ending, Louis was still massaging Buckingham's ego vigorously. On the Duke's departure he presented him with a luxurious sword and belt set with pearls and diamonds.[11] So stunning was the sword, in fact, that not only did the courtiers line up to have a look at it, but a number of its precious stones were stolen, and Buckingham had to replace them at his own expense! Louis also promised to grant Lady Shrewsbury 10,000 *livres* a year and gave an assurance that Buckingham would be awarded a military command in the Low Countries.

By September 1670, when the negotiations were complete, Buckingham made his farewells and left France for England. In his typical, extravagant

The children of Charles I: Mary, James, Charles, Elizabeth and Anne. *(National Portrait Gallery, London)*

Buckingham as a small child in his mother's arms with his sister Mary and his father. *(National Portrait Gallery, London)*

King Charles restored to power. (*The Royal Collection © Her Majesty Queen Elizabeth II*)

GEORGE VILLERS DUKE OF BUCKINGHAM.

Buckingham's special relationship with Charles II gave him a privileged position at the royal court. *(National Portrait Gallery, London)*

The women in Buckingham's life: his wife Mary, left *(Mary Evans Picture Library)*, and the Countess of Shrewsbury *(National Portrait Gallery, London)*, with whom he had one of the most infamous affairs of the century. Lady Shrewsbury's husband died after receiving wounds in a duel with Buckingham.

Opposite: Charles had many extra-marital affairs. Among his mistresses were, clockwise from top right:

Louise de Kéroualle, Duchess of Portsmouth *(Mary Evans Picture Library)*
Both Buckingham and Charles fell for the charms of Frances Stuart, but neither was successful with her. *(National Portrait Gallery, London)*
Hortense Mancini, Duchess of Mazarin *(National Portrait Gallery, London)*
Nell Gwynn *(National Portrait Gallery, London)*
Barbara Villiers, Duchess of Cleveland *(National Portrait Gallery, London)*

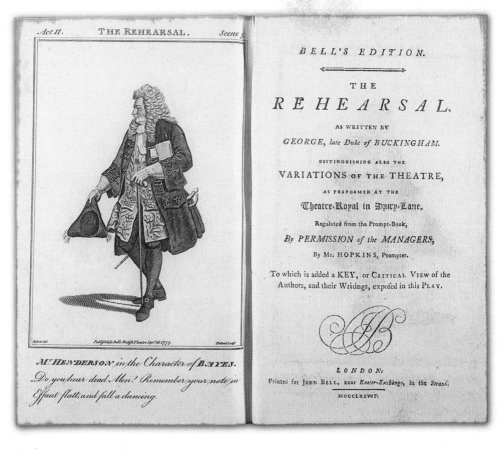

Buckingham's play, *The Rehearsal*, continued to be popular into the next century, as this edition dated 1777 shows. *(Mary Evans Picture Library)*

Opposite: Buckingham had a number of rivals at court, clockwise from top right:

James Butler, 1st Duke of Ormonde *(National Portrait Gallery, London)*
Henry Bennet, 1st Earl of Arlington. *(National Portrait Gallery, London)*
Thomas Osborne, Earl of Danby *(National Portrait Gallery, London)*
Edward Hyde, Earl of Clarendon *(Mary Evans Picture Library)*

John Wilmot, 2nd Earl of Rochester, fellow writer, court wit and good friend of Buckingham. *(National Portrait Gallery, London)*

style he brought fourteen new French servants home with him. A round of discussions now began in England on the terms of the new treaty with France, but Buckingham soon became concerned about the tardiness with which Charles seemed to be finalising it. His anxiety on the matter is clear in a letter sent by him to Louis XIV on 19 November 1670. The letter also demonstrates the high regard in which he held the French King:

Sire, I can no longer help saying to Your Majesty, that nothing ever so disturbed my mind as the handling of this treaty, since our return from Newmarket. There, the King was agreed on all points with Your Majesty. Nothing further was wanting but to draw up the articles we were to sign two days later, and these, I am convinced, could have been written out in less than one. My Lord of Arlington was to finish them in concert with Monsieur l'Ambassadeur, but since then we have had nothing but delays. The first stumbling block was over the islands of Worne and Gorée, which Monsieur l'Ambassadeur has since yielded; but this should not have retarded matters, since the King my master had resolved to sign the Treaty, leaving a blank for the aforesaid islands, on the assurances I gave him of your Majesty's affection for him, and that without doubt, when you had weighed all the reasons, which could be advanced, you would reinstate them yourself. This I told Monsieur l'Ambassadeur, thinking, at first, I had worked wonders, but the next day, instead of arriving at a conclusion, we had another controversy on the preamble of the article touching the Prince of Orange. To begin with, the King my Master assented once more to all your Majesty's envoy demanded, but that was of no profit to us, since time after time he started fresh difficulties, ultimately refusing to sign till his courier had arrived. At this moment, we are debating over one of those two millions, which were to be paid on the signature of the Treaty. During this delay, it has often been predicted to the King my Master that he would shortly have an infallible clue to the intentions of your Majesty, for, if your intentions had really changed, you would hesitate over the payment of the two millions. This prediction, agreeing so absolutely with what has taken place, confirms me in a suspicion which for some time has given me much uneasiness; and I can no longer doubt that the two gentlemen, who should have made all preparations for the conclusion of the Treaty, have plotted to break it off; and that while one suggests scruples to the King my Master, the other does as much with Your Majesty; if I am mistaken pray pardon a weakness which is part of my character. I can not be disinterested for those I revere. I look upon this matter as the only one that can add to the fame of Your Majesty. If we consent to the dishonour that is daily recommended, and indeed thrust upon us, Your Majesty will miss the finest opportunity in the world to employ those talents with which God had endowed you, and which are capable, at the lowest estimate, of ranking you as equal to the greatest in all past history. Sire, I speak as I feel. If I am doing wrong, forgive me and let Your Majesty remember that from the instant I first knew you, my heart has been so filled with admiration for you, that I shall never more experience devotion to any other cause or know any peace till I discover some means whereby I can serve you and thus make you aware of the extent of my gratitude for the many obligations of all kinds that I have received from Your Majesty: From the depths of my heart, I am, Sire, etc.,

Buckingham[12]

Louis replied in a similar manner on 15 December:

My Cousin – I did not hasten to send you back your gentleman, because when he arrived, I was assured that all the difficulties, which had arisen on the other side, were already brought to an end by the orders sent by me a few days before to my Ambassador, bidding him conclude the matter, to the entire satisfaction of the King your master. Yet, I can no longer regret these little obstacles, since they have furnished you with the occasion of giving me a new proof of your friendship, which I prize most highly, while I have an opportunity of reiterating that my friendship for you is as real as I have ever professed, or you could even desire. For the rest, I have committed to Lyonne the task of replying to several points of your letter to me and also one of yours to him; especially with reference to the suspicions you entertained, suspicions indeed, which lay me under the greatest of obligations to you, but which I can assure you are without any foundation, at least as regards my Ambassador, and I wish to think as regards the other person also. In any case, you acted with so much cordiality and energy that it would have been difficult for the business not to have been carried through to a conclusion mutually satisfactory to both of us. I could most ardently have wished that the end had been more quickly attained; but to ensure certainty and security, it has been necessary to proceed with deliberation. And on this I pray God, my cousin, to have you in His most holy keeping.

Louis[13]

Buckingham was further encouraged in his feelings of affection for Louis by the comments made in a letter from the above-named Lyonne, also written on the 15th:

. . . when I presented your letter, His Majesty did me the honour to say in these express terms: 'I am proud when I find the judgment I have formed of a man is correct. You see how little I erred in my estimate of the Duke of Buckingham. I am convinced that he as sincerely loves me, as any man that lives; I doubt whether you yourself have a greater zeal in my interests, for, see in what anxiety the suspicion that our affair might miscarry has plunged him . . .'[14]

The 'public' Treaty of Dover was finally signed in December 1670. It was, of course, essentially a cover-up.[15] Though signed by Buckingham and the four other members of the Cabal, it was rendered null and void in advance by the previous secret treaty. Charles, however, soon began to invent excuses to delay his promised religious conversion to Catholicism, which took place only on his deathbed.

Buckingham never received the military command in the Low Countries he had been promised by Louis XIV. It had been agreed that he would command an army of 6,000 English soldiers in Louis' campaign against the Dutch, but Arlington and his brother-in-law Ossory began to canvass for Ossory to get the command instead. In the end, Arlington lobbied successfully to have the English force reduced to 2,400 men and the command went to Monmouth, with Ossory second in command.[16] When Buckingham vented his anger about this injustice to the King, he was forcibly told by Charles that 'he was worth no more than a dog if he conflicted with the public good'.[17] All of this once again fuelled his rivalry with Arlington.

It is hard to tell how sincere Charles was in his declared intention under the secret treaty to convert to Catholicism as soon as conditions allowed. He was a man whose sense of pragmatism generally overrode spiritual matters, and he would have been acutely aware of how difficult an idea his religious conversion would have been to 'sell' to his subjects. Just as when he swore the Covenant to get the Scots on his side in the war against Cromwell, his agreement to convert at this stage may have been merely an act of political expediency. In any event, at a session of Parliament in 1675 he affirmed 'hand on heart' his commitment to the national Church, from which, he promised, to 'never depart' – even though he would, in fact, do just that on his deathbed. Throughout these dealings he had used his childhood friend Buckingham ruthlessly. Buckingham was devoted to Protestantism and would never have agreed to assisting Charles's conversion to Catholicism. Rumours soon became widespread about Charles's religious agreement with the French, which would seem to make it improbable that Buckingham was unaware of it, although we can point to no firm evidence to prove that he was.

Sixteen

MISTRESS TROUBLE

As the Queen remained childless, many firmly believed that Charles, if given the opportunity, would divorce her. Of course, this belief was reinforced by his interest in and support for the divorce of Lord Roos. Charles, however, always vehemently denied that he had any intention of divorcing Catherine, despite Buckingham's urging him to marry again in order to establish a Protestant succession. According to Burnet, Buckingham proposed a rather extreme solution to the problem:

> . . . if he would give him leave, he would steal her away, and send her to a plantation, where she would be well and carefully looked to, but never heard of any more; so it should be given out that she had deserted; and upon that it would fall in with some principles to carry an act for divorce, grounded upon the pretence of wilful desertion.[1]

Luckily for the Queen, Charles was horrified by Buckingham's suggestion and rejected it roundly. Furthermore, 'he said it was a wicked thing to make a poor lady miserable, only because she was his wife, and had no children by him, which was no fault of hers'.[2]

It was on his return home from Paris in 1670 that Buckingham became embroiled in another débâcle and so won another enemy. Charles had long expressed an interest in Louise de Kéroualle, one of the late Minette's maids of honour. Louise had first come to Charles's attention when she accompanied Minette on the visit to England to finalise the secret treaty. There is a story that when his sister was leaving she urged Charles to select one of her jewels to cherish as a keepsake, to which Charles replied, presumably with humorous intent, that Louise was the only precious item he desired. Minette told him that she had promised Louise's parents that she would look after her.

Louise was the eldest daughter of a Breton noble. Although the family had an ancient and distinguished lineage, they had fallen on bad times financially. Louis encouraged a liaison between Charles and Louise, thinking no doubt of the influence Mademoiselle de Kéroualle might come to have over the King of England. Some believed Minette's dying wish that Louise be well looked after stemmed from her hope that after her death Louise would act as an intermediary between the two royal courts.

Buckingham, too, became actively involved in encouraging the romance. He had previously been active in introducing the King to two other mistresses, Moll Davis and Nell Gwynn. His motives were selfish in that he wanted a new influential friend at court to replace his cousin Barbara, with whom his relations were not good. It was clear to him that Barbara was growing old and her influence was waning. Before he had left for Paris, Buckingham had cleverly contrived a situation wherein Charles paid an unexpected visit to Barbara only to find Jack Churchill leaving hurriedly through a window. Charles is reputed to have shouted out of the window after him: 'I forgive you, for you only do it for your bread.'

Buckingham had agreed to accompany Louise back to England with him, but things went rather bizarrely wrong on the journey and he only brought Louise as far as Dieppe, where he promised to send a royal yacht to fetch her. When the much-anticipated yacht never arrived Louise, understandably, felt much aggrieved. On 19 October 1670 the English Ambassador wrote that 'Mademoiselle Kéroualle hath been at Dieppe these ten days, and hears nothing of the yacht that the Duke of Buckingham . . . was to send for her.'[3]

Louise finally made her way to England and to Charles's court with the help of Arlington, instead of Buckingham. The relationship between Charles and Louise was slow to get going, with neither of them doing the pursuing. Eventually matters did proceed and Charles managed to seduce Louise, aided in his endeavours by Arlington. Mock nuptials were even celebrated between the two lovers at Arlington's Euston estate in October of 1671. Louise soon gave birth to his son.

Charles paid dearly for his relationship with Louise, however, as she became renowned for her luxurious tastes.[4] She was given lavish accommodation at Whitehall, which by the 1670s comprised around forty rooms. With her pension and presents,[5] she represented an estimated cost to the kingdom of £40,000 per year. One famous story tells of how Charles once bought her jewellery to the value of £10,000 as an apology for giving her a dose of venereal disease![6] He also bestowed on her the titles Baroness Petersfield, Countess of Fareham and Duchess of Portsmouth, while Louis XIV of France created her a Duchess in the 1680s. Because of the difficulty of pronouncing her name the common people usually referred to Louise as 'Mrs Carwell'. Although Louise was Charles's newest lover, this does not mean that he accorded her any kind of romantic fidelity: he continued his many casual sexual encounters as well as his relationships with Barbara and Nell. Louise never forgot the way that Buckingham had treated her by deserting her in Dieppe. She bore him a grudge and instead of an ally he now had another enemy in an influential position. The feeling of loathing was, by now, mutual.

Towards the end of the 1660s things were beginning to go wrong for Barbara. The public had for some time enjoyed a love–hate relationship with her. On the one hand, they were fascinated by her, and great crowds gathered to see her whenever they could; but, equally, they were scandalised by her outrageous behaviour and enjoyed the malicious gossip she inspired and the vicious lampoons written about her. Charles realised, after the recent riots, that she was becoming a problem,[7] and decided to distance her from Whitehall – which proved to be a costly business. In 1668 he bought her the luxurious Berkshire House close to St James's Palace, which she later demolished and even sold off the building materials. She later built herself Cleveland House, aptly named after the new title, Duchess of Cleveland, to which Charles had just raised her, along with the titles Countess of Southampton and Baroness of Nonsuch.[8] He also gave her the palace and park of Nonsuch in Surrey, which had formerly been the property of the late Queen Mother.

In 1672 Barbara gave birth to her sixth and final child. This time the father is believed to have been John Churchill, later Duke of Marlborough, rather than Charles. At first Charles was not keen to acknowledge the girl, but later he did so.

In 1705 Barbara's long-suffering husband, Roger Palmer, died, and only four months later she rushed into marriage with a gentleman called Robert Fielding, a cad who had already been married to two wealthy wives. Barbara soon found out that sixteen days before he had married her, he had also married another woman whom he thought to be rich. Ironically, the woman had duped him as she was not who she claimed to be. In any event, Barbara had him charged and tried for bigamy. Although he was found guilty, his punishment didn't amount to much, but Barbara divorced him and he ended up in debtors' prison.

In 1675 yet another mistress arrived at the court of Charles II. Hortense Mancini was the niece of the once powerful French Minister, Cardinal Mazarin. Back in 1659 Charles had been interested in marrying the 14-year-old Hortense, but there had been no enthusiasm for the match at the French court, since at the time Charles was a king without a kingdom and with very little prospect of acquiring one. But times had moved on: Charles now had his kingdom and Hortense had gone from an unhappy marriage to a series of lovers. Her latest 'supporter' had just died and she was in need of new financial support, especially since her husband had frozen all her assets.

Ralph Montague, the English Ambassador to France, was also in search of advancement. He wanted to place a number of influential people close to the King who would be favourable to himself, and felt that Hortense would fit this bill admirably and might even be able to dislodge Louise from her position. He was aided and abetted in this plan by Arlington.

By 1675 Hortense had matured into a strong-minded woman. She is reputed to have been of a wild disposition and liked to 'gamble, eat, shoot, and swim, and was noted for her trick of performing a Spanish dance while accompanying herself on a guitar'.[9] She soon became one of Louise's fiercest rivals. Hortense was also a woman of strong sexual passions, including those of a bisexual nature. It was this passionate side of her character that led to the end of her relationship with Charles. Firstly, there was an incident where she became very close to Anne, the King's daughter by Barbara Villiers. When Anne's husband ordered that she join him at their country estate she refused to be separated from Hortense, the woman she said she loved. In the end, Charles had to insist that she go to her husband. Once there, Anne spent the whole time lying on a bed kissing a portrait of Hortense. Then Hortense had a fling with the Prince of Monaco, who was a guest of Charles. Following a disagreement over this, her relationship with the King changed and it is believed that although they remained friends, they were no longer lovers.

Buckingham's own extra-marital affair was about to burst into public attention once again. Harry Killigrew was back in England. Killigrew had been convicted of rape in France and was only saved from the hangman's noose by the actions of the Queen Mother and Minette who had interceded on his behalf. As soon as he returned home he began once again to speak disrespectfully of Lady Shrewsbury, who this time had resolved to act decisively herself, blaming him for all her troubles — if he had not acted as he had done, she would still be married to Lord Shrewsbury and enjoying her lover in secret.

On the night of 18 May 1669 Killigrew was physically attacked, and, according to Pepys, his attendant murdered as they were travelling in Hammersmith on their way to Killigrew's house at Turnham Green.[10] Killigrew received nine wounds in the attack. The French

Ambassador was one of those who believed the rumour that Lady Shrewsbury had observed the whole event from her six-horse carriage close by and that she had even 'cried out to the assassins to kill the villain'. The Ambassador also pondered on 'the worry and anxiety of the Duke of Buckingham, who is still passionately in love with this virago, whose husband he killed in a duel for having resisted her brow-beatings'.[11]

Such was the scandal caused by the attack that Buckingham felt obliged to speak publicly about it. The Duke of York told Pepys that Buckingham had come into the Queen's bedchamber and announced to the King and Harry Killigrew's father, who happened to be there at the time, that he had it from an unnamed witness that Killigrew had started the fight and that his opponents had only meant to 'cudgel him'. As to the unnamed witness, Pepys writes that 'all the world must know [it] must be his mistress, my Lady Shrewsbury'. The Duke of York expressed himself to be 'the most amazed that ever he was in his life' and said that 'it might cost him [Buckingham] his life in the House of Lords'.[12]

Soon, however, the whole episode was old news. By September Killigrew had recovered from his injuries; he apologised for his actions to both Lady Shrewsbury and the Duke of Buckingham, and was allowed to return to court.[13] The apology notwithstanding, the controversy and scandal in Buckingham's life reached a new low in February 1671 when Lady Shrewsbury gave birth to the Duke's son. It might be expected that he would be rather coy about this event and attempt to hide it, but instead he awarded the child the nominal title of Earl of Coventry, a title he had been given at birth, and held a lavish baptismal ceremony at which Charles was godfather. The King's acceptance of this role seems to suggest that the child's title would soon become official. The infant, named George Villiers after his father and grandfather, sadly died soon afterwards, and the funeral, which was held at Westminster Abbey on 12 March, was no less grand than the baptism.[14] Andrew Marvell mentioned it in a letter saying that the child 'to whom the king stood godfather . . .

died young Earl of Coventry, and was buried in the sepulchre of his fathers'. Rumours abounded to the effect that Buckingham had entered into a bigamous marriage with his mistress. It was said that the ceremony had been conducted by the Duke's chaplain, Dr Sprat.

By 1668 it was widely believed that Buckingham's financial situation was in a parlous state. Pepys, for one, suggests that the Duke was experiencing some financial constraints on his luxurious lifestyle. His income from rent roll was an average of £19,600 per year, in addition to which Charles had granted him a pension of £2,500 for twenty-one years and one of £1,500 for life. From this he had to pay £7,000 a year in interest, £2,000 in fee-farm rents to the King, and wages and pensions to the amount of £6,000.[15] The rest was spent on taxes and living expenses, but by 1671 he had run up large debts in excess of £40,000. Whether his indebtedness and the resultant sale of large amounts of his land were a result of financial mismanagement or, as has been claimed in recent years, a clever financial policy devised by his bankers to convert land into money, is hard to ascertain.[16] Undoubtedly he had a habit of spending vast sums of money, a pursuit in which he was ably assisted by the equally extravagant Lady Shrewsbury. One extravagance was the building of Cliveden House. His desire for a country house near London had prompted him to buy a plot of land at Cliveden, on the Thames. He spent vast resources of time and money building a house there. It was said by Evelyn to have had wonderful views of the 'serpenting' Thames. The diarist also comments on 'the august and stately cloisters, descents, gardens and avenue'. To recover some of the capital spent, on 1 January 1672 he sold York House for £30,000. The purchasers, a firm of builders, demolished it a few years later leaving only the water gate standing near Charing Cross station. On 24 August 1672 he signed a deed of gift giving his glassworks and 'all the stock at Vauxhall' to Lady Shrewsbury in order to protect it from his creditors, while at the same time retaining control of it. A year later he put it up for sale at £4,000.

In November 1671 Buckingham's father-in-law, General Fairfax, died. He was a man for whom the Duke had felt a genuine affection. In his *An Epitaph upon Thomas Lord Fairfax* he writes:

> So blest of all he died, but far more blest were we
> If we were sure to live till we could see
> A man as great in war, as just in peace as he.[17]

Buckingham would not, however, be faithful to the late General's daughter. The affair with Lady Shrewsbury continued. Their relationship, along with Charles's well-publicised romantic adventures with his many mistresses, ensured that the scandalous reputation of the royal court was maintained.

Seventeen

THE REHEARSAL

On 7 December 1671 Buckingham's play *The Rehearsal* was produced at the Drury Lane Theatre. The work, begun in 1663, had been a long time in gestation, perhaps beginning its life as an attack on Sir William Davenant who was then Poet Laureate. The work was interrupted a number of times by, among other things, various political crises and the plague. Buckingham's many collaborators on the work over the years are believed to have included his chaplain Dr Thomas Sprat, Samuel Butler and Martin Clifford.

The finished play became a burlesque or parody of the dramatic convention of seventeenth-century Heroic Drama and was taken by many to be a direct attack upon the work of the new Poet Laureate, John Dryden. Dryden had been appointed to the position in 1668, on Davenant's death, and later became Historiographer Royal. In fact, many contemporary plays, besides those of Dryden, are also satirised in the piece.[1]

This was the premier era for Heroic Drama, a genre which dealt with themes of idealised love and honour, featuring exotic locations and characters of the highest moral standards, often suffering violent emotional conflict. It was usually written in a lofty style and Dryden, in particular, liked to use rhymed heroic verse. In *The Rehearsal* Buckingham retains the style, language, theme and setting of real Heroic Drama but uses a ridiculous plot to make fun of the genre.

The plot involves the central character, Bayes, inviting two people to see the final rehearsal for his new play written in the genre of Heroic Drama, entitled *The Two Kings of Brentford*. The rehearsal reveals Bayes's work to be utter nonsense, with scenes such as those where two kings of the same place are deposed by two usurpers, and a sword fight which ensues between two princes because they are not in love with the same woman. Bayes's play also features ludicrous dances and comical battle scenes. The universal symbol of love, the turtle dove, is replaced by mating pigs. Bayes even admits to plagiarism:

Bayes: When I have anything to invent, I never trouble my head about it, as other men do; but presently turn over this book, and there I have, at one view, all that Perseus, Montaigne, Seneca's tragedies, Horace, Juvenal, Claudian, Pliny, Plutarch's Lives, and the rest, have ever thought upon this subject; and so in a trice, by leaving out a few words, or putting in others of my own, the business is done.[2]

Bayes is a playwright with no real interest in plot – for him, a plot is merely a vehicle for introducing dialogue:

Bayes: . . . what a Devil is the Plot good for, but to bring in fine things?

Understandably, the play ends with Bayes's two invited observers leaving the rehearsal in frustration followed soon afterwards by his disillusioned cast.

It is in *The Rehearsal* that Buckingham gives to the English language the word 'Drawcansir', meaning a blustering, bullying fellow of danger to both friend and enemy. The word comes from the name of a character in the play, who represents a parody of Dryden's character Almanzor from *The Conquest of Granada*. Almanzor is everything Drawcansir is not: a brave hero and a successful lover. Where, in Dryden's play, Almanzor says:

Spight of my self I'le Stay, Fight, Love, Despair;
And I can do all this, because I dare[3]

Drawcansir says in *The Rehearsal*:

I drink, I huff, I strut, look big and stare;
And I can do all this, because I dare[4]

The Rehearsal also has the now famous line, 'Ay, now the plot thickens very much upon us.'

Unfortunately for Dryden and other writers of Heroic Drama, *The Rehearsal* was a great success. Consequently, Buckingham is credited with inflicting serious damage on the genre. 'For a long time his [Bayes's] name and his conversation were as familiar as are those of the Mad Hatter or Mr. Pickwick.'[5] The play continued to be performed for many years,[6] even into the next century the role of Bayes was played eighty-eight times by the famous actor David Garrick. It is argued that as the popularity of the play spread, the standing of Heroic Drama was lessened.[7] It influenced other works such as Fielding's *Pasquin* and Sheridan's *The Critic*.

Recent scholarship has cast doubt on the degree to which Buckingham intended the character of Bayes to be a personal satire of Dryden.[8] As the rivalry between Buckingham and Dryden was so intense during these years, it is not surprising that a number of myths have grown up about it. One dubious story tells of Buckingham and his friends taking Dryden to the opening night of the play and putting him in a side box so that everyone could see his discomfort at watching Bayes, this thinly disguised parody of himself. Also unproven is the story that Buckingham himself took great pains in coaching the actor John Lacy on how best to imitate Dryden. Others have stated that the play contains references to Dryden's mistresses and that Bayes is dressed in black velvet and has a taste for stewed plums and snuff to make him mirror Dryden. Yet another unproven story tells of Buckingham being present at the performance of one of Dryden's plays where a character utters the line, 'My wound is great because it is so small', whereupon, in reply from the audience, Buckingham is reputed to have called out, 'Then t'would be greater were it none at all.'[9]

Whatever the truth of these stories, they indicate the level of interest this rivalry engendered in the popular imagination.[10] However, one scholar has suggested that the real personal target of Buckingham's play may have been Arlington.[11] It can also be argued that to have one's work included in the list of those satirised in *The Rehearsal* may not have signified a bitter personal attack at all – to have been left out might have been more of a slight. For example, the plays of Aphra Behn are included and Buckingham is known to have been an admirer of her work.[12]

In fact, Dryden himself may not at first have regarded the character of Bayes as a personal insult, because just two months after the performance of *The Rehearsal* he was very complimentary about Buckingham's version of *The Chances*.[13] However, perhaps as the years passed, he may have grown tired of his association in the public imagination with this foolish character. This feeling would have been fuelled by events such as Shadwell's publication of an attack on Dryden in 1682, which he entitled *The Medal of John Bayes*. In any event, twenty years after the first performance of *The Rehearsal* Dryden's tone had grown somewhat bitter when he wrote: 'I answered not *The Rehearsal*, because I knew the Author sate to himself when he drew the picture, and was the very Bayes of his own fame.'[14]

Despite Dryden's perceptions, with *The Rehearsal* Buckingham contributed to the development of the burlesque in English theatre. Generally regarded as his best literary work, the play stems from that element in his nature that enjoyed bringing people down to earth. It represents his desire to ridicule pomposity and is inspired by the same need that led to the mimicry with which he so frequently entertained those at the royal court. The play ensured his reputation as a playwright not only in his own century, but also into the eighteenth century, with the publication of twelve editions and hundreds of stage performances.

Eighteen

BLOOD TIES

The issue of fanatical militant Nonconformity continued to be a problem for King Charles. These dissenters had come from a position of strength under Cromwell's rule to the persecution of their religious rights under the restored monarchy. They had been promised 'liberty to tender consciences' under the Declaration of Breda but Clarendon, assisted and encouraged by Bishop Sheldon, had introduced a number of legislative measure intended to curb their freedom. This drove a number of them, known as 'phanaticks', to resort to the use of arms to achieve their religious freedom.

Colonel Thomas Blood was one such.[1] He was born into a Presbyterian family from Derbyshire that had settled in Ireland. The Bloods had done well under Cromwellian rule, but now, with the restoration of the monarchy, Thomas was facing the possible confiscation of his land and the suppression of his religious practice. His first venture into militantism had been a planned attack upon Dublin Castle in 1663, with the intention of taking captive the Duke of Ormonde. Subsequently known as Blood's Plot, the attack did not in fact take place since an informer had infiltrated the group and Ormonde seized them before they could act and had many of them arrested. Blood himself managed to escape, but spent the rest of the 1660s on the run, becoming the kingdom's most wanted man, and the Crown confiscated his land in Ireland as a result of his unlawful actions. The authorities failed to capture him, even though he journeyed incessantly around Britain and even paid a visit to Holland. He made use of a number of disguises and covers, including setting himself up as a physician in Romford for a period. In 1667 he managed to break free one of his fellow Nonconformist rebels, Captain John Mason, as he was being transported by a well-armed troop of soldiers from the Tower of London to stand trial in York.

On the evening of Tuesday 6 December 1670 Ormonde was making his way home from a great banquet that had been held in the Guildhall, London, in honour of the visiting Prince William of Orange. Ormonde, no longer a young man, had decided to leave the festivities early. He was staying in Clarendon House, which had been lent to him by the ex-Chancellor's son.

The Duke's grand coach was brought to a stop at the top of St James's Street by a man on horseback who was shouting that there was a dead man lying on the road. Suddenly Ormonde's coach was surrounded by Colonel Thomas Blood and his armed accomplices.[2] It was an opportunity for which Blood had long waited. The Duke, not recognising the most wanted man in the country, told them that if it was money they were after they could have it. He found himself forced up on to a horse, bound to a member of the gang and heading towards Piccadilly. Blood rode on ahead, some say to prepare a rope for the Duke's hanging at Tyburn.

By this time Ormonde must have realised that he was in deep trouble and began to struggle wildly behind the man to whom he was bound. He managed to dismount them both and continued to fight as they hit the ground heavily. He grabbed the man's sword and broke loose from his binding. Luckily, a number of his servants came running on to the scene at that moment. As Thomas Brooks, the porter at Clarendon House, arrived he heard the kidnappers shout 'Kill the rogue!' before two shots rang out. With this the assailants retreated. The Duke had been saved only by the darkness of the evening. He had not been hit and, although dirty and shaken, after a few days in bed made a full recovery.

The King issued a proclamation on 7 December 1670 requesting information on what he called this 'barbarous and inhumane attempt . . .

upon the person and life of our right trusty, and right entirely beloved cousin and counsellor James Duke of Ormond. . .'.[3] The *London Gazette* also carried an account of the attack, with news of a £1,000 reward.[4] The investigation into the crime revealed that the main culprits were Colonel Blood, acting under his alias of Dr Allen, his son, also named Thomas and acting under the alias of Mr Hunt, and Richard Halliwell or Holloway. Despite the reward and an investigation during which over fifty people were interviewed, none of the suspects was arrested.

Because of the well-known antipathy between the dukes of Buckingham and Ormonde, Buckingham soon began to be suspected of involvement in Blood's outrageous attack upon his adversary. People wondered if Blood had been employed by Buckingham to assassinate Ormonde. A daring kidnap of this kind, where Ormonde was taken in the centre of London as he returned from a society ball, would have appealed to both Blood and Buckingham. As one writer puts it, Buckingham:

> would probably not have considered it ungentlemanlike to slit a rival's throat, by deputy, at a dark corner, but he would have thought it deplorably dull. Whereas, to seize an opponent in the heart of the capital, and in the plenitude of his security, to whirl him to Tyburn, and there, on the gallows to terminate the impeccable career of the *Cavalier sans peur et sans reproche*, was a method of settling accounts, presenting that nice composition of drama and irony dear to the perverted ingenuity of George Villiers.[5]

Certainly Ormonde's son, the Earl of Ossory, believed the rumours of Buckingham's involvement. He confronted the Duke directly on the matter one day as Buckingham stood beside Charles. 'My lord,' he challenged, 'I know well that you are at the bottom of this late attempt of Blood's upon my father; and therefore I give you fair warning; if my father come to a violent end by sword or pistol, if he dies by the hand of a ruffian, or by the more secret way of poison, I shall not be at a loss to know the first author of it; I shall consider you as the assassin; I shall treat you as such; and wherever I meet you I shall pistol you, though you stood behind the king's chair; and I tell it you in his majesty's presence, that you may be sure I shall keep my word.'[6] Perhaps surprised by the directness of Ossory's approach, Buckingham for once was stunned into silence. Ossory's warning may have worked, as no more attempts were made by Blood or anyone else on the life of the Duke of Ormonde.

In May 1671 Blood put into action his most daring deed of all when he attempted to steal the crown jewels from the Tower of London. Ingratiating himself with the Assistant Keeper of the Jewel House at the Tower, Talbot Edwards, he paid Edwards and his family a number of visits and even set up a romantic match between a fictitious nephew of his and Edwards's daughter. On the day chosen for the future lovers to meet, Blood and his accomplices hit old Edwards over the head and made off with the King's state crown, the orb and sceptre. Unfortunately for them, Edwards's son had just arrived home unexpectedly for a visit and he set off in pursuit of the jewel thieves, accompanied by Captain Martin Beckman, who had been invited to the Tower to witness the betrothal of the young lovers.

At one point the two men in pursuit were almost injured by the passing crowds after Blood had had the audacity to point at them and shout 'Stop Thief!' Beckman caught up with Blood on the wharf beside the Thames. Blood fired on him but missed, and was subdued and arrested. So too were his accomplices. At last the almost mythical rogue Colonel Thomas Blood was in captivity, and, it seemed, would pay for his crimes.

Once again Buckingham's name was being associated with Colonel Blood's actions. Had the Duke played a part in this latest deed of Colonel Blood's? Was the theft an attempt to bring attention to the plight of the Nonconformists? Or an attempt to sway opinion in Parliament? Belief in Buckingham's involvement with Blood increased when, much to everyone's amazement, following an audience with Charles, Blood was not hanged but was granted a pardon instead. The rest of his gang were also pardoned, and Blood was even given back his land in Ireland. Buckingham's involvement with Blood would not end with the rumours about his involvement with the theft of the crown jewels. A number of years later their relationship would damage them both![7]

It seems that a deal was cut, probably with Buckingham's assistance. Charles was keen to issue a Declaration of Indulgence under which Nonconformist Protestants and Catholics would be granted limited freedom to practise their religion. Blood would be a great advantage to the regime when dealing with the Nonconformist community. The Declaration was issued in March 1672, permitting Nonconformist preachers who applied for and were granted licences to worship at authorised locations. Blood upheld his part of the bargain as he became very active working as an intermediary processing licences for his co-religionists. He also worked at gaining pardons for those from his community, persuading them not to take a pro-Dutch stance in the forthcoming war, and gathering information useful to the regime.

In his piece entitled *To Mr. Martin Clifford on his Human Reason*, Buckingham argued that 'There is no way, indeed left to make the Reformation flourish, but its espousing sincerely a true and perfect liberty of conscience, that is, that it make the empire of reason sacred. . .'.[8] In reality, however, public opinion turned very quickly against the Declaration of Indulgence. Even those Nonconformists who had gained the right to practise their religion under licence were unhappy about similar freedoms being given to Catholics. When Parliament was summoned on 4 February 1673, Members of the House of Commons drew up a petition calling for the withdrawal of the Declaration. Charles defended it by saying that, as a result of war with the Dutch, it was a necessary way of 'securing peace at home while I had war abroad'. The House made it clear that Charles would not obtain his much needed funds for the Dutch War if the Declaration was not withdrawn. Buckingham, along with Lauderdale and Shaftesbury, urged the King to hold firm, to dissolve Parliament and call a new election. Arlington, on the other hand, wanted him to concede to the wishes of Parliament. By March 1673 Charles felt he had no option but to withdraw the Declaration.

Three weeks after the annulment of the Declaration, the Test Act was passed, which made matters worse for Nonconformists and Catholics. Under this piece of legislation anyone who wished to take public office, use the courts or adopt a child, had to take the oath of allegiance and supremacy, receive communion according to the Anglican rite and declare that they rejected the doctrine of transubstantiation. As a result, James, Duke of York, although excluded from the act, resigned his post as Lord High Admiral.

The fact that Buckingham was freely associating with people from the militant Nonconformist community shows that he was not shy of dealing with dangerous people. He was a man who made many enemies, which placed him in potential danger. No one was surprised in 1667 when the Privy Council investigated claims that there was a plot to assassinate him. In 1668 he made a claim himself that his life was in danger and went around for a time accompanied by an armed guard. It is, of course, understandable that in light of his father's murder, he would be nervous about such things.

In 1670 a rumour was doing the rounds that Ormonde, assisted by the exiled Clarendon, had instigated a plot to murder him. It seems that Buckingham himself was active in disseminating this story, perhaps in an attempt to blacken the reputations of his enemies. According to Buckingham he was saved only by the fact that the would-be assassins were themselves poisoned, making frank confessions on their deathbeds.

Buckingham's links with people such as Blood and his political support for religious toleration on behalf of Nonconformists left him open to accusations of support for militant fanaticism and even sometimes to atheism. This reputation gained him many enemies within the Established Church. But, in reality, he was far from being a fanatical Nonconformist. While in Scotland with Charles in the 1650s it was very clear that he found the austerity, lifestyle and piety of the Presbyterians abhorrent. Both he and Charles found their 'fire and brimstone' sermons and their general way of life extremely trying. His advocacy of religious toleration for Nonconformists, like that of Charles, was based to a large degree on political reality. As he had no principled objection to their form of worship, he felt that it made perfect sense to allow them freedom of conscience in return for political stability.

Nineteen

'DRAW AN ARRANT FOP'

Buckingham's dislike of Henry Bennet, Earl of Arlington, deepened with the passing of the years. Arlington's marriage to Lady Ossory's sister, Isabella von Beerwaert, gave him a link to Ormonde and deepened Buckingham's dislike. After all, by the 1670s Buckingham had eliminated his rivals: Clarendon, Coventry, Barbara and Ormonde. But Arlington was still in power as Secretary of State in the southern office, and during his time there (1662–74) his office was the dominant one. Moreover, his position testified to the esteem in which Charles held him.

A bad scar from an old wound meant that Arlington always wore a strip of black tape across his nose. But he was a talented man who spoke Latin, French and Spanish fluently. The fact that he was somewhat pompous and foppish left him open to Buckingham's ridicule. In his satirical poem, *Advice to a Painter*, this is one of the characteristics to which Buckingham draws attention:

> First draw an arrant fop, from top to toe,
> Whose very looks at first dash shew him so:
> Give him a mean proud Garb, a dapper pace
> A pert dull grin, a black patch 'cross his face,
> Two goggle eyes so clear, though very dead,
> That one may see through them, quite through his head.
> Let every Nod of his, and little wink
> Declare, the Fool would speak, but never think.

Let him all other Fools so far surpass,
That Fools themselves point at him for an Ass.

Arlington, who knew of the existence of the secret treaty, had played Buckingham for a fool during the negotiations for the 1670 Treaty of Dover. When Buckingham went to Dunkirk in the summer of 1671 to talk with the French about some minor aspects of the two countries' relations, Arlington said that he had withdrawn to the country on purpose so that the Duke would think he had control of foreign affairs.

In 1671 there was an argument between the two Houses of Parliament over a new taxation bill. Buckingham and his supporters in the Lords wanted a reduction in the tax being introduced on white sugar. Members of the Commons felt that matters of taxation were outside the remit of the Lords. Buckingham stood up for the privilege of the House of Lords. When the bill failed Arlington was quick to point out to Charles that the Crown had lost a great deal of money as a result, and that Buckingham was to blame.

The next conflict between Buckingham and Arlington centred around the post of Chancellor of the University of Cambridge, which Arlington wanted and Buckingham won in May 1671.[1] Buckingham worked hard canvassing support for his victory. Arlington was warned by Dr Thomas Hill when he wrote that 'There is scarce a man of note in the University who has not been solicited by letters from London by the Duke's friends'.[2] There is no doubt that Buckingham's successful election to this position was made all the sweeter for defeating Arlington to the prize. On 7 June he celebrated the ceremony of his installation at York House, although at the time he had let it to the French Ambassador;[3] it was there that his father had been installed to the same position forty years earlier. The ceremony was a lavish affair with a stately procession entering the house, including, in their multifarious colours, Doctors, Masters of Art and Bachelors of Divinity. Also in attendance were five bishops, including the

Bishop of London and the Bishop of Durham, many earls and barons, and all the University's dignitaries. All were welcomed by the new Chancellor himself resplendent in his new clothes for the occasion. One report said that 'This performance was observed to be remarkable for the great respect showed by the University in the number that appeared and the extraordinary kindness of the duke, both in the grandeur of his treat and the obligingness of his expression and deportment.'[4] In addition to all this ceremony, in October 1671, Charles did the new Chancellor the honour of paying him a state visit at the University. Needless to say, appropriate celebrations were set in train for such a prestigious occasion.

In 1672 Arlington married his only daughter and heiress, Isabella, to Charles's illegitimate son, Henry, Duke of Grafton. It was a match that Buckingham did everything he could to prevent, even going to Charles and proposing the rich Lady Percy as a more suitable wife for the young duke. Charles informed him that it was by then too late to put a stop to the match.

Animosity between the two aristocrats came to a head when Arlington tried to prevent Buckingham from attaining the coveted position of commanding the English troops abroad, a post he had been promised when negotiating the public Treaty of Dover. Arlington used his influence with Charles to obtain a concession from Louis that they send only 2,400 troops instead of the promised 6,000. Then the honour of commanding the troops went to the King's son, the Duke of Monmouth. To add insult to injury, Buckingham's enemy, Ormonde's son, Lord Ossory, was made second in command. The Frenchman Colbert de Choisy was left with the unenviable task of telling Buckingham the news; predictably, he flew into a rage and throughout the following week he refused to attend to any state business. Buckingham vented his anger on Charles and accused Arlington and Montague, the Ambassador in Paris, of plotting against him because it was he who had done so much to foster the close relationship between His Majesty and Louis. As already noted, when he protested strongly to Charles about the matter, the King put him firmly in his place.[5]

In March 1671 war was declared once again on the Dutch and the terms of the Treaty of Dover were published. Buckingham had for a long time been in favour of this war, and to a great extent, his political future would depend upon its outcome. The Captain General and Admiral General of the Dutch forces, William of Orange, Charles's nephew, had troops that would be heavily outnumbered by the combined English and French. William, however, was a serious and determined young man who was not to be taken lightly. (Nonetheless, Buckingham had managed to dent his sober reputation somewhat by getting him drunk at a dinner party on his visit to England a few months earlier. Most uncharacteristically, and much to Buckingham's amusement, the inebriated visitor insisted in staggering off towards the bedrooms of the maids of honour![6])

There was considerable opposition in England to the war. One particular piece of anti-war propaganda was published in the form of a pamphlet entitled *The Present Interest of England Stated*. Buckingham decided to counter these arguments in favour of the war by writing a public letter in 1672 to Thomas Osborne, *A Letter to Sir Thomas Osborn on Reading a Book called the Present Interest of England Stated*:

> The undoubted interest of England is trade, since it is that only which can make us either rich or safe; for without a powerful navy, we should be a prey to our neighbours, and without trade, we could neither have sea-men nor ships. From hence it does follow, that we ought not to suffer any other nations to be our equals at sea, because when they are once our equals, it is but an even lay, whether they or we shall be the superiors. And it would not be a stranger thing that the Dutch should come to be so.[7]

Buckingham remained enthusiastic about the war, and as the Duke of York was preparing the fleet he drove the officials to distraction by giving unending advice and offering suggestions.[8] On 25 May 1672 Buckingham's mind was temporarily deflected from matters of war, however, while he was busily and very effectively involved in fighting a fire in London. The fire began only seven or eight houses away from the Iron Gate at the Tower of London. It spread rapidly leading to a number of deaths and injuries, the burning of eighty houses, the deliberate blowing up of thirty more and the burning of seven ships on the Thames. Buckingham acted bravely and decisively:

> the Duke himself came to the King's stairs on Tower Wharf with a lighter, and took in the engineers, and stood away eastwards, where the fire was most raging. When there, he caused the engines to play on a house on fire some six houses east of St. Katharine's Stairs, and came ashore bringing some persons skilful in blowing up, whom he set to work to blow up some houses east of the fire, making a passage from St. Katharine's Church to the water side, and so round the fire. The number last blown up east of the fire was six . . . In this work the Duke employed himself till eight at night, down to the lower part of the fire by St. Katherine's Church, encouraging the men and giving them money.[9]

Meanwhile, William of Orange's navy had enjoyed a number of successes at sea, but the main events of the war were taking place on land as Louis, with 100,000 men, swept through the Dutch forces. The Dutch sent representatives to England at the beginning of June 1672 to discuss possible peace terms. They met with Buckingham and felt encouraged by the encounter. Charles himself was not entirely happy with the degree of success being achieved by Louis, fearing that the French King could be becoming too powerful.

A few weeks later Charles sent Buckingham and Arlington to the Continent as 'Ambassadors Extraordinary' to negotiate a peace treaty.[10] Lord Halifax, who had been sent earlier to congratulate Louis on the birth of a son, was also involved in the talks. It is said that during this trip Buckingham paid a visit to the Princess Dowager Amalia. One report of their encounter has him telling her that he and his colleagues were 'good Hollanders', and she replying that she only wanted them to be 'good Englishmen'.[11] When he said that they 'did not use Holland as a mistress, but they loved her as a wife', she is said to have retorted sarcastically 'Truly, I think you love us just as you love yours!'

The English representatives had been instructed to demand tough terms for peace, including payment of a substantial war indemnity, an annual payment of £10,000 for the right to fish herring in English waters, the obligation to honour the English flag at sea and full sovereignty to two or three ports. The French demands were just as tough and included the stipulation that a delegation must travel to Paris every year to thank Louis XIV for his mercy.

Buckingham wrote to Charles after his arrival in The Hague telling him that things were going well. 'Though our expectation to find disorder here was very great, yet what we saw when we arrived exceeded all we could imagine. Our first salutation . . . was, God Bless the King of England.'[12] Good reports were coming back in other ways, too. A Richard Watts wrote that 'On the report that the Duke of Buckingham and Lord Arlington were gone for Holland . . . last night a pleasure boat came and delivered a letter to the commander-in-chief in the Downs, it is said that the English colours are up in Amsterdam, and that they with Rotterdam and Zealand have submitted themselves subjects to the King'.[13]

However, the English and French had underestimated William's determination – he would not accept their terms for peace, insisting that he was not interested in their offer of the crown of Holland as he preferred the office of Stadtholder, to which he had been appointed by the Dutch. He warned Buckingham and Arlington that it would be a very awkward situation for England if the Dutch were totally overrun by the French. In fact, Buckingham found his argument so convincing that he decided then and there that they should sign a truce with him.

Arlington was shocked at the Duke's response. Overnight, either as a result of reflection on the matter or following the intervention of his colleagues, Buckingham had a change of mind. At their next meeting he urged William to place himself in his Uncle Charles's hands. When William stated that he would never betray his country, Buckingham asked him, 'Do you not see it is lost?' 'I see it is indeed in great danger,' said William, 'but there is a sure way never to see it lost, and that is to die in the last dyke.'[14]

Buckingham and Arlington left in failure and travelled to Utrecht, where they held meetings with King Louis' ministers. In the end, the only result of the journey was a treaty that was signed at Heeswick between the English and the French promising that neither side would make a separate peace with William. They were home by July 1672.[15]

When Charles opened the new session of Parliament in February 1673 he told Members that the war was being fought for the 'interest as well as the honour of the nation'. He informed them that he needed funds to maintain the war. He was supported by Shaftesbury, who called the Dutch 'the common enemy to all monarchies' saying that they wanted to establish a 'universal empire as great as Rome'.[16] In the end Charles had to drop his Declaration of Indulgence and give his consent to the Test Act before he received any money from Parliament.

In the spring and summer of 1673 Buckingham's mind returned to military matters since he wanted to take part in the action planned for the summer in Holland. In May he was made a Lieutenant-General, under the overall command of the Duke of York.[17] He went to Yorkshire to raise and drill perhaps up to 5,000 men.[18]

Prince Rupert was now appointed Lord High Admiral in place of the Duke of York, who had resigned over the Test Act. By July Rupert was with the fleet awaiting the arrival of Buckingham and his men. On 2 July he wrote to Arlington, as they were preparing to sail, saying that there was no sign of Buckingham's regiment and that he had been informed that the Duke 'intends none shall come'.[19] He wrote again the following day, with growing frustration, saying that the regiment had still not arrived, although he had heard that they had been training every day at Barnett. Buckingham had sent someone to the ships of the fleet demanding his colours and drums. Rupert writes, 'I beseech you to consider how I am to behave myself with this Lieut.-General.'

Buckingham was eventually replaced by the French General Count Schomberg after his soldiers had rioted when their coats were taken from them for use elsewhere.[20] Relations between Schomberg and Prince Rupert deteriorated quickly, even to the extent that at one point Rupert ordered his ship to fire on Schomberg.

When Parliament reconvened Charles once again looked for funds to support the war effort. Shaftesbury again used his oratorial skills in support of this request. Prompted by the opposition of William Coventry, Members were tardy in voting for the needed supply.[21] In fact, feelings towards their ally, France, were beginning to harden considerably. Charles decided to prorogue Parliament in order to allow members time to consider the question.

When the next session began at the beginning of 1674 Charles felt it necessary to scotch rumours by assuring Members that there was no secret agreement between himself and Louis. He told them:

> I know you have heard much of My Alliance with France; and, I believe, it hath been very strangely misrepresented to you, as if there were certain secret articles of dangerous consequence . . . I assure you, there is no other Treaty with France, either before or since, not already printed, which will not be made known.[22]

English involvement in the Dutch War came to an end in February 1674 with the signing of the Treaty of Westminster. The terms agreed were much more lenient than those first proposed to William by Buckingham and Arlington. The Dutch agreed to salute the English flag, they paid a war indemnity, most of which they clawed back in debts, but they refused to pay for the right to fish in English waters.

All in all the war had been a disaster for Charles. In the beginning he hoped that his alliance with King Louis would be hugely beneficial for him and that the Dutch War would bring a quick victory, benefiting England's trade by seriously damaging their main rival. After the war he hoped that his grateful nephew, William of Orange, could be made king of a much weakened country. Instead, the war had turned into a protracted disaster and had damaged Charles's own kingdom financially. He had been forced to withdraw his Declaration of Indulgence and also to concede to the Test Act. He had also managed to increase anti-Catholic feeling in the country by allying himself with Catholic France. To make matters worse, rumours were now rife that Charles had made some kind of secret agreement with the French.

Things were not going well for Buckingham either. Even when he left Whitehall in the autumn of 1673 he was aware that Charles and some of his other ministers were plotting against him, either to force him to toe the line or remove him from power altogether. He secretly turned to France and Louis XIV for comfort, telling Louis's representative that he feared, on the reopening of Parliament, he was to be blamed for the French Treaty. He requested that Louis send over a representative to discuss with him plans for promoting French interests among the Members of Parliament. Louis obliged by sending the Marquis de Ruvigny on the pretext of congratulating the Duke of York on his marriage. Unfortunately for Buckingham, de Ruvigny was ordered to keep Charles informed of every detail of the Duke's proposals.

Buckingham was right: in January 1674 the House of Commons was in combative form. Members wanted answers, and among those from whom they wanted them were Buckingham and Arlington. In Buckingham's case, his close relationship with the French was regarded by many as treacherous. When he saw the Commons proposal that he should be removed from all his employments and from the royal presence and councils for ever, he knew that he would have to come up with a survival strategy. He asked to waive his rights as a peer and to address the House in person so that he could 'inform them in person of some truths relating to the public'.[23] He was informed that during the next session, at ten o'clock the following morning, the House would require 'full and precise answers to a number of questions'.[24]

One account states that before the session started the Duke engaged some Members of the House in conversation and drinking, while in the company of those of a different disposition he received the Sacrament.[25] Before the questioning began, he made a short speech, declaring: 'I hope you will consider the condition I am in, in danger of passing for a vicious person and a betrayer of my country. I have ever had the misfortune of bearing other men's faults.'[26] He did his best to exonerate himself and Shaftesbury, while placing the blame on Arlington. He said 'my Lord Shaftesbury and myself advised not to begin a war without the advice of the Parliament, and the affections of the people; this was my Lord Shaftesbury's opinion and mine, but not my Lord Arlington's.'[27] He probably went too far when he referred before the House to Charles and the Duke of York, without naming them directly, by saying that 'he was weary of the company he was joined with, and knew how to kill a hare with hounds, but could not hunt with lobsters'.[28]

The cross-examination itself was performed by the Speaker of the House, who put eleven questions to the Duke.[29] In the course of his answers he informed Members that the Duke of Ormonde had received 'about five hundred Thousand Pounds' and Lord Arlington not so much, but nevertheless 'a great deal' of money.[30] He also claimed that Arlington was responsible for Schomberg being put in charge of the army and for the army being used 'to awe the Debates and Resolutions of the House of Commons'.[31] Next he was asked about his role in the closing of the Exchequer in 1672, when payments from the Treasury to bankers who had lent money to the government were stopped for a year in order to raise money for the war. It was a move that had brought financial hardship for some. Buckingham countered that he had not agreed with this policy and that, furthermore, it had cost him £3,000 personally. He did admit that he had supported the Declaration of Indulgence, being, 'always of [the] opinion that something was to be done in that nature in matters of Conscience, but no further than the King might do by law'.[32] He also freely admitted of his prime role in the negotiations leading to the Treaty with France. As he answered the questions, he continued to do his best to lay the failures of the preceding few years at the door of Arlington, including the attacking of the Smyrna Fleet, of which he said 'I was utterly against it . . . and incurr'd some anger by it. My Lord Arlington principally moved it.'[33]

When his turn came to defend himself, Arlington attempted to turn the tables by placing the blame right back on Buckingham.[34] While referring to accusations made regarding the violation of the Triple Alliance – the alliance between England, the Netherlands and Sweden against France – he declared, 'I did what I could to further it . . . I was ever against any violation of it. I cannot clear myself without laying something on others, and so must say the Duke of Buckingham was for destroying it.' He also told Members that 'I suppose 'tis well known that the Duke about that time in his common discourse frequently gave out that I was to be turned out, that he would furnish the King with a better Secretary that should drive on another interest'.

Arlington also made sure to mention Buckingham's 'great credit in the French Court'. According to his account, when the King of France was to come to Dunkirk, Buckingham requested to go and meet him there, and although that duty had already been granted to Lord Bellasis, the Duke persisted, desiring 'leave to wait on so great a king since he was come so near'. Arlington told Parliament that in the end Buckingham was permitted to go. Arlington further claimed that while it was not his decision to replace Buckingham and put Schomberg in charge of the English forces, he had agreed with the move, saying that 'The Duke of Buckingham is a person of as great courage as any in the world, but . . . [has] less skill than Schomberg in military matters.' He also claimed that during negotiations with the enemy he and Lord Halifax were 'more moderate' in their demands with the Dutch, whereas 'Buckingham was absolutely against having them moderated in the least'.

In the long run Buckingham's efforts to shift the blame did him no good. The House of Commons voted to remove him 'from all his employments that are held during His Majesty's pleasure and from his presence and councils for ever'.[35] Charles was in no mood to attempt to save his old friend: he was not at all pleased with the revelations and accusations made by Buckingham before the House of Commons. His anger spilled over when he commented to de Ruvigny that 'George Villiers . . . was a worthless fellow who had not only betrayed State secrets but, merely in order to injure his personal enemies, had also seriously misrepresented and distorted matters which had been discussed at the Council Board.'[36] Arlington on the other hand was eventually cleared of all charges against him.

By the mid-1670s a number of significant political changes had taken place. The Duke of York had resigned his commission as Lord High Admiral because of the Test Act. Clifford, a Catholic, had had to give up his post as Lord Treasurer and was replaced by Buckingham's one-time protégé, Thomas Osborne. Shaftesbury was dismissed from the Lord Chancellorship. Buckingham and Arlington had both been subjected to the parliamentary questioning. Buckingham was removed from his positions and Arlington, although cleared, decided to resign as Secretary of State in September 1674, becoming instead Lord Chamberlain of the Household. Parliament was prorogued on 14 February 1674 until 10 November 1674, and again from 10 November to 13 April 1675. Buckingham's period in governmental office was now over: he would have to return to his previous role of Opposition Spokesman. His political difficulties were not his only problem, however – he also had to face attack from another quarter.

Twenty

THE END OF THE AFFAIR

Buckingham's affair with Lady Shrewsbury was about to erupt into the public domain once again. Firstly, in 1673 Buckingham was drawn into a controversy linked with his mistress. On witnessing a fight between two members of the Royal Horse Guards, Lady Shrewsbury's coachman decided that he should intervene, but when his enthusiasm got the better of him and he began to lash one of the soldiers across the face with his whip, the soldier, Mr Ayne, took umbrage and ran him through with his sword, killing him. Onlookers stepped in and Ayne was brought before Buckingham to be questioned about his actions. However, the Duke's rather unprofessional response was to beat the man severely.

Then, in January 1674, when Buckingham was at his lowest point and facing political ruination from the House of Commons, he also came under attack in the House of Lords. The trustees and relatives of the late Earl of Shrewsbury's son presented a petition to the Lords regarding Buckingham's relationship with Lady Shrewsbury.[1] The trustees, Lord Brudenell, Gilbert Talbot, Thomas Talbot, Buno Talbot, Mervin Audeley Touchett and William Talbot, said of the child that he 'becomes every day more sensible of the deplorable death of his father, and of the dishonour caused to his family by the wicked and scandalous life led by George, Duke of Buckingham, with Anna Maria, Countess of Shrewsbury, relict of the late Earl, multiplying new provocations to two noble families by the insolent and shameless manner of their cohabiting together since the death of the late Earl'.[2]

The petitioners said that they would not have complained 'had the offenders employed the usual care to cover their guilt and shame', but on the contrary they had persisted 'in their shameless course of life, in defiance of the laws of God and man, having caused a base son of theirs to be buried in the Abbey church at Westminster, with all solemnities, under the title of Earl of Coventry'.[3] They even alluded to 'conduct even more unnatural than that already ascribed to Lady Shrewsbury'.[4] This may have been a veiled reference to sodomy, that most serious and much laid accusation in the seventeenth century.

This astounding petition silenced the House. Although everyone was aware of Buckingham's behaviour, and many were in similar situations themselves, such a thing should not be drawn attention to in such a way. The Duke of Ormonde spoke in the debate in support of the petition as did the Earl of Bristol. However, Lord Anglesea and Lord Berkshire spoke on behalf of Buckingham. The Duke's supporters managed to secure a resolution whereby he could have eight days to prepare his defence.

Probably suffering from strain, the Duke succumbed to a fever, which laid him low for a number of days.[5] By 14 January he had recovered well and made his reply. He firmly denied that he had brought about the dispute with the Earl of Shrewsbury by 'scandalous and provocative behaviour'. In fact, he claimed, the Earl's jealously had been whipped up by others when, actually, there were very few grounds to justify it. According to Buckingham there had been no 'odious living together before the death of the late Earl'. Lady Shrewsbury, he said, had left her husband and gone to Paris and then to a monastery, but in blaming Buckingham for this the Earl had been misled. According to the Duke, her flight had had nothing to do with him but was, he said in a veiled reference to Harry Killigrew, 'because she thought her honour was not vindicated upon one who had done her a public and barbarous affront'. When the Earl died, Buckingham declared that he felt 'as sensible a grief as any of the gentlemen that subscribed the petition'. And, afterwards, when Lady Shrewsbury's friends and relatives deserted her, he helped her as any 'man of honour' would have done for 'a lady in her condition'.[6]

Buckingham went on to ask 'God's forgiveness and their Lordships' for anything, in this or his whole life, that may have given occasion for scandal. He also promised to 'take care to avoid any reproach of the same nature for the future'. Meanwhile, Buckingham's wife was, according to Lord Conway, 'crying and tearing herself'.[7] Conway stated that she solicited not only on behalf of her husband but also on that of Lady Shrewsbury. The Earl of Cardigan, Lady Shrewsbury's father, also came forward to speak on his daughter's behalf. He informed the House that he had received a letter from his daughter in which she begged not to be made 'desperate'. The father was supported in his appeal by Shaftesbury, who had been working behind the scenes on Buckingham's behalf.

In the end, Buckingham was obliged to acknowledge 'the lewd and miserable life he had led'. He stated that:

> . . . though it was a very heavy burden to lye under the displeasure of the House and the sense of his transgressions, yet he had reason to give God thanks for it, since it had opened his eyes and discovered to him the foulness of his past life, which he was resolved for the future to amend.[8]

A deed was drawn up under which the Duke of Buckingham and Lady Shrewsbury were bound, under penalty of £10,000, not to 'converse or cohabit for the future'.[9] It was also decided that the body of the so-called Earl of Coventry would be permitted to remain in Westminster Abbey.

Once these points had been decided, the Duke requested of the House of Lords that the whole matter should be removed from the records. His request was refused. He then attempted, unsuccessfully, to retract his evidence saying that he 'had owned more than the petitions against him could prove'.[10]

The following Sunday, at the religious service at St Martin-in-the-Fields, the congregation saw Buckingham in all his splendour in the company of his wife.[11] His infamous and notorious love affair with Lady Shrewsbury was over. His emotional suffering may be reflected in his poem *The Lost Mistress, a Complaint against the Countess of* ——

> In love the blessing of my life I closed,
> And in her custody that love disposed.
> In one dear freight all's lost! Of her bereft,
> I have no hope, no second comfort left . . .

Lady Shrewsbury spent a short time in a convent at Dunkirk. Two years later she was married to a Mr George Rodney Bridges, from Somerset. Her parents disapproved of the marriage, which they judged to be beneath her, but she seems to have remained loyal to her husband until her death in 1702.

For Buckingham, this public scandal did not, it is said, mark a new era of loyalty and fidelity to his wife. On the contrary, during the period that followed he moved quickly from one lover to another. As is stated in his Commonplace book: 'To love but one is the monastic life of love, and may justly be suspected of sloth.'[12]

Twenty-one

LIFE IN THE COUNTRY

Buckingham's political career was now in ruins. He was removed from the Privy Council, the Council for Trade and Plantations, the Admiralty Commission and the Lord Lieutenancy of the West Riding. Charles gave instructions in July 1674 that Buckingham be removed from the Chancellorship of the University of Cambridge, and recommended that his own son, Monmouth, be elected in Buckingham's place. Out of favour in this way, Buckingham considered the option of going to live in France. He even sent Ellis Leighton there to sound out King Louis' opinion on the matter. When the signals coming back were none too encouraging, he decided to retreat to the countryside instead.

Charles wanted to dispossess Buckingham of the Master of the Horse without allowing him any compensation from his successor. The Duke had bought the post in 1668 from Albemarle for £20,000. In March the King asked a number of equerries to look into Buckingham's financial handling of his equine duties. Although the Duke had requested and received substantial money to provide equipage, stable provisions and liveries, it seems that half the supplies had not been procured and he had rendered no accounts.[1]

Buckingham wrote a letter to Charles around this time, demonstrating clearly his sense of hurt and betrayal. It also shows how Buckingham could see no fault in his own actions:

May it please Your Majesty, – I desired my Lord Treasurer to beg leave of Your Majesty that I might have the honour to speak with you, which Your Majesty refused. Afterwards he promised to lay before Your Majesty the hardness of my present case, which he tells me he hath done, though I confess I should hardly believe it, if I had not great experience of his honour and truth in general to all men, as well as of his kindness to me in particular. I am not the least surprised at my having enemies about Your Majesty; but I wonder very much after the many observations I have made of Your Majesty's good nature to all the world, that you can find it in your heart to use me with so much cruelty, who have ever loved you better than myself, and preferred the following you abroad in the worst of your misfortunes, before the staying at home to enjoy a plentiful estate.

Pray, sir, what have I done that should make you thus angry with me? Was it my fault that other men did really prejudice Your Majesty's affairs upon the hopes of doing me a mischief? Did I say anything in my defence which could possibly be wrested to a reflection upon Your Majesty? Or if I was forced to reflect upon others, was it anything more than what you yourself gave me leave to do? In case I should be first accused, I beseech Your Majesty examine your own heart well upon this subject, and if those that heard me speak do not clear me from having behaved myself disrespectfully to Your Majesty, I desire no favour from you. I am told the House of Commons have addressed to Your Majesty that I may be deprived of all places which I hold of Your Majesty's pleasure, the severity of which censure I shall not take upon myself now to dispute. But Your Majesty may please to remember that by your gracious permission I bought the place of Master of the Horse, which I hold by patent under the Great Seal during my life, with power of nominating my deputy. It is therefore my most humble request to Your Majesty I may be allowed to name such a deputy as Your Majesty shall approve; that so I may not wholly lose my right to a favour which I purchased by Your Majesty's favour, and which the House of Commons were so far from desiring should be taken from me, that upon the mention of it in the House it was universally agreed to that no man's freehold ought to be invaded, and for that reason the address to Your Majesty was worded accordingly. Your Majesty knows I have often told you that I would depend on no man's favour in the Court but yours, and that nothing could make me desire to stay there but your kindness. These have been always my thoughts and are so still.

If it be upon the score of the House of Commons' address to Your Majesty that you are resolved to remove me from my place, I hope at least you will not be harder to me than the House of Commons were. And if it be only because Your Majesty has a mind the Duke of Monmouth should have it, even in that case I shall not complain of Your Majesty, neither I do not think it strange that you should love him better than me; but I cannot believe Your Majesty would for his sake do any man an injustice.

Consider I beseech you, that I had the honour to be bred up with Your Majesty from a child; that I lost my estate for running from Cambridge, where I was a student, to serve Your Majesty and your Father, at Oxford, when I was not thought of age sufficient to bear arms, and from that reason was sent away from thence to travel. That after the end of the wars, returning into England and having my whole estate restored to me by the Parliament, without composition, a few weeks after my return, there happening to be a design laid to take up arms for Your Majesty, my brother and I engaged in it, and in the engagement he was killed.

That after this the Parliament voted my pardon in case I would return within forty days; that I then being concealed in London, chose rather, with the hazard of my life, to wait upon Your Majesty in the Fleet, where I found you, than to stay, possessed of my estates upon condition of having nothing more to do with Your Majesty's fortunes: That afterwards, when Your Majesty went out of Holland into Scotland, I was offered my composition for £20,000, a sum not considerable to me at that time, my estate being then worth £30,000 a year: That even as Your Majesty's return into England I may justly pretend to some share, since without my Lord Fairfax, by engaging in Yorkshire, Lambert's army had never quitted him, nor the Duke of Albemarle marched out of Scotland; and without me it is sufficiently known to many persons yet alive that my Lord Fairfax had never engaged.

That in all the employments I have had under Your Majesty I have been so far from getting, that I have wasted the best part of my estate in following and waiting upon Your Majesty. All these things being considered, I conceive it will appear but just, that if your Majesty have a desire to make me quit my place I may be allowed to receive for it the full of what it is worth. Were I now as well in my affairs as when I first came into Your Majesty's service, I should never have thought of making this request. Nay, would the condition of my fortune give me leave to yield, I should not dispute with Your Majesty anything you could have a mind to take from me. But my whole estate being mortgaged, and I having lived to this age without being acquainted with any way of getting money, I hope Your Majesty will not be offended if, being forced to part with my freehold, I desire at least to sell it for the payment of my debts.

I humbly ask Your Majesty's pardon for this trouble I have given you, and beg of you to believe that nothing shall ever separate me from my duty and allegiance to Your Majesty; as I cannot despair but that one day Your Majesty will find the difference between those that truly love you and those that serve you only for private ends of their own. – I am, may it please Your Majesty, Your Majesty's most dutiful and most obedient Subject and Servant,

Buckingham.[2]

Buckingham does his best here to play on his long friendship with the King in order to make Charles feel guilty. He reminds him that he was 'bred up' with him 'from a child', and that he fought for the King and his father in the Civil War. He also reminds him that he could have remained on one of his many estates instead of following Charles into exile – of course he does not mention that he eventually deserted Charles on the Continent. He also maintains that he was instrumental in bringing about the Restoration by persuading Fairfax to lend it his support. It is interesting to note that he blames his enemies for driving a wedge between them.

Perhaps, eventually, Charles did feel some guilt over the way Buckingham had been treated, as he agreed that he should be paid for both the titles of Master of the Horse and Gentleman of the Bedchamber. Nevertheless, it seemed to many that this time the rift between them would be permanent. It has been argued that Charles's hope of a conversion to Catholicism was now dead and he no longer needed his overtly Protestant ministers to act as a cover.[3] In any case there was no advantage to him in reviving Buckingham's political career and he was truly angry at Buckingham's behaviour before Parliament. Indeed, their relationship was about to enter one of its most difficult periods. There were many at court, including Arlington, James, Louise, Duchess of Portsmouth, and Thomas Osborne, Buckingham's former protégé, who were resolved to keep the relationship between the two old friends sour and who worked continuously to keep the atmosphere between them poisonous.

For a year Buckingham found ways to occupy himself in the Yorkshire countryside. He went to Burley-on-the-Hill in Rutland, spending a considerable amount of time at the White Horse Inn in Empingham, which was a convenient distance from his mansion. In fact he became such a regular that the landlord became familiar with him and on one occasion, as the Duke called impatiently for another pot of ale, the man is said to have replied, 'Your Grace is in a plaguey hurry; I'll come as soon as I've served my hogs'. Far from being indignant at the landlord's use of such familiar language to a peer of the realm, the incident amused the Duke greatly. He retold it in verse as:

> 'Some ale, some ale!' the impetuous Villiers cried,
> To whom the surly landlord thus replied –
> 'Plague on Your Grace, you treat me as your dog,
> I'll serve Your Lordship when I've served my hog!'

During this period of leisurely country life he requested his friend Lord Rochester to come hunting with him, telling him 'if Your Lordship will give me leave, I shall immediately wait upon you with the best pack of hounds that ever ran upon English ground'. He also alludes, in letters written to Rochester, to his breeding of carp.[4]

In April 1675, although Buckingham had lost all his offices and his relationship with Charles was in tatters, Parliament was about to open and he had decided to return and make his presence felt in opposition to the government. He was determined to make things difficult for all those who had opposed him, including Charles. As he looked around the corridors of power, a bitter Buckingham could see many of his opponents thriving. His old enemy, Harry Killigrew, was now installed as Groom of the Bedchamber with the help of sponsorship from Arlington and Ormonde. All the talk was that Ormonde would soon become Lord Lieutenant of Ireland once again. Arlington had sold his secretaryship but had now bought the post of Lord Chamberlain of the Household.

Even the man whom he had helped at the beginning of his career, Thomas Osborne, was now Earl of Danby, and Lord High Treasurer, the most influential Minister in Parliament. He had been a Deputy-Lieutenant in the West Riding when Buckingham went there as Lord Lieutenant, and the Duke had assisted his career, even helping his election to Parliament. There is no doubt that Danby deserved his career advancements on merit, as he was efficient and diligent in all his roles –

Charles was delighted with him. He had brought a degree of economic stability to the kingdom and was a hard worker who made Charles's life easier. Danby was a stern opponent of both Catholicism and Protestant Nonconformity: the motto of his administration was 'Church, King and State'. On 1 May 1675 these convictions were reflected when Charles signed a declaration expelling Catholic priests from the realm. Buckingham would do all he could to obstruct Danby's policies.

A few days after the reassembling of Parliament, Danby's administration introduced the Non-Resistance Bill, otherwise known as the Test Oath. This piece of legislation was, in a way, an extension of the Test Act of 1673. It stated that all office-holders would be required to take an oath declaring that resistance to the King was unlawful and that they would abstain from all efforts to alter the constitution of the Church and State. Buckingham, Shaftesbury and Halifax were firm opponents of the bill, arguing that it was an abuse of royal power, and they fought it vehemently in the Lords.

The bill was supported not only by the King and a majority in both Houses, but also by the bishops. It was upon the bishops that Buckingham focused his ire. As Andrew Marvell put it: 'Holy Church goes to wrack on all sides. Never were poor men exposed and abused all the session as the bishops were by the duke of Buckingham upon the Test: never the like, nor so infinitely pleasant: and no men were ever grown so odiously ridiculous.'[5]

When rational argument seemed to fail, Buckingham tried the tactic of obstructing the House's business by making 'a famous speech of eloquent, regular, and well-placed nonsense, hoping that might prevail when nothing else would, and so brought confusion into the House'.[6]

By the time the substantially amended bill finally made it through the Lords in May 1675, a disagreement over a constitutional matter had broken out between the two Houses. Dr Shirley had brought a case against Sir John Fagg MP in the Court of Chancery. The case was referred on appeal to the House of Lords, before which Fagg was ordered to appear. The Commons, however, regarded this as a breach of privilege. A major row erupted, reminiscent of the case concerning Skinner versus the East India Company a few years earlier. Charles intervened by summoning both Houses to the Banqueting House on 5 June, but he could find no solution to the dispute, and instead decided to prorogue Parliament on 9 June before the Non-Resistance bill could go before the House of Commons again.

Not surprisingly during this time Buckingham and Charles remained estranged from each other, and the Duke was not received at court. For the period of the prorogation he went back to the country. The loss of all his appointments along with his estrangement from Charles and Lady Shrewsbury began to take their toll upon him. He was drinking heavily and was informally separated from his wife.

Parliament reconvened in October 1675, and Buckingham soon returned to the subject of religious toleration for Protestant Nonconformists. In November he made a speech to the Lords asking leave to bring in 'a bill for the ease of Protestant Dissenters'.[7]

My Lords,

There is a thing called property (whatever some men may think) that the people of England are fondest of. It is that they will never part with, and is that His Majesty in his speech has promised to take particular care of. This, my Lords, in my opinion, can never be done, without an indulgence to all Protestant dissenters.

It is certainly a very uneasy kind of life to any man, that has either Christian charity, good nature, or humanity, to see his fellow-subjects daily abused, divested of their liberties and birth-rights, and miserably thrown out of their possessions and freeholds, only because they cannot agree with others in some opinions and niceties of religion, which their consciences will not give them leave to consent to, and, which even by the consent of those who would impose them, are in no ways necessary to salvation.

But, my Lords, besides this, and all that may be said upon it, in order to the improvement of our trade, and increase of the wealth, strength and greatness of this nation (which with your leave I shall presume to discourse of at some other time), there is methinks in this notion of persecution, a very gross mistake, both as to the point of government, and religion.

There is so as to the point of government, because it makes every man's safety depend on the wrong place, not upon the governors, or man's living well towards the civil government, established by law; but upon his being transported with zeal for every opinion that's held by those that have power in the Church that's in fashion.

And I conceive it's a mistake in religion, for that it is positively against the express doctrine and example of Jesus Christ; Nay, my Lords, as to our Protestant religion, there is something in it yet worse; for we Protestants maintain, that none of those opinions which Christians here differ about, are infallible; and therefore in us it is somewhat an inexcusable conception, that men ought to be deprived of their inheritance, and all their certain conveniences and advantages of life, because they will not agree with us in our uncertain opinions of religion.

My humble motion to your Lordships therefore is, that you will give me leave to bring in a Bill of Indulgence to all dissenting Protestants. I know very well, that every peer of this realm has a right to bring into Parliament any Bill which he conceives to be useful to this nation. But I thought it more respectful to your Lordships to ask your leave for it before; and I cannot think that doing of it, will be any prejudice to the Bill, because I am confident, the reason, the prudence, and the charitableness of it, will be able to justify it to this House and the whole world.[8]

He was granted leave to introduce his bill.[9] In the end, however, events overtook him when Parliament was prorogued as a result of the continuing controversy over Shirley versus Fagg.

Shaftesbury made sure to raise the Shirley–Fagg issue once again in the House of Lords, even though Charles had urged them all, at the opening of the session, to postpone such constitutional issues in favour of public bills. The main aim of Shaftesbury and Buckingham at this time was to force a dissolution of Parliament. A conference that was held between the two Houses on 19 November to discuss Shirley versus Fagg ended in deadlock once again. The following day a motion was introduced to the Lords seeking to address the King in favour of the dissolution of Parliament. Danby had the motion defeated by a margin of two votes. Buckingham, Shaftesbury and nineteen others entered a protest against this decision stating, 'We do humbly conceive, that it is according to the ancient laws and Statutes of this Realm, that there should be frequent and new Parliaments; and that the Practice of several Hundred Years hath been accordingly.'[10] Charles had had enough, and prorogued Parliament again. Buckingham had not had the time to introduce his bill for religious toleration. This time the prorogation was to last for fifteen months.

Before the last session of Parliament Charles had been back negotiating in secret with the French. Louis, who did not want an anti-French Parliament in Westminster, agreed that if Charles's Parliament proved difficult, Charles would dissolve it and in return would receive around £100,000 from France. During the fifteen-month prorogation, even though Parliament had not been dissolved, Louis agreed to pay the money in quarterly instalments.[11] During this period Louis and Charles also agreed 'not to help their common enemies nor to sign agreements with other countries without one another's consent'.[12]

By now, the propaganda war between those who wanted Parliament dissolved and those who did not was in full swing. In March 1676 a warrant was issued to the Surveyor of the Presses to seize all copies of two speeches made by the Earl of Shaftesbury and the Duke of Buckingham and to bring before a Justice of the Peace all the printers and publishers of same.[13] In October 1676 the authorities received intelligence from an informer that Buckingham had 'taken a cup of tea and drunk a health to another Parliament or a new parliament, and to all those honest gentlemen of it that would give the King no money'.[14]

When Parliament was finally reassembled on 15 February 1677 Buckingham had only just recovered from an attack of gout in time to attend. Parliament was now divided firmly between two groups. There was the so-called 'Country Party', which consisted of Shaftesbury, Buckingham and their supporters, who wanted a dissolution of Parliament and were determined to do all they could to bring it about. They were opposed by the government side, known as the Court Party led by Danby.

Buckingham, along with Shaftesbury, Halifax and Monmouth, was also a member of the Green Ribbon Club. This was a private political club, from which the future Whig party would eventually be formed.[15] The club drew people from many backgrounds united in their opposition both to the Court Party and Catholicism. These gentlemen politicians met regularly at the corner of Fleet Street and Chancery Lane in the King's Head tavern, drank claret and sherry, and discussed politics:

> . . . gentlemen appeared on the balcony without hats or swords, sometimes without their periwigs, smoking long clay pipes and interchanging jokes and slogans with the crowd below when they were not directing the clerical work that their political activities entailed.[16]

Danby and the Court Party feared that a dissolution might lead to a new Parliament that might look more favourably upon Protestant Dissenters.[17] The Country Party agreed with this analysis, and that is exactly why they wanted to force a dissolution.

At the opening of Parliament, following the speeches of Charles and Lord Chancellor Finch, Buckingham rose to speak, dressed in a wonderful suit of blue.[18] He argued that under two statutes of Edward III,

Parliament ought to meet at least once every year, and since the recent prorogation had lasted fifteen months, Parliament was, in effect, dissolved. He told the Lords:

The Question, which in my opinion does now lie before your Lordships, is not, what we are to do, but, whether at this time we can do anything as a Parliament. It being very clear to me, that the Parliament is dissolved. And if in this opinion I have the misfortune to be mistaken, I have another misfortune joined to it, a desire to maintain this argument with all the judges and lawyers in England, and leave it afterwards to your Lordships to decide, whether I am in the right or no. This, my Lords, I speak not out of arrogance, but in my own justification. Because if I were not thoroughly convinced, that what I have now to urge, were grounded upon the fundamental laws of England, and that the not pressing it at this time, might prove to be of utmost consequence, both to his Majesty and the whole nation, I should have been loath to start a notion, which perhaps may not be very agreeable to some people. And yet, my Lords, when I consider where I am, who I now speak to, and what was spoken in the place about the time of the last prorogation, I can hardly believe that what I have to say, will be distasteful to your Lordships.

I remember very well how your Lordships were then displeased with the House of Commons, and I remember too as well, what reasons they gave you to be so. It is not so long since, but that I suppose your Lordships may easily call to mind, that after several odd passages between us, your Lordships were so incensed, that a motion was made here, for to address to his Majesty, about the dissolution of this Parliament. And tho it fail'd of being carried in the affirmative by two or three voices, yet this in the debate was remarkable, that it prevail'd with much the major part of your Lordships that were here present, and was only overpower'd by the proxies of those Lords who never heard the arguments. What change there has been since either in their behaviour, or in the state of our affairs, that should make your Lordships change your opinion, I have not yet heard. And therefore, if I can make it appear (as I presume I shall) that by law the Parliament is dissolved, I presume your Lordships might not to be offended at me for it.

I have often wondered how it should come to pass, that this House of Commons, in which there are so many honest, and so many worthy gentlemen, should yet be less respectful to your Lordships, as certainly they have been, than any House of Commons that ever were chosen in England; and yet if the matter be a little enquired into, the reason of it will plainly appear. For my Lords, the very nature of the House of Commons is changed: They do not think now that they are an assembly that are due to return to their own homes, and become private men again (as by the laws of the land and the ancient constitution of Parliaments they ought to be) but they look upon themselves as a standing Senate, and as a number of men picked out to be legislators for the rest of their whole lives. And if that be the case my Lords, they have reason to believe themselves our equals.

But, my Lords, it is a dangerous thing to try new experiments in a government, men do not foresee the ill consequences that must happen when they go about to alter those essential parts of it, upon which the whole frame of the Government depends, as now in our case, the customs and constitutions of Parliament. For all Governments are artificial things, and every part of them has a dependance one upon another. And as in clocks and watches, if you should put great wheels in the place of little ones, and the little wheels in the place of great ones, all the fabric would stand still: So we cannot alter any one part of a government without prejudicing the motions of the whole. If this, my Lords, were well considered, people would be more cautious how they went out of the old, honest, English way and method of proceedings. But it is not my business to find faults, and therefore if your Lordships will give me leave, I shall go on to show you, why, in my opinion, we are no Parliament.

The ground of this opinion of mine is taken from the ancient and unquestionable statutes of this realm, and give me leave to tell your Lordships by the way, that statutes are not like women, for they are not one jot the worse for being old.

According to him it was 'as plain as a pike-staff'.

Here now, my Lords, there is not left the least colour or shadow for any further mistake, for it is plainly declared, that the Kings of England must call a Parliament once within a year . . .

The laws have reposed so great a trust, and so great a power in the hands of a Parliament, that every circumstance relating to the manner of their electing, meeting and proceeding, is look'd after with the nicest circumspection imaginable . . .

He brought his speech to a close with:

Nothing can be more dangerous to a King or a people, than that laws should be made by an assembly, of which there can be a doubt whether they have power to make Laws or no: And it would be in us so much the more unexcusable, if we should overlook this danger, since there is for it so easy a remedy; A remedy which the Law requires, and which all the Nation longs for, THE CALLING OF A NEW PARLIAMENT.

It is that only can put his Majesty into a possibility of receiving supplies; That can secure your Lordships the honour of sitting in this House like Peers, and of being serviceable to your King and country; and that can restore to all the people of England their undoubted rights of choosing men frequently to represent their grievances in Parliament. Without this all we can do would be in vain; the nation might languish a while, but must perish at last: We should become a burden to ourselves, and a prey to our Neighbours.

My Motion therefore to your Lordships shall be, that we humbly address ourselves to his Majesty, and beg of him, for his own sake, as well as for all the people's sakes, to give as speedily a new Parliament. That so we may unanimously, before it is too late, use our utmost endeavours for his Majesty's service, and for the safety, the welfare, and the glory of the English nation.[19]

Buckingham had now placed himself in direct opposition to Charles, who was furious. Although his motion that Parliament be dissolved was rejected, Lord Frescheville, one of Danby's associates, called for him to be brought to the Bar of the House to answer for his words.[20] Danby called for Shaftesbury, Salisbury and Wharton, all of whom had supported the motion, to be treated similarly. Shaftesbury decried this as an attack upon liberty and free speech.

On 16 February all four Lords were asked to withdraw from the House as a discussion was held on what should be done. Buckingham's part in the affair was debated first. After some discussion it was decided that he be required to make the following acknowledgement at the Bar: 'I do acknowledge that my endeavouring that this Parliament is dissolved was an unadvised action, for which I humbly beg pardon of His Majesty and this honourable House.'[21] However, when the House sought the return of the Duke, he had disappeared. It was ordered that the Gentleman Usher of the Black Rod should take him into custody the following morning and bring him to the Bar.[22]

A similar treatment was decided upon for the other three Lords, who refused to use the required words of apology and were sent to the Tower of London for high contempt. Buckingham, it was reported, had been seen leaving in a small boat.

On the following day, 17 February 1677, Black Rod informed the House that he had been to the Duke of Buckingham's house and that his servants could give him no information, having not seen the Duke since the morning before. Consequently, the House ordered 'That, in case the Duke render not himself this noon, his Majesty be desired to issue a proclamation for stopping the ports and apprehending him, wherever he should be found, and bring him to the Tower, there to remain a prisoner, till he should be delivered by due course of law.' At this point, to much amazement, Buckingham walked calmly into the chamber of the House of Lords and sat in his usual place. There was uproar, with shouts of 'To the Bar!' The Duke informed the Peers that he had gone home the night before merely to put his house in order. He was ordered to withdraw and brought to the Bar by Black Rod. When shown the required formula of words to be used in the apology, he said that although he asked their pardon if he had offended his Majesty and the House, he could 'not ask pardon for thinking and speaking his thoughts'.[23] As he could not apologise in the required manner, he was committed to the Tower of London, where he joined Shaftesbury, Wharton and Salisbury. On 23 May 1677 Parliament was prorogued until 16 July.

Since he had suffered two ague fits the day before, Buckingham asked that he be transported to the Tower over land so that he would not be made worse by the dampness of a river passage. This request was granted and he travelled there 'in two of his own coaches and a great retinue of his footmen, all in gallant new liveries, and six hackney coaches following them'.[24] For his stay there he requested, and was granted, a cook and one other servant. He also arranged to have 'his laboratory in the Tower, in which he . . . [spent] his time in chemistry'.[25]

It was ordered that the incarcerated peers were not to be allowed to communicate with each other and that any visitors should be scrutinised carefully and have the prior permission of the House of Lords.[26] Sir John Robinson, Lieutenant of the Tower, reported to Charles that a number of people had arrived with the Duke of Buckingham and had to be turned away because of the Lords' ruling. He even said that 'the Lords' ladies were here, which was very troublesome. I told them they must get the Lords' order or your Majesty's before they came in.'[27] The ruling on communication seems not to have worked completely at first, since on their first Sunday it was said that 'the four lords met at divine service, and made use of that time to talk all the service while'. Efforts were made to prevent this afterwards.[28]

If Buckingham had been hoping for a big public outcry on his imprisonment, as there had been in 1667 during the Heydon affair, he was disappointed. No crowds cheered him on his way to the Tower this time. However, he soon began to rally influential people into lobbying on his behalf. One of these was Lord Middlesex, who presented a petition from the Duke to the King. On reading the document Charles was not satisfied and commented that 'though there was great humility used to himself there was no reparation to the Lords'.[29] Buckingham enlisted the help of his friends Lord Rochester and Nell Gwynn.

Next Buckingham wrote to Charles seeking a temporary release on the spurious excuse of having to see his builder at Cliveden, the work on his house being at so critical a point. But it is clear that his real reason was to speak to the King in secret:

> May it please Your Majesty,
>
> I cannot but tell Your majesty I am so perfectly overjoyed at the kindness you have been pleased to express of me to my Lord Middlesex that I shall be satisfied in mine own mind whether I come out to-day or not. But there is a necessity of speaking to you immediately in order to your own service and it is necessary also that it be done with all kind of privacy . . . it is most certain that a little mistake in my builders at Clifden may cost me above ten thousand pounds because I shall certainly pull it down again if it be not to my mind; so that there is a very just pretence for Your Majesty's giving me leave to go out for two days. And yet going out upon the

condition he proposes it, which is to have him ['Sir John' scratched out] always with me, I shall be in as ill company and as much a prisoner as I was before; (which will give great satisfaction to some well-natured people about Your Majesty), and I may easily then have the happiness of speaking to Your Majesty without its being known.

Pray I beseech Your Majesty to believe that I would rather be hanged than be thus earnest in this business if I did not know I should please you when I speak with you. And I am not such a beast as to make you hate me as long as you live by telling you a flim-flam story, in order to the getting a thing for which I shall not be one jot the better. My design is to let you see that I love you, and I am sure I shall convince you of it.[30]

The 'Sir John' referred to in the letter is Sir John Robinson, Lieutenant of the Tower of London, and indeed Sir John did accompany Buckingham when Charles granted him permission to go and see the building work for two days in June 1677.[31] We do not know if Charles and Buckingham had a discussion, but they probably did since on 22 July Buckingham received a warrant for his release until 22 August on the grounds that he had 'contracted a very dangerous distemper by his confinement'.[32] He went directly to stay at the lodgings of his friend Rochester at Whitehall.

His permanent release from the Tower was granted in August when he signed a declaration of penitence for his efforts to bring about a dissolution of Parliament.[33] He said that:

being now deeply sensible of his great indiscretion, unadvisedness and rashness, he most humbly submits himself to his Majesty and hopes that the past actions of his life will so far extenuate this as to make him a fit subject for the clemency of his Majesty and that House, to whom he is heartily sorry to have given so just occasion of displeasure, and earnestly begs his Majesty's and their pardon.[34]

Buckingham heard that Shaftesbury, who had probably heard of his communication with Charles, had referred to him as 'a man inconstant and giddy'. On the Duke's departure from the Tower the following conversation was heard to have taken place between them: Shaftesbury, calling from a window said, 'What, my Lord, are you going to leave us?' Buckingham replied, 'Ah, my Lord, such giddy-headed fellows as I can never stay long in a place.'[35]

Buckingham's penance was not over, however. In January 1678 he had to go before the House of Lords and read a statement which included the words: 'I do acknowledge that my endeavouring to maintain that the Parliament is dissolved was an ill advised action, for which I humbly beg the pardon of the King's Majesty and of this most honourable House.'[36] While Salisbury and Wharton had been released in July 1677, Shaftesbury was not given his freedom until February 1678.[37]

The incarceration of its leaders had left the Country Party in a very weakened condition, and they never again attempted to force a dissolution of Parliament.[38] Buckingham had been somewhat chastised, but his involvement at the highest level of political intrigue was not yet over. Now that he had his freedom, Nell Gwynn and Rochester were working together for his readmission to the royal court.[39] It was inevitable that this would happen. Charles and Buckingham had betrayed each other on a number of occasions, had had serious and bitter arguments, but through it all there was still a great deal of love and attachment between them. An emotional letter written by Buckingham to Charles demonstrates the ironic double-sidedness of their relationship:

I am so surprised with what Mrs Nelly has told me, that I know not in the world what to say. The more sensible grief I had in being put away from Your Majesty, was not the losing my place, but the being shut out of Your Majesty's kindness. And if the aspiring to that be a fault, it is at least a more pardonable one than the aspiring to wealth and the making one's own fortune. What has made this inclination more violent in me, than perhaps it is in other people, is the honour I had of being bred up with Your Majesty from a child; for those affections are ever strongest in men, which begin in their youngest years. And therefore I beseech Your Majesty to believe me when I say, that I have ever loved you more than all the rest of mankind; and that I have not only once chosen to follow you in misfortune rather than be in ever so great plenty any other way, but that I would willingly do so again tomorrow, if Your Majesty could take it kindly of me.

What should I say? I am not one that pretends to a preciseness in devotion, but yet I am sure Your Majesty never found me to be a knave and I wish that all the curses imaginable may fall upon me, if I tell you a lie; or if I would tell you a lie to save my life. I have lived long enough in the world, not to care much for it, and have met with so much ungratefulness from almost all mankind, that the pleasure of conversing with man is one quite taken from me. Yet I beseech Your Majesty to believe, that the grief which in my whole life did ever sit nearest to my heart, was the loss of Your Majesty's kindness. You that have been a lover yourself, know what it is to think oneself ill-used by a mistress that one loves extremely and it is that only I can truly compare my great misfortune to. Yet there was besides my own misfortune in it, a great deal of art used to make me believe that Your Majesty hated me, and I can hardly forgive them that did it, since it was done with as much undutifulness to Your Majesty, as ingratitude to me.

But why should I say any more of this matter? What you have been pleased to say to Mrs Nelly, is ten thousand times more than ever I can deserve. Could you make a question whether I can love you or no? Oh Christ sir for heavens sake know that I would as willingly die tomorrow to do your majesty's service, as any of those about you would have me dead, to satisfy their envy and their ill nature. I am really in that ecstasy of joy, and so truly satisfied with my condition, since I am persuaded your Majesty has a kindness for me, that I would willingly stay here all my life if your Majesty can think it may be for your service. Though I confess I should be very glad to throw myself at your majesty's feet, and give you humble thanks for the goodness you have been pleased to show me. In short sir, do with me what you please, I will absolutely be governed by you . . .[40]

Once again their relationship recovered. As early as August Charles and Buckingham were enjoying themselves at Rochester's lodgings, which fuelled rumours of a return to favour:

The great discourse of the town is that the Duke of Bucks shall be restored to favour, and be Lord Steward of the Household in place of Duke of Ormond; but of this they are very silent at court, only his sacred Majesty and his Grace (I hear) were very merry one night at Lord Rochester's lodgings, which, I conceive, created this discourse.[41]

With Shaftesbury still languishing in the Tower of London, Buckingham was welcomed back at court. His reappearance at Whitehall made many people feel uneasy about the extent to which his relations with Charles had been repaired. They remembered 1667 when he had returned from a period of estrangement to become stronger than ever. They were well aware of the special bond from childhood that existed between the two men. Some, like Danby and Monmouth, complained to the King directly about the matter. The Duke of York was concerned about it too, and felt the need to reassure William of Orange by writing: 'I believe you will have been surprised with the news of the Duke of Buckingham's having leave to come to court. I am sure I was, for I knew nothing of it, till he had been with his Majesty, but his Majesty knows him too well to let him do any harm.'[42]

For his part, Buckingham believed that unscrupulous methods were being used to discredit him. He wrote to Rochester that lies were being spread about them and that a 'treasonable lampoone' had been written, which was to be attributed to Rochester's own pen.[43] It was now that the effects of Buckingham's abandonment of the Duchess of Portsmouth in Dieppe, and their subsequent poor relationship, worked against him. She had influence with Charles and she did not want to see Buckingham restored to favour.

The King, on the other hand, seems to have been delighted at the return of his roguish friend. While watching *Macbeth* at the theatre he is quoted as having said: 'Pray, what is the meaning that we never see a rogue in a play but oddsfish! they always clap him in a black periwig, when it is well known one of the greatest rogues in England wears a fair one?'[44] Buckingham, who was still High Steward of Oxford, also received an impressive reception when he visited there around the beginning of November 1677. William Temple writes:

> He was met and attended by a numerous train of citizens on horseback into the city, the bells all speaking his welcome . . . After a short speech by the town clerk he was conducted to the Council chamber, and thence to dinner, which was exceeding rich and plentiful of all sorts of wines and music. He highly commended all things and expressed a high sense of their kindness and a readiness to serve the city. After drinking the healths of his Majesty and all others of the royal family he took his leave about 7 in the evening towards London . . .[45]

Meanwhile, the war between the French and the Dutch continued on the Continent and Charles found himself in the role of a peace mediator. By 1677, however, he was faced with a Parliament that was becoming increasingly anti-French. Danby also favoured taking a stand against France. Charles was in an awkward position. He told the French Ambassador: 'You see how I suffer. I put myself in trouble with my subjects for love of the French King. I am resolved to keep my promises to him; but I beg him to help me a little and make peace before winter.'[46]

On 23 May an address was approved by the House of Commons to ask the King 'to enter into a league, offensive and defensive, with the States-General of the United Provinces . . .'.[47] A few days later Charles rebuked them for trespassing upon his royal prerogative by attempting to dictate foreign policy. As Charles was unwilling to fight a war without adequate resources and which, in any case, he did not believe he could win, it was clear to him that the best solution would be to broker a peace between the two warring parties.

It was a peace that proved difficult to achieve. Charles had prorogued Parliament on 28 May 1677, and when it was due to reconvene on 16 July he wanted to prorogue it once again. He needed French money to enable him to do so. After long negotiations he managed to secure merely a promise of £145,000 from the French, in return for not holding another Parliament until the following May.[48]

Meanwhile, Danby had been working hard to arrange a marriage between William of Orange and the 15-year-old Princess Mary, daughter of the Duke of York and granddaughter of the late Earl of Clarendon. In October William arrived on a visit to England. The marriage was quickly arranged, although Mary is said to have 'wept all that afternoon and the following day'.[49] The couple were married on 4 November 1677.

Louis XIV was furious about the marriage. He told the Duke of York, 'You have given your daughter to my mortal enemy,'[50] and he promptly stopped Charles's 'latest subsidy'. Louis knew who to blame and became determined to support financially anyone who could destroy Danby; Buckingham, as an enemy of Danby, was in contact with and receiving funds from Paul Barrillon, Louis' new representative in England.

Before the newlyweds left England, Charles hammered out a set of proposals under which William could accept peace with France – but these were rejected by Louis. By January 1678 Laurence Hyde signed a treaty with the Dutch promising to compel the French to accept the peace terms.

Since Louis had withdrawn his subsidy, Charles summoned Parliament in January 1678 instead of in May as agreed with the French. At the opening of the session on 28 January he pleased most of those listening by telling them that

> I have used all the means possible, by a mediation, to have procured an honourable and safe peace for Christendom; knowing how preferable such a peace would have been to any war, and especially to this Kingdom; which must necessarily own the vast benefits it has received by peace, whilst its neighbours only have yet smarted by the war: But, finding it no longer to be hoped for by fair means, it shall not be my fault, if that be not obtained by force which cannot be had otherwise.[51]

Charles was bluffing and dearly hoping that Louis would see sense and accept peace terms. But this did not happen, and the call for war with France was growing ever louder, especially in the House of Commons, which voted for the money that would allow Charles to go to war. France, watching the relationship of England and the Dutch develop, finally sent Charles the first instalment of the promised money.

In March 1678 the Commons sent an address to Charles calling for war to be declared on France at once. The Lords agreed that he should be addressed to declare war on France, but they were split over whether it should be declared immediately or as soon as possible. Buckingham and Shaftesbury were among those who argued for speedy action. Danby argued that the King did not have the means to go to war immediately. Deadlock ensued and Parliament was adjourned.

In May the Commons, now unhappy with the original agreement with the Dutch, voted that the King be asked to conclude alliances to carry on a war against France. Charles was finally helped out of his awkward situation by the Dutch and the French agreeing a peace treaty. Many in Parliament were disappointed at missing the opportunity of going to war with France. Charles also agreed to the French terms, signed a treaty with the French and was promised more money.

In the interest of bringing about the dissolution of Danby's anti-French and anti-toleration Parliament, Louis granted Charles 6 million *livres* a year for three years and also gave £10,000 to the Country Party. Louis promised Shaftesbury and his colleagues that he would respect their religion if they were successful. Buckingham went on a secret visit to make the arrangements. In 1678 he visited the French court wearing a dark wig and without his star.[52] But Danby's spies were on to him. When he returned, in an attempt to improve relations, he entertained Louise, Duchess of Portsmouth, at Cliveden. In September 1678 he was staying with Nell Gwynn in Pall Mall. Danby's supporters were much concerned by stories of great merriment being had between Buckingham and the King. The King was said to have been reduced to tears of laughter at the Duke's imitation of Lady Danby. After all, one observer said of Buckingham that 'His particular talent consisted in turning into ridicule whatever was ridiculous in other people, and in taking them off, even in their presence, without their perceiving it.'[53] On a visit of the Duchess of York to one of Buckingham's evenings of entertainment her servants became so drunk that her coach overturned.

Charles and Buckingham had come through a particularly difficult time in their relationship, as bad, perhaps, as when Buckingham had deserted Charles in exile. His behaviour in the wake of the Dutch War and his various attempts to disrupt the work of Parliament had been trying enough, but his attempt to defy Charles and launch an attack upon the royal prerogative by having Parliament dissolved was the worst.

It is possible to speculate on why Buckingham had decided to go so far in his opposition to Charles. Undoubtedly, he had been frustrated for some time by the fact that he was not being appointed to the high political appointments to which he felt he was entitled. But one has to wonder if, by now, he had found out about the secret treaty with the

French and how Charles had used him as a cover. Was his extreme opposition to Charles in Parliament a result of the anger he felt about being fooled and used in this way? We cannot be sure.

In the end, though, Buckingham had to relent, apologise and seek Charles's forgiveness. His latest period in the Tower of London seems to have taught him a lesson. He managed to repair his relationship with Charles, and part of that process may well have included an undertaking not to repeat his behaviour. In any event, we can notice an attempt not to be so publicly involved with the efforts of the Country Party in Parliament from that point on. There is a distinct cooling, too, in his relations with Shaftesbury. When Shaftesbury and the others push for the exclusion of James, Duke of York, from the succession, Buckingham takes no part in the parliamentary debates. He would not challenge Charles so publicly again.

Twenty-two

THE POPISH PLOT

The Popish Plot erupted when Titus Oates announced that he had details of a plot by which the kingdom was to be invaded by a Catholic army from the Continent, the King assassinated and the Pope made Lord of England and Ireland. It was even said at the time that a large number of monks had already been shipped in from Jerusalem to sing at the celebrations once the Catholics had seized power.[1] A list had been drawn up, Oates claimed, specifying names of prominent Protestants to be executed, including that of the Duke of Buckingham. Oates declared the plot to be the brainchild of Jesuit priests and said that it had come to his attention while he posed as a Catholic convert in two Jesuit seminaries.

It was indeed true that Oates had been admitted to the seminaries at Valladolid and St Omers, but he had been rejected by both. Earlier in his life he had been expelled from Merchant Taylors School in London, sent down from Cambridge, imprisoned for perjury while a curate and once dismissed for misconduct as a navy chaplain. Although the Popish Plot was no more than a creation of his villainous imagination, it had the effect of spreading fear and suspicion throughout the land and resulted in a widespread wave of anti-Catholic sentiment.

Oates was assisted in his story by Israel Tonge, another rogue, who had been a fellow of Oxford and had earned a doctorate in Divinity. Tonge descended into a spiral of insanity, blaming the Catholics for everything including the starting of the Great Fire of 1666. He was now convinced that they were intending to take over the country. Oates made sure that the fanatical Tonge found a document containing details of a plot to assassinate the King and to raise a Catholic rebellion. Tonge managed to arrange a meeting with Charles through the offices of his friend Christopher Kirkby, who knew the King through their mutual association with the Royal Society. Charles listened to him with an air of scepticism and then directed that the papers be brought to Danby. Danby, equally unimpressed by the quality of the evidence, told Tonge that he would need more. Oates went on to forge five incriminating letters, which he then sent to the Jesuit confessor of the Duke of York, in the mistaken belief that they would be intercepted by the authorities. They were not, but on receiving them, the priest handed them over to the Duke of York. They were then investigated by the Privy Council.

Charles opened the proceedings of the Privy Council and ordered that the incriminating letters be produced. At first no one seemed convinced by them. Neither Charles nor the Duke of York stayed for the afternoon session when Oates gave his evidence, preferring instead to go to the races at Newmarket. But Oates put on a good performance, convincing many of those present that there might be some substance to his story of royal assassinations, Catholic uprisings and the mass murder of Protestants. The Council ordered that the Jesuits named by Oates should be rounded up that very night.

Then a horrific event occurred that added to the widespread fear. Sir Edmund Bury Godfrey was a businessman and Justice of the Peace in the London parish of St Martin-in-the-Fields. Ironically, he was known to have had a favourable attitude towards Catholics. On 1 September 1678 he heard a sworn deposition of evidence from Titus Oates. Then, on 17 October, Sir Godfrey's dead body was found lying in a ditch near Primrose Hill. He had been stabbed with his own sword and had strangulation marks on his neck. His clothes were covered in candle wax, which was intended to suggest the involvement of priests in his murder. An associate of Oates called William Bedloe claimed that he had been offered £4,000 by Catholics to dispose of Sir Godfrey's body. Bedloe was nothing more than an opportunist.

The level of suspicion and paranoia caused by the Popish Plot increased and Charles failed to prevent Parliament from getting involved. Oates was summoned to the Bar of the House and from there he once again got the chance to spread his stories. The House of Commons was fooled into believing that the Catholics were plotting to assassinate the King and destroy Protestantism throughout the country.

Although Buckingham and Shaftesbury did not believe in the Popish Plot, they may have considered that it furthered their political interests. After all, perhaps it would cause such a crisis that it would assist in achieving a number of their aims, such as the dissolution of Parliament, the defeat of Catholicism or the succession of a Protestant heir. On the other hand, Buckingham was not happy about the timing of attacks made upon the Queen. William Bedloe claimed that Godfrey had been murdered in the Queen's own house. Oates himself claimed that she was heavily involved with the Jesuits and even made a statement to the House of Commons saying, 'I do accuse the Queen for conspiring the death of the King.'[2] Buckingham is reputed to have said that 'This rascal Oates will spoil our business – it is not yet time to bring the Queen forward.'[3]

One of those named by Oates as a conspirator was Edward Coleman, a former secretary to the Duke of York. Coleman was arrested and his papers seized – they were found to contain a number of letters written to Jesuits in France in which he yearned for the return of Catholicism to England, and in particular the future reign of the Duke of York. They contained no word of rebellion or the assassination of Charles, but they were enough to justify his execution.

Many Catholics were now being removed from positions of authority and trust. The new Test Act was passed, which excluded all Catholics from membership of Parliament, although Danby managed to get the Duke of York excepted from its provisions. Many Catholics were arrested and some executed. In most of the terror tales of a Catholic takeover, the Duke of York was the one named as the potential king of the new Catholic kingdom. Hysteria about his role in the future of the country grew to unprecedented levels. In November 1678 Shaftesbury 'requested the Lords to dismiss the Duke of York from the Privy Council'. Two days later Lord Russell moved the same resolution in the Commons. Shaftesbury also had William Sacheverell ask in the House of Commons whether the King and Parliament might between them dispose of the succession. The Duke of York declared that he would take no further part in public business.

From its earliest stages, Charles had never believed in the veracity of the plot. He remained convinced that the whole thing was a tissue of lies, and told the French Ambassador that Oates was 'a wicked man', and that 'he did not believe the accusations had any foundation in truth'.[4] He is reported to have laughed when Oates named a man called Bellasis as Commander-in-Chief of the Catholic army when, in fact, Charles knew the poor man to be bedridden. Neither was the King satisfied with many of the answers he received from his questions to Oates. In particular, when Charles asked him where the Jesuit College in Paris was situated, Oates replied that it was near the Louvre. Charles commented wryly that 'he was as much out as if he had said Gresham College stood in Westminster'.[5]

As the effects of the Popish Plot were being felt, Buckingham was appointed to a subcommittee that was to investigate the authenticity of Titus Oates's claims. As part of his work for the committee he was involved in a number of interrogations. The subcommittee looked into claims made by Bedloe that a clerk of Samuel Pepys's, named Samuel Atkins, had been involved in the murder of Sir Edmund Bury Godfrey. The committee, and Buckingham in particular, tried to get Atkins to say that Pepys was no friend of Godfrey's. They failed in the end to implicate the diarist and had to be content with imprisoning Atkins, who was sent to Newgate where he underwent some further interrogation.

An informant interviewed before a Lords' committee claimed that Buckingham had said to her, 'if you were a man, I would sheath my sword in your heart's blood, for you have undone all the business by endeavouring to take off the report that Sir Edmund was murdered by the Papists, as if he murdered himself'.[6]

James Netterville, a prisoner in the Marshalsea, became determined to swear that the Popish Plot had actually originated with Shaftesbury and Buckingham's party. Netterville was a Catholic Irishman who had been a clerk in the Court of Claims in Dublin. He had also been one of Danby's informers.[7] On one occasion when he was brought before the Privy Council charged with seditious talk overheard at St James's Park, he got into a fight outside the Council chamber and was then impertinent to the King – for which behaviour he was sent to Newgate Prison.

Netterville offered another Irishman, Captain Bury, £400 to £500 if he would assist in blaming the Popish Plot on the Opposition. However, unfortunately for Netterville, Bury went straight to Colonel Thomas Blood with the information. Blood told Bury to find out who was supplying the money. Bury came back with the name of Russell, a servant to the French Ambassador. When Netterville subsequently confessed his side of the story to a Catholic priest it differed in that he claimed that the intention had actually been to bribe Blood himself with £500. In the end, Charles took no notice of the supposed evidence.

Barillon, the French Ambassador, remained in frequent contact with Buckingham. In November 1678 Buckingham told Barillon that London citizens must be armed against the militia under the control of Danby and even requested money from Louis for the purpose; but he was refused.[8] At one stage, in the midst of all this fervour created by the Popish Plot, Buckingham told the French that there was a plot in hand to assassinate Louis and once again looked for money from them. No answer seems to have been received to this request.

Thomas Dangerfield was another figure who found himself drawn into the machinations of the Popish Plot. He had spent a considerable proportion of his adult life in gaol, having engaged in a variety of crimes from the counterfeit of coins to, some said, the robbery of his own father. Elizabeth Cellier was a Catholic midwife who had once had a relationship of some kind with Sir Edmund Bury Godfrey.[9] In 1679 she was among a number of Catholics who were keen to counter the effects of the Popish Plot by spreading similar rumours about Protestants.

Dangerfield and Cellier joined forces. With Cellier's help Dangerfield got out of prison and went to work immediately spreading rumours of the formation of a rebel army by the Opposition, implicating Shaftesbury and Buckingham. He even produced documents to back up his claims, which he had probably forged himself. Other prominent Protestants, such as Colonel Thomas Blood and Sir William Waller, were also implicated by this information. Dangerfield received encouragement and money from the Duke of York and got as far as showing his evidence to the King who passed him on to Secretary of State Coventry.

Next, Dangerfield produced more documentary evidence in the form of incriminating letters, which he claimed had been stolen from Shaftesbury.[10] He then tried, unsuccessfully, to persuade Coventry to have a search carried out at the house of Buckingham's steward, Colonel Roderick Mansell. Undeterred, Dangerfield persisted in spreading malicious rumours about the Protestant army. In October 1679 he met Thomas Curtis at the Hoop Tavern, Fish Street Hill. Curtis was a former Member of Parliament from Lancashire who by now spent most of his time drinking. Dangerfield bought him food and liquor and persuaded him that there would be a reward in it if he could ask around and get some of the rebel army commissions that were on offer. Before long Curtis found himself at the Heaven Tavern in Old Palace Yard, Westminster, where he spoke to the barmaid, Jane Bradley, about the army. Unfortunately for Curtis, Mrs Bradley was a loyal informant of Colonel Thomas Blood, to whom she passed the information. Blood asked Mrs Bradley to find out more information from Curtis and at the same time informed the King. Eventually Curtis was brought before a justice of the peace and committed to the Gatehouse Gaol.

While all this was going on, Dangerfield had not been idle. He managed to get himself admitted, under false pretences, to the house of

Colonel Mansell, where he planted some forged incriminating documents behind the Colonel's bedstead. He then informed customs officials that he had information to the effect that there were smuggled goods hidden in Mansell's house. He even accompanied the officials on their search of the house and when they were about to give up, he miraculously pulled the forged papers from the bedstead with the words 'Here is treason!'[11]

Colonel Mansell went directly to the Privy Council to plead his innocence, and Dangerfield, when put under pressure, betrayed Mrs Cellier and turned informer. When Mrs Cellier's house was searched an incriminating 'paper book ty'd with ribbons' was found hidden at the bottom of a tub of meal.[12] This plot consequently became known as the Meal-Tub Plot. The document, which may well have been planted by Dangerfield, contained an outline of the whole plot against the Protestants and particularly of Mrs Cellier's part in it. Luckily for her, Dangerfield's testimony was not accepted and Mrs Cellier was acquitted. In 1685 Dangerfield was convicted of libel as a result of a piece of writing entitled *Narrative,* for which he was pilloried and whipped. He died some time afterwards as a result of a blow to the eye from a barrister's cane.

In 1679 five Jesuit priests were put to death. In 1680 one of five Catholic Lords who had been arrested as a result of the Popish Plot, Lord Stafford, was tried, found guilty and executed. Of the other four, Powis, Arundel and Bellasis remained in prison for another five years and one, Petre, died before being released.[13] Oliver Plunkett, the Archbishop of Armagh, was brought from Ireland on very flimsy evidence and executed in 1681.[14]

There were other atrocities, but by the 1680s the hysteria of the Popish Plot was beginning to subside. With Bedloe's death in 1680 the plotters lost one of their most effective witnesses. Titus Oates had a writ of *scandalum magnatum* brought against him by the Duke of York in 1684 for uttering scandalous words about him: Oates had referred to him as 'that traitor James, Duke of York' at dinner in the Bishop of Ely's house in 1680. He was ordered to pay £100,000. He could not pay such a sum and was thrown in the debtors' section of the King's Bench Prison. Other legal actions against him followed and Oates's whole tangle of lies began to unravel.

Oates's eventual punishment makes incredible reading. On Monday he had to walk through the Courts of Justice in Westminster Hall wearing a notice describing his offence, before standing in the pillory for an hour, where an estimated crowd of 10,000 people pelted him with rotten eggs. On Tuesday he went through the same treatment but this time at the Royal Exchange. On Wednesday he was whipped the mile and a half from Aldgate to Newgate. On Thursday he got a day's rest. On Friday, as he was being whipped the two miles from Newgate to Tyburn, he fell unconscious from the exertion and was dragged on a sled. He was then imprisoned for the rest of his life. But on four occasions each and every year he was forced to stand for an hour in the pillory at various locations around London.[15] He was later freed in the wake of the revolution of 1688, received a pension from William III and died in 1705.

Oates's Popish Plot had been successful in creating an almost unprecedented degree of hysteria and anti-Catholic feeling in the country. It led to a political climate in which the very nature of the succession to the throne would be subject to attack.

Twenty-three

THE FALL OF DANBY

The return of Buckingham to Charles's court after his latest period in the Tower of London infuriated Danby, who had hoped that this time the Duke would be removed from the scene for ever. Consequently, the antagonism between them grew to new levels. Although Buckingham had been Danby's supporter in the early years, it has been said that Danby now 'determined to blacken Buckingham's character on an entirely new basis'.[1]

The bitterness between the rivals is clear in Buckingham's *Upon the Installment of Sir Thomas Osborn, and the late Duke of Newcastle*, written about Danby and Newcastle's investiture into the order of the Garter. The ceremony took place in April 1677 while Buckingham was in the Tower. In his poem he has the voice of St George attack Danby personally:

> Go get a Shroud to match your Face and Breath,
> Be drest, as well as look and smell, like death.
> 'Twas that alone at first which Nature meant,
> Your Loathsome Carcass still should represent
> For so unlively and so Nauseous too,
> Is every thing you either say or do . . .

It was to take three years before an attack could be mounted on Buckingham, but before then Danby himself fell from political power thanks to the actions of Ralph Montague, the English Ambassador to France. Montague was no stranger to controversy – in fact, his animosity for Buckingham had already boiled over one day in December 1673 when the Duke, on entering the King's withdrawing room, had pushed the Ambassador out of his way. Montague was annoyed, and when Buckingham refused to apologise, demanded satisfaction in the traditional way. Although Montague wanted the matter settled then and there, Buckingham had him agree to a meeting the following day. When the King heard of this he banned the duel and had Montague incarcerated in the Tower of London for a short period. This time Buckingham did not suffer at all for his actions.[2]

Barbara went to Paris in the late 1670s as a result of financial difficulties resulting from her and John Churchill's extravagancies. While there, she had an affair with Montague. It may have been a mistake for him to have had an affair with Barbara, which ended in 1678, but it was an even greater mistake to embark upon one with her daughter, Anne. Barbara was in England already complaining of her former lover to Charles while Montague was engaging in his fling with Anne. Barbara was furious when she found out and their relationship deteriorated still further. Barbara began to blacken Montague's reputation with Charles. Among other accusations, she told Charles that Montague had been plotting to have Danby removed and to take his place. It was even said that she told him that Montague had planned to bribe a favourite astrologer of Charles's in Paris into making predictions that suited himself. The corrupt astrologer would predict that unless Danby and Louise, Duchess of Portsmouth, were removed from power he would face grave danger. When Montague came to England to defend himself, he found that he had been removed from all his positions.

Montague's response was to secure his election to the House of Commons at a by-election, from where he could fight back. Having tried unsuccessfully to prevent his election, Charles and Danby then moved to have him arrested, which Montague fought on the grounds of parliamentary privilege. They seized his papers, but he had hidden the most important ones. On 19 December Montague produced some incriminating documents at the House of Commons that showed Danby to have been involved in secret negotiations with Louis XIV. The following day the House of Commons drew up articles of impeachment against Danby, accusing him of planning to overthrow the constitution with the help of a standing army and French money. It is, of course, very possible that the French, perhaps through Louise de Kéroualle, had bribed Montague in order to bring Danby down and force a dissolution of Parliament.[3]

Danby was now in the firing line. Although by this time Buckingham hated Danby just as much as he had hated both Clarendon and Ormonde in earlier years, and was no doubt very eager to become associated with his impeachment, he had to be careful about his involvement in this quarrel. Danby had already threatened him 'with a counter charge of a personal nature' if he was involved in any attack upon him[4] and also made the rather ominous comment to Ormonde's son, Lord Ossory, that he was 'not out of hopes of procuring something very material against the Duke'.[5] Buckingham did not speak at Danby's impeachment, but he did use the Earl of Carnarvon, whom he plied with drink, as his mouthpiece. The House gave Danby time to prepare his reply. But on 30 December 1678 Charles prorogued Parliament. He then gave Danby instructions to negotiate with some members of the Country Party, including Lord Holles and Richard Hampden. An agreement was reached that Charles would dissolve Parliament and disband the army in return for the necessary money and an additional supply. It was also agreed that Danby would resign.

The Parliament that had been in existence for nearly eighteen years was finally dissolved on 24 January 1679. With the fever in the country running so high against Catholics, Charles told James that if he did not convert back to the Church of England, he would have to go abroad. Elections were held and a new Parliament opened on 6 March 1679. A few days into the session Charles asked for Danby's resignation, gave him a free pardon under the Great Seal for all offences committed by him before 27 February 1679, a pension of £5,000 a year and raised him to the rank of marquess.

But the new House of Commons did not want Danby to get off so lightly. In fact the elections had produced an even deeper opposition to him. While the Lords attempted to have him banished, the Commons would have none of it. In March they reminded the Lords that the impeachment proceedings still stood against him and that he should be placed in custody. On 22 March Charles called both Houses together and assured them that Danby was innocent in regard to the letter written to Montague as it had been written under his own instruction.[6] He also reminded them that he had already given his Lord High Treasurer a full pardon, 'which was no more than he had formerly done to Lord Buckingham and Lord Shaftesbury, when they left his service'.[7]

Charles was not confident that he would be successful in controlling Parliament, so he advised Danby to go abroad. He was right. The Commons ordered that Danby be placed under arrest. After some disagreement, both Houses agreed that if Danby did not give himself up by the specified date, a bill of attainder would be submitted to the King. But Danby had not taken Charles's advice, and on 16 April presented himself to Black Rod and was sent to the Tower of London. He would stay there for five years, until released by Charles in 1684.

In the wake of the Danby era, Charles decided to form a completely new kind of Privy Council. He appointed thirty members, half of whom received ministerial appointments. In order to give an impression of balance, and hoping that he might be less divisive on the inside, Charles appointed Shaftesbury Lord President of the Council – the aim of this strategy was to give the appearance that the King was open to the views of the opposition and perhaps also to control Shaftesbury. Ultimately, however, the move would fail to lessen the divisive influence of Shaftesbury, who was planning to challenge the very succession to the throne. Significantly, Buckingham, who had been absent for most of the Parliamentary session, was not included in the new Privy Council.

Twenty-four

THE EXCLUSION CRISIS

The paranoia engendered by the Popish Plot brought to the fore Protestant fears about James, Duke of York, the Catholic heir to the throne. Since Charles had no legitimate children, his brother James was rightfully next in line. James's marriage in 1673 to the Catholic Mary of Modena had only made matters worse. By the end of the 1670s Shaftesbury had decided that the time had now come to have the Duke of York excluded from his right of succession.

Buckingham agreed with Shaftesbury that James should be excluded. There were even ridiculous rumours circulating at the time that Buckingham was prepared to lead a rebellion himself.[1] Buckingham and James had never seen eye to eye, as was obvious when James blocked his efforts to get a command during the Dutch War. There had been various attempts to reconcile them through the years. In 1670, for example, there is mention of reconciliation in a letter written partly in cipher: 'All James's old friends are using their best industry to make Mr. Gorgis [Buckingham] and Mr. James friends'.[2] Because of his upbringing, Buckingham did not stand in awe of either Charles or James. In fact, Barillon, the French Ambassador, stated that he had heard Buckingham make the argument many times that he had a legitimate claim to the throne himself through his mother's connections with the House of Plantagenet.[3] Burnet said that Buckingham once summed up Charles and James by saying that 'The King could see things if he would, and the duke would see things if he could.'[4] The animosity that James felt for Buckingham may have been rooted in feelings of jealousy over the way

Charles seemed to regard him as a brother; James knew that Charles did not feel the same way about him as he did about Buckingham.

But Buckingham hesitated in supporting Shaftesbury's campaign. Firstly, he did not agree that Monmouth, Charles's illegitimate son with Lucy Walter, was a suitable alternative to James. He said that the young duke thought 'the world was made only for him'.[5] He favoured the idea of Charles's divorce from the Queen and remarriage as a means of producing an heir and thereby blocking James's succession. Secondly, he knew better than most how determined Charles was to prevent anyone tampering with the succession. Whatever his personal feelings about James, towards the end of his reign, through many crises, Charles would show himself to be resolute in his determination to fight any moves to have his brother excluded. It was a determination not driven by a liking for James, or even by a belief that his brother would make a great king – in fact, Charles once commented to William of Orange that James would not hold on to the throne for more than four years. His determination that James should become king was driven by a belief in the sanctity of the royal prerogative. Parliament, he believed, had no right to interfere with the succession. Knowing of such firmly held beliefs, Buckingham had no intention of publicly opposing Charles. He had learned his lesson from his recent attempts to prorogue Parliament.

Supporters of Monmouth had for a long time been spreading the rumour that Charles had actually married Lucy Walter, thus making Monmouth his legitimate heir. In 1679 Charles felt obliged to deny this rumour. He formally announced in Council that he had never been married to any other woman but the Queen. A statement dated March 1679 read:

> For the voiding of any dispute which may happen in time to come concerning the succession to the Crown, I do here declare in the presence of Almighty God, that I never gave nor made any contract of marriage, nor was married to any woman whatsoever, but to my present wife Queen Catherine now living.[6]

In April 1679 the whole issue came to a head when the House of Commons was asked to vote that 'The Duke of York, being a Papist, and the hopes of his coming as such to the Crown, have given the greatest countenance and encouragement to the present conspiracies and designs of the Papists against the King and the Protestant Religion.' It was passed unanimously and James's automatic right to become king after Charles's death was under attack. In an attempt at compromise, Charles told his Privy Council that he was prepared to agree to certain constitutional limitations being put on the monarchy in the case of a Catholic king succeeding to the throne. In such an instance, he would agree to changes in the law which would necessitate Parliament being automatically reassembled on the accession of the monarch and the Catholic king having no control over appointments to judicial or ecclesiastical positions.

These proposals for limitations on the succession were put to the House of Commons by Lord Finch, the Lord Chancellor, to what at first seemed to be a positive response. In the days following, though, Shaftesbury's supporters in the Commons managed to work up opposition to the proposals. They did not want compromise, they were bent on exclusion. A few days later an Exclusion Bill was proposed. On its second reading in the Commons on 21 May it was carried by 207 votes to 128. On 27 May Charles prorogued Parliament until 14 August. In July he dissolved it once again, with elections to be held in August and September. These would be the first elections to be held on what one could call an early form of party lines.

Then, on 20 August, fears about the succession were given new immediacy. The day before Charles had been as physically active as usual: he had played a game of tennis and gone for a long walk along the river at Windsor. But this morning he felt ill. On the 21st he was worse, with what was probably a case of malaria. Doctors arrived and began to apply the standard seventeenth-century treatments of purging and 'blooding'. The King's illness looked serious enough for the Duke of York to return from Brussels. Buckingham was one of those who believed the King had been poisoned – at least that is what he told the French.[7] In the end Charles recovered, but opponents of the Duke of York had been given a scare.

It soon became clear that the elections were not going well for Charles and that a House of Commons in favour of exclusion was being elected. He sent the Duke of York to Scotland to get him out of the way. When Shaftesbury heard about this, as Lord President of the Council, he called together a meeting of the Privy Council on 7 October to discuss the development. He objected to James being sent to Scotland and said that the Council should have been consulted on the matter. Charles came to the decision that he was not going to have a meeting of the new Parliament that year and also that he had had enough of Shaftesbury. He dismissed him from his post as President and prorogued Parliament until 16 January 1680.

On 23 September Buckingham also found himself in trouble when a warrant was issued for his arrest on the grounds of engaging in treasonable practices.[8] This charge was based on some comments he had reportedly made regarding Lord Chief Justice Scroggs. Buckingham had allegedly accused Scroggs of 'favouring the Papists' and implied that he had been acting on the King's instructions. Buckingham disappeared for a while until the issue had blown over.

There was an overwhelming degree of anti-Papist sentiment to the annual November celebrations of 1679. The day of celebration was moved from Guy Fawkes Day to 17 November, the Accession Day of Queen Elizabeth. Buckingham was instrumental in the organisation of the festivities, which cost almost £2,500 to mount. The climax was the ritual burning of a magnificent wax figure of the pope.[9]

When Monmouth, who had been abroad, arrived back in England without permission, the King was furious and dismissed him from all his offices. On 10 December Charles announced to the Privy Council that he would not now call Parliament until the following November, although he chose to do this by means of a number of short prorogations. The Duke of York was recalled to London.

The next move by those who wanted to force the exclusion of the Duke of York was to have petitions drawn up for the recalling of Parliament. The exclusionists began to be known as 'Whiggamores' or Whigs, after a group of Scottish fanatical Covenanters whose rebellion had been put down by Monmouth in June 1679, while those who objected to the petitions became known as Tories. Although petitioning in this way was illegal under a 1661 Act and a royal declaration of 1679, Charles was presented with a number of petitions in January 1680 calling on him to meet his Parliament at once.

In December 1679 Buckingham had gone on a trip to France, telling Charles that its purpose was to 'effect an alliance between France and England'; its real purpose may have been to secretly raise funds for the Country Party.

In May 1680 Charles suffered another short bout of illness, which again alarmed the exclusionists. The Whigs decided to have bills of indictment presented at the Grand Jury of Middlesex against the Duke of York as a popish recusant and Louise de Kéroualle, Duchess of Portsmouth, as a common whore. Lord Chief Justice Scroggs made sure the case came to nothing, but although the attempt had failed, it was a clear indication to Charles of just how determined the Country Party would be to attack the succession when Parliament next met.

Before Parliament met on 21 October 1680 Charles felt it wise to send the Duke of York back to Scotland. Once the new session began it soon became clear that even more MPs had now been swayed to the side of exclusion. The Whigs were divided, however, between those who wanted Monmouth to succeed and those who wanted Mary, the Duke of York's Protestant daughter and her husband, William of Orange, to assume the throne.

On 2 November the debate on the Exclusion Bill began in the House of Commons and by the 11th had received its third reading. It was sent to the Lords a few days later. With Charles in attendance throughout the debate, the bill was finally rejected by sixty-three votes to thirty.[10] The controversy rumbled on until Charles prorogued Parliament on 10 January 1681, and on 18 January Parliament was dissolved.

Following the elections, Charles called for the new Parliament to be held on 21 March 1681, but this time in Oxford where, perhaps, he hoped the atmosphere might be calmer. Once again, Buckingham did not attend. Much to Charles's frustration, the question of exclusion soon reappeared. On 26 March the House of Commons appointed a committee to draw up a bill for James's exclusion.[11] On 28 March Charles dissolved the Oxford Parliament. He would never call another.

Charles now decided to fight back in another way. On the morning of 2 July, Shaftesbury was arrested at his house in London, brought before Charles and the Privy Council and accused of treason. He protested his innocence and requested to know who were the witnesses against him, which was denied. He was brought to the Tower of London. On a search of his house the only evidence found against him was a Bill of Association, which included a list of people who were to be asked to protect the King and prevent the Catholic succession. Shaftesbury asked to be released from the Tower on the grounds of ill-health, but was permitted only to leave for short coach trips with his wife. He persuaded Arlington to intercede with Charles on his behalf, offering to go to the colony of Carolina if released; but to no avail.

Finally, Shaftesbury came before a Grand Jury at the Old Bailey, which endeavoured to see if he had any case to answer. The heavily Whig-influenced jury decided that he did not, and a verdict of *Ignoramus* was entered on 24 November 1681. Charles was not pleased, complaining of 'the hard measure done him by Lord Shaftesbury's jury'.[12]

In the summer of 1682 Monmouth threatened to challenge the Marquess of Halifax to a duel: Charles refused to see him and ordered his courtiers to act likewise. This only had the effect of making Monmouth draw even closer to Shaftesbury. In September he was arrested in Stafford for disturbing the public peace while attempting to raise support for the exclusionist cause. He was granted bail but refused an audience at court.

By this time Shaftesbury had lost the will to struggle on and moved to Amsterdam, where he died in January 1683. The Whig opposition was, by now, effectively shattered.

Charles continued to hear evidence from around the country of growing support for Monmouth. There was a riot in Oxford where the mob shouted 'a Monmouth, a Monmouth!' In the spring of 1683 the Rye House Plot became public. This alleged plot consisted of a plan to assassinate the King and the Duke of York as they passed a property known as the Rye House situated in Hertfordshire, on the road from Newmarket to London. The King's entourage was to be stopped by a large group of men and both he and James were to be killed. A number of risings would then follow the assassinations. But a fire in Newmarket that year meant that the King returned to London earlier than anticipated, so it is very hard to tell whether there was any truth in the plot, or whether it would have been successful. A number of people were executed for their alleged involvement in the plot, on very flimsy evidence, including Algernon Sydney and Lord William Russell. Others, such as Captain Richard Rumbold, the owner of the Rye House, fled the country.

A reward of £500 was offered for the capture of Monmouth. In the end, however, having written letters to his father and his uncle assuring them that he would never take part in any plot to murder them, Monmouth was reunited with Charles and the legal proceedings against him were dropped. But father and son promptly fell out again when Monmouth agreed to sign a letter in which he admitted the existence of the plot and then, after talking to his friends, withdrew his assent. Charles was furious once again and excluded him from court. Monmouth decided it prudent to flee the country in case legal action would be brought against him again. In the event, he was to stay away from England for most of the rest of Charles's reign. This enabled Charles and his government to capitalise on the Rye House Plot by sending out a message that they were prepared to take firm action against their opponents.

Buckingham had avoided overt involvement in the exclusion crisis probably because he did not want to see Monmouth installed as the new heir to the throne, and, most of all, because he knew how much Charles would resent any move to tamper with the succession. He was careful not to fall victim to Charles's anger again. Although it is hard to know how active he was behind the scenes, his policy of staying out of the crisis meant that he avoided its repercussions and managed to keep his friendship with Charles intact. However, in the midst of this constitutional crisis, he was threatened by a very personal and dangerous accusation.

Twenty-five

A CHARGE OF
A PERSONAL NATURE

In 1680 an attempt was made to bring a charge against Buckingham that could be described as both 'of a personal nature' and 'very material', as Danby had threatened some years earlier: a plot was in hand to accuse him of the capital crime of sodomy. This accusation, often made in the seventeenth century to discredit an enemy, was made on a number of occasions against Buckingham in particular. It was a charge he dismissed, saying, 'I was never such a virtuoso in my lusts.'[1] Samuel Butler wrote of him:

[The Duke of Buckingham] is one that has studied the whole body of vice . . . His appetite to his pleasure is diseased and crazy . . . Perpetual surfeits of pleasure have filled his mind with bad and vicious humours . . .[2]

We do not know for sure if Danby was the instigator of this particular plot. The Lord Treasurer was committed to the Tower of London at the time, but it could have been supervised by his steward, Edward Christian. Christian was a disgruntled ex-employee of Buckingham, whom the Duke had dismissed for embezzlement of estate funds.

Another man named as one of the chief instigators of the plot was Buckingham's one-time ally, Colonel Thomas Blood. This particular rumour began when two Irishmen, Philemon Coddan and Samuel Ryther, came forward claiming that they had been engaged by Blood to give evidence that Buckingham had committed sodomy with a woman called Sarah Harwood and subsequently forced her to go to France. They also said that a young man called Philip Le Mar was to swear that he too had been sodomised by the Duke. Le Mar's mother was also to be a witness against him. Also supporting their story was an employee of Buckingham's called Jenks.

Coddan and Ryther claimed that a number of meetings had taken place in preparation for the accusation. They also claimed that large amounts of money were offered to two additional characters, Maurice Hickey and Thomas Curtis, to persuade them to cooperate with the plot. They produced a statement, which they said had been prepared for them to sign, in which the Duke of Buckingham's crimes were described in detail. It read:

Whereas Samuel Ryther and Philemon Coddan gentlemen, in St. Martins Parish in the Fields, do hereby confess and declare, That Sarah Harwood of the City of London, gentlewoman, did confess before us, that the Lord Duke of Buckingham was with his privy members as far in both her privy parts as he could go with forcible entrance, stopping her breath, and that the said Lord Duke of Buckingham hath since conveyed the said Sarah Harwood out of the way, by which means the King lost his evidence. And do further declare, that since that time, the said Duke did order the said Sarah to be murdered, and since the time is murdered or sold beyond Sea. And do further declare, that the said Duke hath committed the said Sin of Sodomy, with several more, which we are ready to prove, when we are required as the Kings Evidence.

When presented with this document, according to their story, Ryther absconded with it and they brought it to Buckingham's solicitor, Mr Whitaker. They were then brought before Sir William Waller, a Justice of the Peace, to tell their story.

It is very difficult to tell who was telling the truth and who was trying to frame whom. In the end, the Grand Jury found the evidence against Buckingham contradictory and inadequate, and so he was cleared with a verdict of *Ignoramus*. Blood was summoned before Waller but vehemently protested his innocence in the whole affair. In addition to Blood, a number of people were put on trial, including Maurice Hickey, Thomas Curtis, Edward Christian and Mrs Bradley of the Heaven Tavern. They were charged with:

> . . . unlawfully, unjustly . . . devilishly and corruptly, by unlawful ways and means between themselves, have practised, conspired, intended and designed, to dispoil and deprive his Grace the Duke of Buckingham, then and there one of the Peers and Grandees of this Kingdom of England, not only of his honour, estimation and reputation, but also to take his life away, and destroy his life and dignity of Dukeship. And to cause the said George Duke of Buckingham, to be taken, arrested and condemned to death, for detestable crimes and offences of sodomy and buggery, by him supposed to be committed, with one Sarah Harwood, and divers other persons, against the order of nature. And also for inticing or transporting of the said Sarah Harwood beyond sea, to suppress and take off their evidences, of and concerning the crimes of sodomy and buggery aforesaid.[3]

The case generated a huge sensation at the time, with one observer remarking that 'The business of the Duke of Buckingham is now become the only discourse of the town.'[4] Blood, Christian, Curtis and Hickey were all found guilty, fined and imprisoned. Philip Le Mar and his mother were also tried. Someone seems to have attempted to force Le Mar to change his story by drugging him, which resulted in his being too ill to attend his trial.[5] One newsletter commented, 'It's discoursed that who have any ways been tampering with Le Marr or abetting to it, will be made public exemplaries for such their ill practices.'[6] Despite his illness, Le Mar and his mother were found guilty. Le Mar died soon afterwards and on 19 June 1680 his mother was forced to stand in the pillory where she was 'severely dealt with by the people throwing dirt and rotten eggs at her'.[7] Mrs Bradley of the Heaven Tavern was found to be innocent of any involvement in the affair.

The career of William Waller, JP, was ruined by the débâcle. Although he had managed to damage his enemy, Thomas Blood, his conduct during the affair, which included tampering with witnesses, bribery, and spending a whole night drinking with Maurice Hickey when the man was supposed to be in gaol, gave the King a convenient excuse to remove his commission as a Justice. He later fled to the Netherlands.[8] It is interesting to note that in 1685 Coddan received a position as a tide surveyor in Plymouth, which may have been a reward for his involvement in the affair.[9] Buckingham however brought a charge of *scandalum magnatum* against Colonel Blood and was awarded £10,000 in damages. Of course Blood was unable to pay. The affair ruined him financially and he died soon afterwards, on 24 August 1680.

This is not the first time that Buckingham had used a charge of *scandalum magnatum* to ruin someone. In July 1680, the Duke had been involved in another action of *scandalum magnatum*, which he brought against a barber called Henry Howard. That time he had been awarded £1,000 in damages.[10] More than two years later the poor man was still in prison, unable to pay the damages.[11]

Buckingham's reputation had been damaged by these accusations and even more by the publication in 1681 of John Dryden's bitterly satirical masterpiece *Absalom and Achitophel*. In this poem, written in heroic style, Dryden deals with the issues of the day by using biblical characters and themes. He recalls the rebellion of Absalom against his father King David.[12] Dryden represents Monmouth as Absalom, the beautiful and much loved child who rebelled against his father:

> Of all this numerous progeny was none
> So beautiful, so brave, as Absalom:

Achitophel, Absalom's adviser who commits suicide in the Bible version, is Shaftesbury:

> Of these the false Achitophel was first;
> A name to all succeeding ages cursed:
> For close designs, and crooked counsels fit;
> Sagacious, bold, and turbulent of wit;

In *Absalom and Achitophel* Dryden gets his revenge for the satirical *The Rehearsal* by parodying Buckingham for posterity as the biblical character Zimri. The name is taken from two figures called Zimri in the Bible: one lustful and blasphemous, the other a conspirator and regicide.[13] Dryden intended them both to stand for Buckingham:

> Some of their chiefs were princes of the land:
> In the first rank of these did Zimri stand;
> A man so various, that he seemed to be
> Not one, but all mankind's epitome:
> Stiff in opinions, always in the wrong;
> Was everything by starts, and nothing long;
> But, in the course of one revolving moon,
> Was Chymist, fiddler, statesman, and buffoon:
> Then all for women, painting, rhyming, drinking,
> Besides ten thousand freaks that died in thinking.
> Blest madman, who could every hour employ,
> With something new to wish, or to enjoy!
> Railing and praising were his usual themes;
> And both (to show his judgement) in extremes:
> So over-violent, or over-civil,

That every man, with him, was God or Devil.
In squandering wealth was his peculiar art:
Nothing went unrewarded but desert.
Beggared by fools, whom still he found too late,
He had his jest, and they had his estate.
He laughed himself from court; then sought relief
By forming parties, but could ne'er be chief;
For, spite of him, the weight of business fell
On Absalom and wise Achitophel:
Thus, wicked but in will, of means bereft,
He left not faction, but of that was left.

Although it was said that Buckingham sent Dryden a congratulatory letter and a gift of £500 on publication of *Absalom and Achitophel*, he was irked by the personal satire. The verse *To Dryden* in his Commonplace book contains the words, *'thy ill made Resemblance wasts my fame'*.[14]

Dryden was not the only person in the literary world to have a dispute with Buckingham. On another occasion when the Duke organised a group of supporters to hiss the *United Kingdom* by Edward Howard off the stage, such was the ire of the playwright's family that they lay in wait afterwards with the intention of doing the Duke serious harm. Buckingham was only saved that night by the confusion caused in the theatre house by his supporters, which allowed him to escape.

Twenty-six

THE DEATHS

On Sunday 1 February 1685, Charles enjoyed a supper of goose eggs. He then spent an enjoyable evening in company with the Duchess of Portsmouth, among others. The following morning he looked and felt ill, and spoke only with difficulty, and as he sat down to be shaved he suffered a fit. The doctors immediately began to bleed him. The treatment continued but on Wednesday he suffered further convulsions. By the afternoon he seemed much improved and even managed to talk with visitors for several hours – so much so that the *London Gazette* announced on the following day that he was out of danger.

By Thursday, however, his condition had deteriorated once again. It was only then, as he lay dying, that Charles would fulfil his long-time wish of converting to Catholicism. Father John Huddlestone, a priest he had known from the Civil War, was smuggled into his room. With only the Earl of Bath and Lord Feversham present in the room, Charles declared that he wished to die a Catholic, confessed his sins, and was anointed.

As evening drew into night he said farewell to his Queen, held a long conversation with his brother James, whom he asked to look after the Duchess of Portsmouth and not to let 'poor Nelly starve'. He also blessed those of his sons who were in attendance. On Friday 6 February 1685 between eleven-thirty and noon King Charles II died. His funeral took place on 14 February and he was buried in a vault in the south aisle of Henry VII's Chapel at Westminster Abbey. Queen Catherine returned to

Portugal in 1692, where she died in 1705. Her great rival, Barbara Villiers, died a few years later, in 1709.

During the 1680s Buckingham had gradually begun to play less and less of a role in politics. In November 1680 he made a speech to the House of Lords in which he called for a committee drawn from both Houses to 'consider the state of the nation with regard to Popery'.[1] He was beginning to decline physically, and it was noticed that he looked ill.

Nell Gwynn had asked him to wear new shoes and a new wig when calling on her so that he would not stink the place out.[2] 'The Duke of Buckingham has a set of false teeth and wears a feather. I think when a fellow has come to that, it is no matter what he does or is', wrote Lady Harvey to her brother Ralph Montague.[3] Henry Savile said that Buckingham was 'out at heels and stunk most grievously'.[4]

In March 1681 Buckingham was given the freedom of London. The attacks on him had not ceased, however, as in May of that year Captain Bury was tried, fined and imprisoned for conspiring against him.[5] By 1682 his political life may have been over and he may have been dirty and his health in decline, but whenever he travelled to London to see Charles the old rumours of a return to power resurfaced. One letter-writer in March 1682 says that 'My Lord Duke of Bucks is said to be restored into his Majesty's favour', while another account from 1683 speaks of 'the reconciliation of the Duke of Buckingham'.[6] In 1684 yet another writer heard that the Duke was to 'go into the West Indies as Vice Roy'.[7]

Neither had his feisty spirit been completely vanquished. In 1683 he was sued by his bailiff, John Goodchild, for assault. Goodchild claimed that the Duke had broken into his house with a party of men armed with blunderbusses. Buckingham admitted that he had indeed entered Goodchild's house, but only after returning from Lincolnshire to find no hay for his horses and no food for himself or his servants. He claimed that he had only a switch in his hand at the time, but that he would never travel without a blunderbuss. He was bound over for £1,500 to keep the peace with Goodchild.[8]

The activities of his servants had not grown any quieter either. In 1681 one was found murdered on a street in London.[9] In February 1682 one of his servants was stabbed by another, and in the same year his cook was executed for the murder of a cook who was on the staff of the Earl of Feversham.[10]

In 1610 Beaumont and Fletcher wrote a play entitled *Philaster: or, Love Lies a-Bleeding*. A revised version of this play, completed in 1683 and called *The Restauration: or, Right Will Take Place*, is generally believed to be the work of Buckingham. The theme is one of love frustrated. However, the play did not make it to the stage and is not highly regarded in terms of its literary merit.

As they neared the end of their lives, the old friends, Charles and Buckingham, were back together. In the summer before Charles's death Buckingham travelled with him on a yacht to Portsmouth along with James and three of Charles's sons: Richmond, Grafton and St Albans.[11] They entered the harbour to be greeted by the sound of a gun salute and the ringing of church bells, and afterwards attended a lavish reception given by the Mayor. After Charles's death everything was different for Buckingham. As one writer has put it, 'As long as Charles was alive Buckingham had nothing to fear; he could . . . return to Court whenever he pleased.'[12]

The coronation of King James II turned out to be Buckingham's final public engagement. In marked contrast to Charles's coronation, Buckingham now held no privileges and so did not carry any of the regalia. Instead, he walked alone in procession wearing his garter robes and carrying his coronet. His relationship with James saw no improvement during the final years of his life.

In 1685 Buckingham published a piece entitled *A Short Discourse upon the Reasonableness of Men's having a Religion, or Worship of God*, in which he once again made the case for liberty of conscience in matters of religion:

It does highly concern every man, to examine seriously, which is the best way of worshipping and serving this God; That is, which is the best religion . . . I must leave every man to take pains, in seeking out, and choosing for himself; he only being answerable to God Almighty for his own soul.[13]

It is interesting to note that this time, with a Catholic king upon the throne, he is careful not to exclude Catholics from his desire for religious toleration.

Nothing can be more anti-Christian, nor more contrary to sense and reason, than to trouble and molest our fellow-Christians, because they cannot be exactly of our minds, in all the things relating to the worship of God.

The arguments set out in the *Short Discourse* prompted much debate and led to the publication of a number of replies. One such reply was an anonymous piece entitled *A Short Answer to His Grace of Buckingham's Paper* to which Buckingham wrote another, even shorter, reply. His answer was addressed to 'My Nameless, Angry, Harmless, Humble Servant', to whom he said: 'I perceive you do as little understand any part of what I have written, though I thought it had been so plain a style, that a child of six years old might very well have done it.'[14]

Monmouth returned to England in 1685 to mount a military challenge against his uncle, King James II – and paid for it with his life. Monmouth's army was defeated at the battle of Sedgemoor in July and Monmouth himself was soon captured and beheaded. Buckingham's play, *The Battle of Sedgmoor Rehearsed at Whitehall: A Farce*, believed to have been written shortly after the event, is an unmerciful satire on the Earl of Feversham, the commander of the Royalist forces that day. Although the Royalists won the battle, Buckingham used his play to draw attention to their serious military blunders.

In November 1685 Buckingham suffered a grievous loss in the death of his sister Mall. The last few years of his life were spent mostly in

Yorkshire at Castle Helmsley and Fairfax House. He still enjoyed engaging in country pursuits such as fishing and hunting. His interest in hunting is testified to in an old Yorkshire song from the time that goes:

> Oh! with the Duke of Buckingham
> And other noble gentlemen,
> Oh! But we had some fine hunting![15]

On 14 April 1687 Buckingham went out hunting with horses and hounds. The hunt neared its end with a three-hour run during which the Duke's horse dropped dead. The fox went to ground and Buckingham helped with the digging. But, by the time a new horse had arrived, Buckingham felt too ill to make the journey to York and decided instead to stay at the farmhouse of one of his tenants, at Kirkby Moorside. This sudden onset of illness was blamed by many upon the fact that the Duke had spent a considerable amount of time that day sitting on damp grass. The relatively spartan surroundings in which he was to spend his final hours are exaggerated by Pope in his *Moral Essays*:

> In the worst inn's worse room, with mat half hung,
> The floors of plaster and the walls of dung,
> On once a flock-bed, but repaired with straw,
> With tape-tied curtains, never meant to draw,
> The George and Garter dangling from that bed,
> Where tawdry yellow strove with dirty red,
> Great Villiers lies.

He developed a fever and his stomach became swollen and inflamed. He had been suffering for a day and a night when his cousin James Douglas, Earl of Arran, arrived to see him.[16] He told Arran that he was sure he was in no danger of his life and that he would be up and about again in a few days. Arran, on the other hand, believed that the Duke was dying. He sent to York for Dr Whaler who, after his examination, confirmed Arran's fears. Arran decided that he would have to tell Buckingham the truth.

Still the Duke would not accept his approaching death, saying, 'It is not as you apprehend. In a day or two I shall be well.'[17] Since Arran was worried that he would die without preparing his soul and clearing his conscience, he sent for the clergyman, the Revd Gibson, in the company of whom he once again told Buckingham bluntly that he should prepare for his death.

For the next six or seven hours Arran and the clergyman tried to encourage him to make his peace with God and declare his heir. He would do neither. At one stage, Arran even resorted to offering to send for a Catholic priest, to which Buckingham said: 'No, no – I am not one of that persuasion. I will hear no more of it.'[18] He also rejected the intercession of a Presbyterian with the words, 'No, those fellows always made me sick with their whine and cant.'

Finally the following morning he consented to a visit from the village parson, Mr Shepard. When the parson asked, 'what is your Grace's religion?' His answer was: 'It is an insignificant question. I have been a shame and a disgrace to all religions – but if you can do me any good, do.' Later that evening he received the last sacraments of the Church of England.

In the course of the afternoon the Revd Gibson had asked him if he had made a will, to which he replied that he had not. Revd Gibson then called out the names of a number of suitable beneficiaries, including that of Arran, to each of which the Duke gave a negative reply. By the time Brian Fairfax arrived at his bedside the Duke was no longer able to speak but only held on to Brian's hand. The 2nd Duke of Buckingham died at eleven o'clock on 16 April 1687. In his pocket was found a commonplace book containing a number of verses, aphorisms and one unfinished play. With no legitimate heirs, all titles that he had inherited from his father lapsed with him.

As the end of his life approached, Buckingham had written the following poignant words:

> To what a situation am I now reduced! Is this odious little hut a suitable lodging for a prince? . . . I am afflicted with poverty and haunted by remorse; despised by my country, and I fear forsaken by my God. I am forsaken by all my acquaintances, neglected by the friends of my bosom. . .[19]

The Duke's body lay at Helmsley Castle for six weeks. A magnificent funeral was organised, paid for by King James II. At midnight on 21 June 1687 his body was laid to rest in the family vault in King Henry VII's Chapel at Westminster Abbey beside his father, his two brothers and the son born to Lady Shrewsbury. His wife Mary lived on until 1704, when she died at the age of 66. *To the Memory of the Illustrious Prince, George Duke of Buckingham* was written in his honour by Aphra Behn:

> Thy Witt, a Torrent for the Banks too strong,
> In twenty smaller Rills o're-flow'd the dam . . .[20]

EPILOGUE

King Charles II and George Villiers, 2nd Duke of Buckingham, were two of the most intriguing, illustrious, influential and scandalous figures of the seventeenth century. Like us all, their personalities were forged by the circumstances of their lives. They both had fathers who were political leaders and had suffered violent deaths. They both regarded Charles I as a father figure. They also shared the typical childhood and education of a royal household, until that protected world, and the future that had been assured them, was shattered by civil war and the usurpation of the monarchy. They suffered together through the psychologically and financially challenging years of exile, at least until Buckingham's return to England. Following the Restoration of the monarchy, they spent the rest of their lives together at Charles's royal court, at the highest level of political decision-making.

They were men of their era. The seventeenth century was a time of uncertainty. The historical period in which they lived was an era of change, not least political and religious change. The people had undergone the political transition from a monarchy to a commonwealth, a protectorate and back to a monarchy again. They saw the ascendancy of the Episcopalian church dismantled and the Puritan model take its place, and later the whole process reversed again with all the resultant conflict. This was also a time of philosophical change from the certainty of unquestioned theological belief to the growth of scientific reason. All these changes wrought a society that was fractured, strained and, in many ways, confused. The leaders of that society, such as Charles and Buckingham, had to deal with the pressures caused by such change.

Charles has earned the sobriquet 'the Merry Monarch' as a result of his reputation as a carefree pursuer of pleasure. It is true that he did pursue pleasure, but he was also a shrewd political operator who managed to survive through difficult times. He was aware, on his return from exile, that circumstances for the monarchy would never be the same again. His father had been executed by his subjects and with that event the nature of absolute monarchy had changed for ever. Throughout his reign he suffered the lingering fear that if he were not politically adroit he could suffer the same fate as his father. The story of his father's life and death, coupled with his own experiences of hard times, had taught him that in order to survive in the cut-throat world of politics he would have to be opportunistic, flexible, duplicitous, ruthless, manipulative and clever. He would have to know when to stand firm and when to bend. For example, when Parliament refused to assent to his Declarations of Indulgence for Nonconformists and Catholics, he backed down: but on the question of the succession of James to the throne he refused to relent. He was similarly intransigent on his right to summon, prorogue and dissolve parliaments. In order to pursue his aims he was untrustworthy with his ministers and devious in his foreign policy. He was criticised by contemporaries for being lazy, and as regards paperwork and administration there is some truth in that claim. He was, however, in charge of a system of administration that was highly centralised. He rose most mornings at five or six and regularly attended meetings of the Privy Council, the Foreign Affairs Committee and the House of Lords.[1] But, most importantly, he knew how to get things done when they had to be done. He was a pragmatist who always did just enough to get a job done and no more.

Charles was likeable, amusing, tolerant and forgiving. He once declared that he was prepared to forgive anyone in his kingdom that day, except for the horse that had thrown him in the morning.[2] He was a man of lively interests. Evelyn writes of discussing with him subjects as diverse as 'shipping, architecture, bee-keeping, gardening, and urban pollution'.[3] He had a keen interest in a range of subjects, such as science, naval matters, astronomy, music, theatre and equestrianism. He was well known for his pursuit of physical exercise, regularly taking brisk walks around St James's Park with his spaniels, and engaging in early morning swims and games of real tennis.

Buckingham, like Charles, could be manipulative, devious and untrustworthy. He was capable of intense rivalries, such as those with Clarendon, Ormonde and Arlington. He was unscupulous in his attacks on his enemies, often ridiculing them through the use of mimicry, verse and drama. As Burnet said of him, 'He had the art of treating persons or things in a ridculous manner beyond any man of the age.'[4] On the other hand, the tables were turned when Dryden characterised him for ever as Zimri in *Absalom and Achitophel*. In the pursuit of his aims he did not shy away from recourse to those who operated outside the law, such as Thomas Blood.

Yet, like Charles, he was also a man capable of great charm and wit, who was liked by a great number of people including Abraham Cowley, Martin Clifford, Ellis Leighton, the so-called court wits such as Rochester, and Charles himself. He was gifted artistically, with admirable skills in literature, theatre and music. He was intelligent and had many talents that enabled him to fulfil a number of roles beyond that of a leading political figure. He was a farmer, a soldier, a glass manufacturer, a scientist, a playwright, a poet, an actor, a musician, a composer and a patron of the arts, among other things. His reputation as a polymath was widespread. In 1671 the French King asked his chief minister if he could write him a play. When the minister told him that he didn't possess such talents, King Louis told him that in England Buckingham had got 'a great deal of honour by writing a farce'.[5] His most famous work, *The Rehearsal*, made a significant contribution to the development of burlesque in the English theatre.

He argued, on a number of occasions, for liberty of conscience on behalf of Protestant Nonconformists. He genuinely believed that Protestants had the right to choose their form of worship, although it was only when there was a Catholic king on the throne that he extended this right to Catholics. His support for liberty of conscience led to him being labelled as an atheist and a promoter of radicalism by those who disagreed with the concept. His connections with people like Thomas Blood contributed to this reputation.

Buckingham could be inconsistent and was always willing to change his policy for practical reasons. Dryden refers to this trait when he writes that he 'Was everything by starts and nothing long', and Butler when he says 'He is as inconstant as the Moon'.[6] Buckingham resembled Charles in this tendency to change course. One obvious example was the U-turn he took when he decided to return to England in the 1650s. That decision meant that he made peace with the very forces against whom he had fought in the Civil War and by whom his brother had been killed. Other inconsistencies, which he felt were necessary for reasons of political expediency, were his opposition to Catholicism at home and his keenness to have the primary Catholic state, France, as an ally – and, as already mentioned, his advocacy of religious toleration for Catholics for the first time when the Catholic King James II was on the throne.

Although he appointed Buckingham to his Privy Council, Charles never promoted him to the key political positions of Lord Chancellor, Lord Treasurer or Secretary of State. Charles was aware of his faults – the tendency to be inconsistent, the inability to develop long-term political policies and the lack of a diligent work ethic. As a result of his special influence with Charles, his unusual upbringing, and the fact that he took some credit for bringing about the Restoration, Buckingham did not work hard at building a political career in the way that Arlington and Danby did. Instead, he felt that high office was his birthright. His relatively poor record of attendance at Parliament and the Privy Council attests to his lack of diligence, as does his lacklustre efforts at everyday administration in the North Riding. Charles also refused to appoint him to the military commands that he so desired. He would not put him in command of the army marching to meet Cromwell in the 1650s and also refused to countermand James's order during the second Dutch War, that Buckingham not be given command of a ship or attend the councils of war. The fact that he never managed to rise to the high political rank enjoyed by his late father was a cause of frustration and anger to Buckingham throughout his life. He felt let down by Charles. But, mostly, he tended to blame his failures at political advancement on the intervention of his enemies such as Clarendon, Ormonde and Arlington.

Both Charles's and Buckingham's relationships with women caused frequent public scandal. Of course, the stories of Charles and his many mistresses are legendary. Everyone knew of Barbara, Louise, Nell and the others. Buckingham, although not as promiscuous as Charles, also managed to scandalise seventeenth-century polite society with his romantic life. His affair with Lady Shrewsbury, which led to the death of her husband and his public humiliation before the House of Lords, was widely reported. Both Charles and Buckingham fathered illegitimate children, in Charles's case many of them, in Buckingham's case just the one, short-lived, child with Lady Shrewsbury. Yet neither managed to conceive a legitimate heir. On more than one occasion they found themselves attracted to the same woman. One such notable case was that of Frances Stuart, who ultimately rejected both of them. There were even rumours that Buckingham had enjoyed illicit relations with Charles's chief mistress and his own cousin, Barbara Villiers. There were similar rumours about Buckingham and Nell Gwynn, who had to 'box' the Duke's ears on at least one occasion when he was becoming too familiar with her.[7]

It was as Charles and Buckingham played their children's games in the gardens of various royal places, and later suffered as young men in exile, that the relationship between them began its development into one that would endure for years to come, albeit through many difficult times. The fact that they possessed a number of personality traits in common, such as active imaginations, lively intellects, many interests beyond politics and a fondness for having fun, was the bond that held the structure of their relationship together throughout the years. They enjoyed each other's company.

Theirs was a friendship that suffered from bouts of anger, betrayal and dishonesty. Even though they had been together since childhood and despite Buckingham's being a member of Charles's Privy Council in exile, Buckingham eventually deserted him and returned to Cromwell's England when it seemed unlikely that the monarchy would ever be restored. This was a big blow to Charles's trust in his childhood friend. Yet, soon after the Restoration, their relationship was revived and Buckingham was made a Gentleman of the Bedchamber, reappointed to the Privy Council and made Lord Lieutenant of the West Riding.

Charles, in turn, can be said to have betrayed Buckingham when he sent him to treat with the French in the late 1660s while the secret treaty was already being negotiated. Under the terms of that secret treaty Charles made a commitment to convert to Catholicism, a move that Buckingham would have wholeheartedly opposed. Having the 'public' treaty negotiated by Buckingham, who was a recognised advocate of Protestantism and an opponent of Catholicism, was an admirable cover for the secret treaty. Towards the end of his career, Buckingham once again found himself in conflict with Charles when he aligned himself with Shaftesbury and the Country Party in opposition to the King and the Court Party. He also publicly challenged Charles's wishes by attempting to have Parliament dissolved, and as a result found himself thrown into the Tower of London.

They were many such occasions in their lives when Charles and Buckingham were genuinely angry with each other. Yet, for all the times of trouble, their friendship had an enduring quality and they were inevitably, in the end, reconciled to each other. Even as they approached the end of their lives, they were back on friendly terms, enjoying a trip to Portsmouth in 1684 just a few months before Charles's death. The bond between them was so strong and the memories of happy times spent together in their youth so enduring that they could never abandon each other.

NOTES

ABBREVIATIONS

BL	British Library
Burghclere, *Buckingham*	*George Villiers, 2nd Duke of Buckingham 1628–1687: A Study in the History of the Restoration*
Burghclere, *Ormonde*	*The Life of James, First Duke of Ormonde, 1610–1688*
Clarendon, *History*	Clarendon, Edward, Earl of, *History of the Rebellion and Civil Wars in England* (1888 edition, edited by MacRay)
Clarendon, *Life*	Clarendon, Edward, Earl of, *The Life of Edward, Earl of Clarendon, . . . in which is included a Continuation of his History of the Grand Rebellion, written by Himself* (1827)
CSP	Calendar of State Papers
HCJ	House of Commons Journal
HLJ	House of Lords Journal
HMC	Historical Manuscripts Commission
Pepys	The Diary of Samuel Pepys
TNA	The National Archives (formerly Public Record Office)

Preface

1 W. Burghclere, *George Villiers, 2nd Duke of Buckingham 1628–1687: A Study in the History of the Restoration* (London: John Murray, 1903), p. 85, quoting Brian Fairfax.

Chapter One

1 R. Lockyer, *Buckingham: The Life and Political Career of George Villiers, First Duke of Buckingham 1592–1628* (London and New York: Longman, 1981), p. 452; S.R. Gardiner,

A History of England under the Duke of Buckingham and Charles I, 1624–1628 (London, Longman, Green & Co., 1857), vol. 2, p. 335; H.W. Chapman, *Great Villiers: A Study of George Villiers Second Duke of Buckingham 1628–1687* (London, Secker & Warburg, 1949), p. 3.

2 Lockyer, *Buckingham: The Life*, p. 459.

3 HMC, Mar and Kellie MSS, Supplement Report (1930), p. 56.

4 J. Morrill, *Stuart Britain: A Very Short Introduction* (Oxford University Press, 2000), p. 29.

5 Clarendon, *History*, vol. 1, p. 37.

6 Sir Edward Coke speaking in the House of Commons.

12 J.H. Wilson, *A Rake and His Times: George Villiers 2nd Duke of Buckingham* (London: Frederick Muller, 1954), p. 7.

13 Fraser, *King Charles II*, p. 16.

14 Clarendon, *History*, vol. 3, p. 381.

15 CSP, Domestic, 1635–6, p. 342.

16 See S.A. Strong (ed.), *A Catalogue of Letters and Other Historical Documents at Welbeck* (London, 1903), pp. 188–9.

17 Fraser, *King Charles II*, p. 19.

18 HCJ, vol. 2, 24 June 1641.

19 HCJ, vol. 2, 1 June 1642.

20 See HLJ, vol. 4, 30 October 1641; HLJ, vol. 4, 14 January 1642.

21 CSP, Domestic, 1639, p. 509.

22 Clarendon, *Life*, I, p. 51.

Chapter Two

1 Burghclere, *Buckingham*, p. 8.

2 Lockyer, *Buckingham: The Life*, pp. 457, 460.

3 *Ibid.*, p. 461.

4 Bagwell, p. 87.

5 Burghclere, *Buckingham*, p. 10.

6 *Ibid.*, pp. 16, 17.

7 I am using the terms Anglican and Anglicanism throughout although they did not come into general use until after 1660. See N. Davies, *The Isles, A History* (London: Macmillan, 1999), p. 559.

8 P. Gregg, *King Charles I* (London: J.M. Dent & Sons, 1981), p. 157.

9 A. Fraser, *King Charles II* (London: Arrow, 1998), p. 3.

10 *Ibid.*, p. 11.

11 Chapman, *Great Villiers*, p. 11.

Chapter Three

1 Chapman, *Great Villiers*, p. 22.

2 J.H. O'Neill, *George Villiers, Second Duke of Buckingham* (Boston: Twayne, 1984), p. 2; Wilson, *A Rake and His Times*, pp. 15, 16.

3 Fraser, *King Charles II*, p. 22.

4 T. Reilly, *Cromwell: An Honourable Enemy* (Co. Kerry, Ireland: Brandon, 1999), p. 16 for the 4 million acres.

5 Davies, *The Isles, A History*, p. 579.

6 JHL, vol. 8, 31 October 1646.

7 Fraser, *King Charles II*, p. 37.

8 Clarendon, *History*, vol. 4, pp. 21–3; Fraser, *King Charles II*, p. 37; D. Wilson, *All the King's Women* (London: Hutchinson, 2003), pp. 39, 40.

9 A. Bryant, *King Charles II* (London: Longman, Green & Co.), p. 47.

10 Fraser, *King Charles II*, pp. 38–40.

11 Both Fraser (*King Charles II*, p. 43) and D. Wilson (*All the King's Women*, pp. 43, 44) doubt the validity of this.

12 S. Coote, *Royal Survivor: A Life of Charles II* (London: Hodder & Stoughton, 1999), p. 57.

13 Fraser, *King Charles II*, p. 49.

14 Burnet, *History of My Own Time*.

15 From D. Wilson, *All the King's Women*, p. 98 quoting *Mercurius Politicus* 8–15 January 1652, from J. Raymond (ed.), *Making the News, an Anthology of the Newsbooks of Revolutionary England 1641–1660* (Moreton-in-Marsh: 1993), p. 277.

16 Burnet, *History of My Own Time*.

17 Fraser, *King Charles II*, p. 50.

18 JHL, vol. 9, 7 April 1647.

19 See G. Hopkins, *Constant Delights: Rakes, Rogues and Scandal in Restoration England* (London: Robson, 2002), p. 4.

20 Ludlow Memoirs, vol. 1. p. 255.

21 Chapman, *Great Villiers*, p. 42.

22 Marvell's authorship is usually questioned because of the poem's strong Royalist sympathies.

23 Chapman, *Great Villiers*, p. 42.

24 *Ibid.*, p. 43.

25 Burghclere, *Buckingham*, p. 26.

26 Although the spelling 'Ormond' was generally used prior to his being raised to the dukedom in 1661, in the interest of simplicity I have used the spelling 'Ormonde' throughout.

27 Fraser, *King Charles II*, p. 78.

28 Chapman, *Great Villiers*, p. 48.

Chapter Four

1 Chapman, *Great Villiers*, p. 46.

2 W. Burghclere, *The Life of James, First Duke of Ormonde, 1610–1688* (London: John Murray, 1912), vol. 1, p. 407.

3 Bryant, *King Charles II*, p. 59.

4 Burghclere, *Ormonde*, vol. 1, pp. 446, 447.

5 Chapman, *Great Villiers*, p. 47.

6 Burghclere, *Buckingham*, p. 27.

7 Lockyer, *Buckingham: The Life*, p. 462.

8 Burnet, *History of My Own Time*, vol. 1, p. 182; Wilson, *A Rake and His Times*, p. 17 disagrees that Buckingham ever sought the philosopher's stone.

9 Burghclere, *Buckingham*, p. 28.

10 Bryant, *King Charles II*, p. 47, tells us that Burnet first made this accusation; however, he disagrees with it, citing lack of evidence as his reason. See also Coote, *Royal Survivor*, pp. 53, 54.

11 Fraser, *King Charles II*, p. 65.

12 Burghclere, *Buckingham*, pp. 28–30.

13 *Ibid.*, p. 33 quoting Newnham MSS, Earl of Denbigh. Basil, Earl of Denbigh, to his mother.

14 C. Phipps (ed.), *Buckingham: Public and Private Man. The Prose, Poems and Commonplace Book of George Villiers, Second Duke of Buckingham (1628–1687)* (New York and London: Garland, 1985), p. 5.

15 Chapman, *Great Villiers*, p. 60.

16 Burghclere, *Buckingham*, p. 56; Chapman, *Great Villiers*, p. 86.

17 Clarendon MSS, No. 457, 12 December 1650, Henry Nash to William Edgeman.

18 HMC, Portland MSS, vol. 2, pp. 137–8, Buckingham to Newcastle, 5 December 1650.

19 Chapman, *Great Villiers*, p. 65.

20 Adapted. See Clarendon, *History*, vol. 5, pp. 187, 188; Burghclere, *Buckingham*, pp. 49, 50; Chapman, *Great Villiers*, p. 67.

21 Clarendon, *History*, vol. 5, p. 188.

22 Burghclere, *Buckingham*, pp. 56, 57.

23 Sir J. Reresby's *Memoirs*, p. 73.

24 Clarendon MSS, No. 672, Hyde to Nicholas, 2 March 1652.

25 *Ibid*. According to Chapman, *Great Villiers*, p. 73, this was a threat she often made when her children misbehaved in some way.

26 Burghclere, *Buckingham*, pp. 59, 60 and Chapman, *Great Villiers*, p. 73, quoting F. Peck, *Desiderata Curiosa*, p. 160, Nicholas Oudart to Mr Harding, 30 May 1652.

27 *Ibid*.

28 Chapman, *Great Villiers*, p. 75.

29 *Ibid.*, p. 76.

30 Burghclere, *Buckingham*, p. 65.

31 *Ibid.*; Chapman, *Great Villiers*, p. 77.

32 Burghclere, *Buckingham*, p. 65.

33 *Ibid.*, pp. 65, 66; Clarendon MSS, 2, 1199.

34 Burghclere, *Buckingham*, pp. 69, 70.

35 *Ibid.*, p. 75.

36 Nicholas Papers, vol. 2, p. 9, 1654, Lord Hatton to Nicholas.

37 Burghclere, *Buckingham*, pp. 72–3.

38 *Ibid.*, p. 73; Chapman, *Great Villiers*, p. 84.

39 Burghclere, *Buckingham*, pp. 73, 74.

40 R. Hutton, *Charles II*, p. 97; Hopkins, *Constant Delights*, pp. 10, 11.

41 *A Collection of the State Papers of John Thurloe*, vol. 5, p. 645.

Chapter Five

1 Burghclere, *Buckingham*, p. 79.

2 George Villiers, Second Duke of Buckingham, *An Epitaph upon Thomas Lord Fairfax*.

3 CSP, Domestic, 1657–8, p. 9, Lady Conway to M. Mayet, 13–23 June.

4 For description of Mary Fairfax see Burghclere, *Buckingham*, p. 86, and Chapman, *Great Villiers*, p. 95; for the quote on Buckingham's appearance, see Burghclere, *Buckingham*, p. 85, quoting Brian Fairfax.

5 HMC, 15th Report, Part 2, p. 48, 25 August 1657.

6 BM Add. MSS 27872, fo.1; Phipps, *Buckingham: Public and Private Man*, p. 327; Burghclere, *Buckingham*, pp. 88, 89.

7 CSP, Domestic, 1656–7, p. 349, Hyde to Nicholas, 20–30 April.

8 Burghclere, *Buckingham*, p. 84.

9 Westminster Registers, p. 255.

10 Burghclere, *Buckingham*, p. 91; Chapman, *Great Villiers*, p. 97.

11 Calendar of Clarendon State Papers, ed. W. MacRay, vol. 3, p. 372, Hyde to Nicholas, 12 October.

12 CSP, Domestic, 1657–8, p. 9, Lady Conway to M. Mayet, 13–23 June.

13 Chapman, *Great Villiers*, p. 98.

14 *State Papers of John Thurloe*, vol. 7, p. 344, Colonel Gibbon to Secretary Thurloe, August 1658, Rochester.

15 Fairfax Papers, vol. 4, p. 253.

16 See CSP, Domestic, 1658–9,
    pp. 125, 145; the quote is from
    Burghclere, *Buckingham*, p. 97.
17 BL, Add. MSS 28937, fo. 58.
18 HCJ, vol. 7, 21 February 1659.
19 Dryden, J., *Absalom and Achitophel:
    A Poem.*
20 Burghclere, *Buckingham*, p. 101.
21 HCJ, vol. 7, 23 February 1659.
22 *Ibid.*
23 Burghclere, *Buckingham*, p. 102.
24 Bodleian Library, Clarendon MSS 60,
    fo. 219v, Moore to Hyde, 11 March.
25 Calendar of Clarendon State Papers,
    ed. W. MacRay, vol. 4, pp. 187, 188,
    Hyde to Cooper, 14 April–4 May.

Chapter Six

1   HMC, 6th Report, Part I, p. 466.
2   Burghclere, *Buckingham*, p. 108.
3   *Ibid.*, p. 111.
4   Evelyn, *Diary*, vol. 3, p. 246, 29 May
    1660.
5   Burghclere, *Buckingham*, p. 113.
6   Chapman, *Great Villiers*, p. 102.
7   CSP, Domestic, vol. 3, 1663–4, p. 612.
8   The new development would include a
    number of streets and lanes called
    George, Villiers, Duke, Of and
    Buckingham. Later Duke Street became
    part of John Adam Street, George Street
    became York Buildings, Of Alley
    became York Place, while Villiers and
    Buckingham Streets still exist.
9   It was demolished after his death and
    became the site of the Admiralty
    Buildings.
10 Burghclere, *Buckingham*, p. 119.

11 *Ibid.*, p. 121.
12 Burnet, *History of My Own Time*, vol. 2,
    p. 172.
13 D. Wilson, *All the King's Women*, p. 155.
14 Burghclere, *Buckingham*, p. 122;
    Chapman, *Great Villiers*, p. 111.
15 Chapman, *Great Villiers*, p. 114.
16 Evelyn, *Diary*, vol. 3, pp. 320, 321.
17 Bryant (ed.), *Letters of Charles II*, pp. 116–17.
18 Pepys, 7 September 1662.
19 D. Wilson, *All the King's Women*, p. 195.

Chapter Seven

1   BL, Add MS 19253, fo. 16.
2   D. Wilson, *All the King's Women*, p. 145.
3   Pepys, 7 November 1666,
    1 December 1666.
4   CSP, Domestic, vol. 3, 1663–4, p. 160.
5   Pepys, 31 December 1662.
6   *Ibid.*, 23 August 1662.
7   T.H. Lister, *Life and Administration of
    Edward, First Earl of Clarendon* (1838),
    vol. 3, p. 244.
8   D. Wilson, *All the King's Women*, p. 188.
9   Hopkins, *Constant Delights*, p. 96;
    D. Wilson, *All the King's Women*, p. 337.
10 Hopkins, *Constant Delights*, p. 97.
11 *Ibid.*, p. 98.
12 *Ibid.*, p. 94.
13 *Ibid.*, p. 92, quoting from Francis
    Fane's *Commonplace Book*.
14 Chapman, *Great Villiers*, p. 183.

Chapter Eight

1   Hutton, p. 149.
2   Pepys, 31 May 1662.
3   For links with Penn see Burghclere,
    Buckingham, p. 128.

4   See Chapter 4.
5   CSP, Domestic, vol. 2, 1661–2, p. 431.
6   CSP, Domestic, vol. 3, 1663–4,
    pp. 289, 296.
7   Burghclere, *Buckingham*, p. 126.
8   CSP, Domestic, vol. 3, 1663–4, p. 296.
9   *Ibid.*, p. 301.
10 Burghclere, *Buckingham*, pp. 128, 129.
11 *Ibid.*, p. 129.
12 *Ibid.*, p. 129.
13 CSP, Domestic, vol. 3, 1663–4, p. 352.
14 *Ibid.*, p. 507.

Chapter Nine

1   Lister, *Life and Administration*, vol. 3,
    p. 228.
2   *On Charles II's Mistress Winifred Wells*:
    for the text see Phipps, *Buckingham:
    Public and Private Man*, p. 142.
3   Fraser, *King Charles II*, p. 285.
4   Minette to Charles, 4 January 1662 in
    R. Norrington (commentary), *My
    Dearest Minette. The Letters between
    Charles II and his Sister Henrietta,
    Duchesse d'Orléans* (London and Chester
    Springs: Peter Owen, 1996), pp. 53, 54.
5   Pepys, 13 July 1663.
6   Burghclere, *Buckingham*, p. 134.
7   *Memoirs of the Count de Grammont*,
    Chapter 7.
8   Pepys, 8 February 1663.
9   *Ibid.*, February 1663.
10 Pepys mentions them working
    together on 6 November 1663.
11 D. Wilson, *All the King's Women*,
    pp. 193, 194.
12 Chapman, *Great Villiers*, p. 121.
13 *Ibid.*

14 Pepys, 6 November 1663.
15 CSP, Domestic, vol. 3, 1663–4,
    p. 301.
16 For an example of Charles's poetry, see
    Bryant, *King Charles II*, pp. 169, 170.
17 D. Wilson, *All the King's Women*, p. 212.
18 Charles to Minette, 26 August 1667, in
    Norrington, *My Dearest Minette*, p. 138.
19 Charles to Minette, 7 May 1668, in
    Norrington, *My Dearest Minette*, p. 151.
20 D. Parker, *Nell Gwyn* (Stroud: Sutton,
    2001), p. 81; Fraser, *King Charles II*,
    p. 287.
21 Pepys, 26 October 1667.
22 Chapman, *Great Villiers*, p. 185;
    Parker, *Nell Gwyn*, p. 116.
23 Wilson, *A Rake and His Times*, p. 15.
24 J. Macpherson (ed.), *Original Papers
    containing the Secret History of Great
    Britain from the Restoration to the
    Accession of the House of Hanover*, 2nd
    edn (1776), vol. 1, p. 25.
25 *Memoirs of the Count de Grammont*,
    Chapter 10.
26 Burghclere, *Buckingham*, pp. 136, 137;
    Hopkins, *Constant Delights*, p. 127.
27 Burghclere, *Buckingham*, p. 306.
28 G. Greene, *Lord Rochester's Monkey*
    (New York: Viking, 1974), pp. 92–5;
    Hopkins, *Constant Delights*, p. 143
    describes the tale as 'spurious'.
29 CSP, Domestic, vol. 2, 1661–2,
    p. 552.
30 Burghclere, *Buckingham*, p. 164.
31 *Ibid.*, pp. 165–6, quoting from
    Despatches of M. de Comminges;
    HMC, 7th Report, p. 484.
32 Burghclere, *Buckingham*, p. 166.

33 *Ibid.*, p. 166; CSP, Domestic, vol. 3, pp. 101, 102.

34 CSP, Domestic, vol. 14, October 1672–February 1673, p. 34.

35 Fraser, *King Charles II*, p. 194.

36 *Ibid.*, pp. 193, 194.

37 D. Sobel, *Longitude* (London: Fourth Estate, 1998), pp. 30–3.

38 Wilson, *A Rake and His Times*, p. 18, from Thomas Birch, *History of the Royal Society* (1756), vol. 1, pp. 26, 35.

39 CSP, Domestic, vol. 3, 1663–4, pp. 186, 187.

40 Evelyn, *Diary*, vol. 2, p. 322, 19 September 1676.

41 Chapman, *Great Villiers*, note, p. 125.

42 CSP, Domestic, vol. 5, 1665–6, p. 354, Ent. Book 23, p. 77.

43 CSP, Domestic, vol. 9, October 1668–December 1669, p. 422.

44 Pepys, 5 February 1667.

45 Dryden, *Defense of the Epilogue: or, an Essay on the Dramatic Poetry of the Last Age.*

46 Fraser, *King Charles II*, p. 292.

47 The Bilsdale Fox Hunt in the Yorkshire Dales is believed to have been founded by Buckingham and to be the oldest in England.

Chapter Ten

1 Charles to Minette, 19 September 1664, in Norrington, *My Dearest Minette*, pp. 90, 91.

2 Pepys, 30 April 1664.

3 CSP, Domestic, vol. 4, 1664–5, p. 301.

4 *Ibid.*, p. 313.

5 *Ibid.*, pp. 319, 320.

6 *Ibid.*, pp. 301, 320.

7 Burghclere, *Buckingham*, p. 146.

8 *Ibid.*

9 CSP, Domestic, vol. 5, 1665–6, p. 512.

10 *Ibid.*, p. 562.

11 CSP, Domestic, vol. 4, 1664–5, pp. 497, 498.

12 CSP, Domestic, vol. 5, 1665–6, p. 121.

13 *Ibid.*, p. 534.

14 6 September 1666 as quoted in Burghclere, *Buckingham*, pp. 154, 155, from C.J. Smith, *Historical and Literary Curiosities*.

Chapter Eleven

1 Arlington to Ormonde, 11 September 1666, Carte MSS 46, fo. 365.

2 Coventry to Ormonde, September 1666, Carte MSS 47, fo. 464.

3 CSP, Domestic, vol. 5, 1665–6, p. 186.

4 HLJ, vol. 12, 29 October 1666.

5 Burghclere, *Buckingham*, pp. 159, 160 quoting from *Miscellanea Aulica*, p. 424, 20 October 1666, Arlington to Ormonde.

6 HLJ, vol. 12, 29 October 1666; Carte, vol. 4, p. 270; Burghclere, *Buckingham*, pp. 158–60; Burghclere, *Ormonde*, vol. 2, pp. 125, 126.

7 HLJ, vol. 12, 31 October 1666.

8 *Ibid.*, 19 November 1666.

9 *Ibid.*, 19 December 1666.

10 Burghclere, *Buckingham*, p. 161.

11 HLJ, vol. 12, 19 December 1666.

12 *Ibid.*, 22 December 1666.

13 *Ibid.*, 22 December 1666; Burghclere, *Buckingham*, pp. 160, 161; Chapman, *Great Villiers*, pp. 131, 132.

14 Anglesea to Ormond, Carte MSS 217, fos. 362–3.

15 Burghclere, *Buckingham*, p. 162;
    Wilson, *A Rake and His Times*, p. 55.
16 Burghclere, *Buckingham*, p. 167;
    Clarendon, *Life*, vol. 3, p. 203.
17 See Chapter 18.
18 Burghclere, *Ormonde*, vol. 2, p. 135.
19 CSP, Domestic, vol. 6, 1666–7,
    pp. 428, 429.
20 Wilson, *A Rake and His Times*, p. 19.
21 Carte, vol. 4, p. 293.
22 Burghclere, *Buckingham*, pp. 169, 170.
23 Carte, vol. 4, p. 293.
24 For altercation with Dorchester see
    p. 85.
25 Burghclere, *Buckingham*, p. 171.
26 Carte, vol. 4, pp. 293–5; Burghclere,
    Ormonde, vol. 2, p. 135; Burghclere,
    Buckingham, p. 170.
27 A. Marshall, *Intelligence and Espionage
    in the Reign of Charles II, 1660–1685*
    (Cambridge University Press, 1994),
    p. 166.
28 CSP, Domestic, vol. 6, 1666–7, p. 532.
29 Pepys, 3 March 1667; CSP, Domestic,
    vol. 6, 1666–7, p. 552; Burghclere,
    Buckingham, p. 173.
30 Burghclere, *Buckingham*, p. 174.
31 CSP, Domestic, vol. 6, 1666–7, p. 552.
32 *Ibid.*, p. 560.
33 See Burghclere, *Buckingham*, p. 174.
34 CSP, Domestic, vol. 6, 1666–7, p. 555.
35 Pepys, 13 March 1667.
36 CSP, Domestic, vol. 7, 1667, p. 11
37 Burghclere, *Buckingham*, p. 174.
38 *Ibid.*, p. 175.
39 BL, Add. MS 27872, fo. 6; Burghclere,
    Buckingham, p. 175; Phipps, *Buckingham:
    Public and Private Man*, pp. 13, 14.

40 CSP, Domestic, vol. 6, 1666–7, p. 552.
41 *Ibid.*, p. 555.
42 CSP, Domestic, vol. 7, 1667, p. 11.
43 Carte, vol. 4, p. 295.
44 Carte MSS 48, fo. 488, Ormonde to
    Clarendon, Dublin, March 1666.
45 Burghclere, *Buckingham*, p. 179.
46 CSP, Domestic, vol. 7, 1667, p. 240;
    Burghclere, *Buckingham*, p. 179.
47 CSP, Domestic, vol. 7, 1667, p. 221.
48 *Ibid.*, p. 246.
49 Pepys, 28 June 1667.
50 Burghclere, *Buckingham*, p. 181.
51 *Ibid.*
52 Chapman, *Great Villiers*, p. 137,
    quoting Pepys.
53 Burghclere, *Buckingham*, p. 182.
54 CSP, Domestic, vol. 7, 1667, p. 294.
55 *Ibid.*, p. 427.

Chapter Twelve

1   Burghclere, *Ormonde*, vol. 2, p. 135.
2   Pepys, 12 July 1667.
3   Wilson, *A Rake and His Times*, p. 81.
4   *Ibid.*
5   *Ibid.*
6   D. Wilson, *All the King's Women*,
    pp. 212, 213, 220–1.
7   Bryant, *King Charles II*, p. 192.
8   HMC, 14th Report, Part 9, p. 370,
    Lindsey MSS, Chas Bertie to his
    brother [in-law], Sir Thomas Osborne.
9   Chapman, *Great Villiers*, p. 141,
    quoting Reresby.
10 Burghclere, *Buckingham*, p. 188.
    Hutton (pp. 254, 258, 259, 280)
    disagrees. He argues that Buckingham
    was never that powerful and that the

real power lay with Arlington; see also Fraser, *King Charles II*, pp. 255, 256: 'Nor did Buckingham assume that total leadership which Clarendon had once enjoyed.'

11 Norrington, *My Dearest Minette*, pp. 146, 147.

12 A. Marshall, T*he Age of Faction: Court Politics, 1660–1702* (Manchester University Press, 1999), p. 104.

13 CSP, Domestic, vol. 8, November 1667–September 1668, p. 32; HLJ, vol. 12, 20 November 1667.

14 Burghclere, *Buckingham*, p. 187.

Chapter Thirteen

1 Wilson, *A Rake and His Times*, p. 13.

2 *Ibid.*, pp. 14, 15.

3 *Memoirs of the Count de Grammont*, Chapter 9.

4 *Ibid.*, Chapter 6.

5 HCM, 7th Report, p. 484; *Memoirs of the Count de Grammont*, Chapter 6.

6 For date see Hopkins, *Constant Delights*, p. 230.

7 As quoted in Burghclere, *Buckingham*, p. 153.

8 Hopkins, *Constant Delights*, p. 231.

9 *Commonplace Book*, p. 12, no. 41; Phipps, *Buckingham: Public and Private Man*, p. 170.

10 Chapman, *Great Villiers*, p. 126.

11 *Ibid.*, p. 129.

12 Wilson, *A Rake and His Times*, p. 79.

13 Pepys, 22 July 1667.

14 Charles to Minette, 17 October 1667, in Norrington, *My Dearest Minette*, p. 139.

15 Savile Correspondence, H. Savile to Sir George Savile as quoted in Burghclere, *Buckingham*, p. 192.

16 Pepys, 17 January 1668.

17 Burghclere, *Buckingham*, p. 195, quoting St Evrémond to Waller, Lett. 4, quoted in *Rochester, and Other Literary Rakes*, p. 94; Hopkins, *Constant Delights*, p. 235, quoting St Evrémond.

18 CSP, Domestic, vol. 8, November 1667–September 1668, p. 192.

19 *Ibid.*, pp. 193, 198, 205, 233, 234.

20 Burghclere, *Buckingham*, pp. 196, 197.

21 CSP, Domestic, vol. 8, November 1667–September 1668, p. 192

22 Pepys, 15 May 1668.

23 Hopkins, *Constant Delights*, p. 240, quoting G. Thorn-Drury, *Poems of Waller*, vol. 1, p. lxvi.

24 CSP, Domestic, vol. 8, November 1667–September 1668, p. 238.

25 For example Lord Keeper Bridgeman as recorded in CSP, Domestic, vol. 8, November 1667–September 1668, pp. 494, 495.

26 CSP, Domestic, vol. 8, November 1667–September 1668, pp. 411, 435.

27 *Ibid.*, p. 259.

28 Pepys, 21 December 1667.

Chapter Fourteen

1 Bagwell, p. 87.

2 Carte, vol. 4, p. 311.

3 *Ibid.*, p.153.

4 *Ibid.*

5 Burghclere, *Ormonde*, vol. 2, p. 141.

6 Bagwell, pp. 86, 87; Wilson, *A Rake and His Times*, p. 108.

7 CSP, Domestic, vol. 8, November 1667–September 1668, p. 564.

8 Burghclere, *Ormonde*, vol. 2, p. 146.

9 *Ibid.*, p. 155.

10 Carte, vol. 4, p. 352.

11 Pepys, 12 February 1669.

12 Wilson, *A Rake and His Times*, p. 117.

13 Norrington, *My Dearest Minette*, p. 171, Charles to Minette, 7 March 1669.

14 Carte MSS 48, fo. 254v, Bodleian Library, Ormonde to Ossory, 25 February.

15 Bagwell, p. 89.

16 Carte, vol. 4, p. 352.

17 CSP, Domestic, vol. 10, 1670, p. 45.

18 See Chapter 18.

19 Pepys, 23 October 1668.

20 See Chapter 11.

21 This play was missing for 300 years until a copy was discovered in Washington and published by Arthur H. Scouten and Robert D. Hume in 1976 (see bibliography). Experts disagree as to the influence exerted by Buckingham on the play. Scouten and Hume believe that he may only have been responsible for the scene found objectionable by Coventry (see also *Times Literary Supplement*, 18 September 1973). Others, such as O'Neill, argue that his input to the play was much greater.

22 Pepys, 4 July 1668.

23 CSP, Domestic, vol. 9, October 1668–December 1669, p. 222.

24 Pepys, 6 March 1669.

25 *Ibid.*, 4 March 1669.

26 Charles to Minette, 7 March 1669, in Norrington, *My Dearest Minette*, p. 171.

27 Burghclere, *Buckingham*, pp. 206–9.

28 Pepys, 4 March 1669.

29 CSP, Domestic, vol. 9, October 1668–December 1669, p. 224.

30 A. Swatland, *The House of Lords in the Reign of Charles II* (Studies in Modern British History, Cambridge University Press, 2002), p. 131.

31 *Ibid.*, p. 132.

32 The Duke of Buckingham's Speech in a Late Conference: Skinner vs The East India Company, 1668, BL, 8122.g.9.

33 Swatland, *The House of Lords*, p. 131.

34 Coote, *Royal Survivor*, p. 231.

35 CSP, Domestic, vol. 6, 1666–7, p. 335.

36 Fraser, *King Charles II*, p. 259; Bryant, *King Charles II*, p. 209.

37 Burghclere, *Buckingham*, p. 213.

Chapter Fifteen

1 Charles to Minette, 25 April 1669, in Norrington, *My Dearest Minette*, pp. 175, 176.

2 Burghclere, *Buckingham*, p. 205.

3 Ibid., p. 212.

4 Bryant, *King Charles II*, p. 211; Chapman, *Great Villiers*, p. 156; Wilson, *A Rake and His Times*, p. 134.

5 Burghclere, *Buckingham*, p. 219.

6 D. Wilson, *All the King's Women*, p. 268, makes the point that modern medical analysis would suggest that she actually died of peritonitis.

7 Burghclere, *Buckingham*, pp. 221, 222.

8   *Ibid.*, p. 223.

9   *Ibid.*, p. 224.

10   *Ibid.*, pp. 224, 225.

11   CSP, Domestic, vol. 10, 1670, p. 390.

12   Burghclere, *Buckingham*, pp. 233–5.

13   *Ibid.*, pp. 235, 236.

14   *Ibid.*, pp. 236, 237

15   Fraser, *King Charles II*, p. 275.

16   CSP, Domestic, vol. 16, 1 November 1673–28 February 1675, p. 104.

17   Hutton, p. 280.

Chapter Sixteen

1   Burnet, *History of My Own Time*, vol. 2, p. 473.

2   *Ibid.*

3   Burghclere, *Buckingham*, p. 230.

4   Bryant, *King Charles II*, pp. 237, 239.

5   Hutton, pp. 335, 336.

6   *Ibid.*

7   See Chapter 7.

8   CSP, Domestic, vol. 10, 1670, p. 357.

9   Hutton, p. 336.

10   Pepys, 19 May 1669.

11   Hopkins, *Constant Delights*, pp. 241, 242.

12   Pepys, 19 May 1669.

13   Wilson, *A Rake and His Times*, p. 128.

14   Burghclere, *Buckingham*, p. 244.

15   Pepys, 14 February 1669.

16   See F.T. Melton, 'A Rake Refinanced: The Fortune of George Villiers, 2nd Duke of Buckingham, 1671–1685', *Huntington Library Quarterly* 51 (1988), 297–318. Melton argues that Buckingham was not in such a dire financial situation as was widely believed. He says that the policy of selling land and using land as security against loans was simply a ploy of his banker, Robert Clayton, to turn land into money. When the Duke died, there was plenty of equity in his estates to pay off all creditors.

17   George Villiers, Second Duke of Buckingham, *An Epitaph upon Thomas Lord Fairfax*.

Chapter Seventeen

1   O'Neill, *George Villiers*, p. 103, says that thirty-seven plays are parodied of which seven of Dryden's are included in the 1671 edition, with another added in an expanded edition of 1675.

2   *The Rehearsal*, 1.1, 124–36.

3   *The Conquest of Granada*, Pt. 2.

4   *The Rehearsal*, 4.1.248–9.

5   Chapman, *Great Villiers*, p. 180.

6   E. Albert, *A History of English Literature* (Surrey: Nelson, 1984), p. 178; Donaldson, in R. Lonsdale, *Dryden to Johnson* (London: Sphere, 1987), p. 189.

7   Chapman, *Great Villiers*, p. 179, disagrees that it had such an effect, saying that 'There was no charm powerful enough to destroy the Heroic Drama, which continued to flourish long after Buckingham was in his grave.'

8   See O'Neill, *George Villiers*, pp. 102–10.

9   Burghclere, *Buckingham*, p. 257; Chapman, *Great Villiers*, p. 179.

10   O'Neill, *George Villiers*, pp. 103–5, points out that most of these stories come from people who were not present. For example, the story of

Dryden being brought to the theatre was written by Davies in his *Dramatic Miscellanies* (1783) more than 100 years after the event.

11 George McFadden, 'Political Satire in *The Rehearsal*', in the *Yearbook of English Studies* 4 (1974), 120–8.

12 M. Duffy, *The Passionate Shepherdess: The Life of Aphra Behn 1640–1689* (London: Phoenix, 2000), pp. 122, 123.

13 O'Neill, *George Villiers*, p. 106.

14 Dryden, *Discourse Concerning the Origin and Progress of Satire*, 1693.

Chapter Eighteen

1 For the story of Colonel Thomas Blood see D. Hanrahan, *Colonel Blood: The Man Who Stole the Crown Jewels* (Stroud: Sutton, 2003).

2 I use the term Colonel here although it seems that it was only after this attack on Ormonde that Blood began to use this title.

3 *By the King: A proclamation. Charles R. whereas upon Tuesday, the sixth of this instant December, between the hours of six and seven in the evening, a barbarous and inhumane attempt was made upon the person and life of our right trusty and right entirely beloved cousin, and counsellor, James Duke of Ormond, etc.* (London: Printed by the asssigns of John Bill, and Christopher Barker, 1670).

4 *London Gazette*, 5–8 December 1670.

5 Burghclere, *Ormonde*, vol. 2, p. 187.

6 M. Petherick, *Restoration Rogues* (London: Hollis & Carter, 1951), p. 33; Burghclere, *Buckingham*, p. 242.

7 See Chapter 25.

8 The Duke of Buckingham, *To Mr Martin Clifford on his Human Reason*, 1672.

Chapter Nineteen

1 CSP, Domestic, vol. 11, January–November 1671, p. 237.

2 *Ibid.*, p. 223.

3 *Ibid.*, p. 306.

4 *Ibid.*

5 See Chapter 15.

6 Coote, *Royal Survivor*, p. 269.

7 *A Letter to Sir Thomas Osborn, One of His Majesties Privy Council, Upon the Reading of a Book Called the Present Interest of England Stated*, 1672.

8 Burghclere, *Buckingham*, p. 262.

9 CSP, Domestic, vol. 13, 18 May–30 September 1672, pp. 80–2.

10 *Ibid.*, pp. 262, 263.

11 Burghclere, *Buckingham*, p. 268.

12 Letter written on 25 June 1672, quoted in Burghclere, *Buckingham*, pp. 265–8.

13 CSP, Domestic, vol. 13, 18 May–30 September 1672, p. 276.

14 Burghclere, *Buckingham*, p. 271.

15 CSP, Domestic, vol. 13, 18 May–30 September 1672, p. 371.

16 Coote, *Royal Survivor*, p. 277.

17 CSP, Domestic, vol. 15, 1 March–31 October 1673, pp. 243, 268.

18 *Ibid.*, pp. 258, 268, 264.

19 *Ibid.*, p. 416.

20 Coote, *Royal Survivor*, p. 281.

21 *Ibid.*, p. 184.

22 HCJ, vol. 9, 7 January 1674.

23 *Ibid.*, 13 January 1674.

24 Burghclere, *Buckingham*, p. 283.

25 *Ibid.*, p. 283; Chapman, *Great Villiers*, pp. 205, 206.

26 'The History and Proceedings of the House of Commons', vol. 1, 1660–80 (1742), The Second Parliament of Charles II, Thirteenth Session – begins 7/1/1674.

27 *Ibid.*

28 Burghclere, *Buckingham*, p. 282; Chapman, *Great Villiers*, p. 207.

29 HCJ, vol. 9, 14 January 1674; 'The History and Proceedings of the House of Commons', vol.1, 1660–80 (1742), The Second Parliament of Charles II, Thirteenth Session – begins 7/1/1674.

30 *Ibid.*

31 *Ibid.*

32 *Ibid.*

33 *Ibid.*

34 CSP, Domestic, vol. 16, 1 November 1673–28 February 1675, pp. 103–6.

35 Burghclere, *Buckingham*, p. 288.

36 Ruvigny to Pomponne, 15 January 1674.

Chapter Twenty

1 HLJ, vol. 12, 7, 14, 15, 20, 26 January, 6 February 1674.

2 HMC, 9th Report, Part I, Appendix, pp. 35–7.

3 *Ibid.*

4 Burghclere, *Buckingham*, p. 291.

5 CSP, Domestic, vol. 16, 1 November 1673–28 February 1675, p. 149; Chapman, *Great Villiers*, p. 210.

6 HMC, 9th Report, Part I, Appendix, pp. 35–7.

7 Essex Papers, vol. 1. p. 160, Lord Conway to Earl of Essex, 10 January 1673–4.

8 Burghclere, *Buckingham*, p. 296; Chapman, *Great Villiers*, p. 212.

9 HMC, 9th Report, Part I, Appendix, pp. 35–7.

10 Chapman, *Great Villiers*, p. 212.

11 Essex Papers, Lord Angier to Lord Essex, vol. 1, pp. 167, 174.

12 *Commonplace Book*, p. 65, no. 272; Phipps, *Buckingham: Public and Private Man*, p. 193. It should be noted that Harold Love in his *Restoration Verse* (p. 326: see bibliography) regards Buckingham's authorship of this commonplace book as 'doubtful'.

Chapter Twenty-one

1 CSP, Domestic, vol. 16, 1 November 1673–28 February 1675, p. 188.

2 As quoted in Burghclere, *Buckingham*, pp. 298–301 from *Correspondence*, vol. 4, p. 249.

3 Wilson, *A Rake and His Times*, p. 200.

4 Burghclere, *Buckingham*, pp. 304–6.

5 Ibid., p. 307; Chapman, *Great Villiers*, p. 221.

6 Burghclere, *Buckingham*, p. 308.

7 CSP, Domestic, vol. 17, 1 March 1675– 29 February 1676, p. 404.

8 The Duke of Buckingham's Speech in the House of Lords, November 1675, BL, 8122.e.2.

9 CSP, Domestic, vol. 17, 1 March 1675–29 February 1676, p. 404; Phipps, *Buckingham: Public and Private Man*, p. 103.

10 JHL, vol. 13, 20 November 1675.

11 M. Ashley, *Charles II* (Herts: Panther, 1973), p. 215.

12 *Ibid.*, pp. 213, 215; Chapman, *Great Villiers*, p. 231; Fraser, *King Charles II*, p. 336.

13 CSP, Domestic, vol. 18, 1 March 1676–28 February 1677, p. 51.

14 *Ibid.*, p. 353.

15 The name the 'Green Ribbon Club' was not used until 1679; Chapman, *Great Villiers*, p. 228; Fraser, *King Charles II*, pp. 337, 338.

16 Chapman, *Great Villiers*, p. 228.

17 Swatland, *The House of Lords*, pp. 246, 247.

18 Chapman, *Great Villiers*, p. 232.

19 Buckingham's speech given in the House of Lords, 15 February 1677.

20 Swatland, *The House of Lords*, p. 222.

21 CSP, Domestic, vol. 18, 1 March 1676–28 February 1677, pp. 555, 556; Burghclere, *Buckingham*, p. 318; Chapman, *Great Villiers*, p. 234.

22 CSP, Domestic, vol. 18, 1 March 1676–28 February 1677, pp. 555, 556.

23 *Ibid.*, p. 556.

24 HMC, 7th Report, Part 1, p. 468.

25 *Ibid.*, p. 469.

26 CSP, Domestic, vol. 18, 1 March 1676–28 February 1677, p. 556.

27 *Ibid.*, p. 564.

28 Burghclere, *Buckingham*, p. 322.

29 *Ibid.*, 324.

30 Add. MSS, 27872, fo. 34, Duke of Buckingham to Charles II.

31 CSP, Domestic, vol. 19, 1 March 1676–28 February 1678, p. 205.

32 *Ibid.*, p. 260.

33 *Ibid.*, p. 292.

34 *Ibid.*, p. 290.

35 Burghclere, *Buckingham*, p. 330.

36 CSP, Domestic, vol. 19, 1 March 1677–28 February 1678, p. 606.

37 *Ibid.*, pp. 262, 274; Fraser, *King Charles II*, p. 350.

38 Swatland, *The House of Lords*, p. 248.

39 Chapman, *Great Villiers*, p. 237.

40 BL, Add. MSS, 27872, fos. 20–2, Duke of Buckingham to Charles II; Burghclere, *Buckingham*, pp. 325, 326; Chapman, *Great Villiers*, pp. 237, 238; Phipps, *Buckingham: Public and Private Man*, pp. 328, 329.

41 HMC, 7th Report, Part 1, p. 469.

42 CSP, Domestic, vol. 19, 1 March 1677–28 February 1678, p. 640.

43 Burghclere, *Buckingham*, p. 331.

44 Chapman, *Great Villiers*, p. 238.

45 CSP, Domestic, vol. 19, 1 March 1677–28 February 1678, p. 441.

46 Ashley, *Charles II*, p. 222, quoting from Courtin to Louis XIV, 12/22 April 1677.

47 Ashley, *Charles II*, p. 223.

48 Fraser, *King Charles II*, p. 347.

49 Ashley, p. 228, quoting from 'Diary of Dr Edward Lake', Camden Society, 1846, p. 5.

50 Fraser, *King Charles II*, p. 349.

51 JHC, vol. 9, 28 January 1678.

52 Chapman, *Great Villiers*, p. 245.

53 Burnet, *History of My Own Time*, vol. 1, p. 182; *Memoirs of the Count de Grammont*, 1:137.

Chapter Twenty-two

1 Bryant, *King Charles II*, p. 272.

2 J. Kenyon, *The Popish Plot* (London: Phoenix, 2000), p. 130.

3 Chapman, *Great Villiers*, p. 249.

4   Kenyon, *The Popish Plot*, p. 84.

5   Bryant, *King Charles II*, p. 272.

6   CSP, Domestic, vol. 24, 1 January–30 June 1683, p. 127.

7   Marshall, *Intelligence and Espionage*, p. 211.

8   Chapman, *Great Villiers*, p. 253.

9   Marshall, *Intelligence and Espionage*, p. 241.

10 Coventry Papers, vol. 2, fos. 441–2.

11 Burghclere, *Buckingham*, p. 374.

12 *Ibid.*, p. 375.

13 Fraser, *King Charles II*, p. 400.

14 *Ibid.*, p. 400; Kenyon, *The Popish Plot*, p. 234.

15 Kenyon, *The Popish Plot*, pp. 293, 294.

Chapter Twenty-three

1   Chapman, *Great Villiers*, p. 239.

2   CSP, Domestic, vol. 16, 1 November 1673–28 February 1675, p. 43.

3   Chapman, *Great Villiers*, pp. 253, 254.

4   Burghclere, *Buckingham*, p. 363.

5   HMC, Ormonde, vol. 4, pp. 328–9; Marshall, *Intelligence and Espionage*, p. 217.

6   CSP, Domestic, vol. 21, 1 January 1679–31 August 1680, p. 106.

7   *Ibid.*

Chapter Twenty-four

1   Burghclere, *Buckingham*, p. 352; CSP, Domestic, vol. 25, 1 July–30 September 1683, p. 12.

2   CSP, Domestic, vol. 10, 1670, p. 45.

3   *Archives des Affaires Estrangers*, no. 135, fo. 40, 13 July 1679.

4   Burnet, *History of My Own Time*, vol. 1, p. 295.

5   Fraser, *King Charles II*, p. 371.

6   *Ibid.*, p. 387.

7   Dispatch from Paul Barillon, 4–14 September, TNA, 31/3/143, fo. 61.

8   Burghclere, *Buckingham*, pp. 370, 371; Chapman, *Great Villiers*, p. 256.

9   Fraser, *King Charles II*, p. 385.

10 Ashley, *Charles II*, p. 275; Fraser, *King Charles II*, p. 394.

11 HCJ, vol. 9, 26 March 1681.

12 Ashley, *Charles II*, p. 295, quoting Reresby Memoirs, 19 November 1681.

Chapter Twenty-five

1   HMC, Ormonde, vol. 4, pp. 328, 329.

2   From Samuel Butler's *Character of a Duke of Bucks*.

3   The Narrative of Col. Thomas Blood, pp. 24–8.

4   CSP, Domestic, 1 January 1679–31 August 1680, p. 431.

5   *Ibid.*, p. 489.

6   *Ibid.*, p. 432.

7   *Ibid.*, p. 521.

8   Marshall, *Intelligence and Espionage*, pp. 221, 223.

9   A. Marshall, 'Colonel Thomas Blood and the Restoration Political Scene', in *Historical Journal* 32/3 (1989), 573, gives the following references: CSP, Domestic, 1682, pp. 47–8; CSP, Domestic, 1690–1, p. 458; Calendar of Treasury Books, 1685, Pt. 1, pp. 116, 149.

10 CSP, Domestic, vol. 21, 1 January 1679–
    31 August 1680, pp. 575, 576.

11 CSP, Domestic, vol. 23, 1 January–
    31 December 1682, p. 615.

12 2 Samuel: 13–18.

13 Numbers 15; 1 Kings 16: 8–20;
    2 Kings 9: 31.

14 Burghclere, *Buckingham*, p. 261; for
    full text of *To Dryden*, see Phipps,
    Buckingham: Public and Private Man,
    p. 168.

Chapter Twenty-six

1 Chapman, *Great Villiers*, p. 264.

2 *Ibid.*, p. 240. This was in 1679.

3 *Ibid.*

4 *Ibid.*, pp. 240, 241.

5 *Ibid.*, p. 164.

6 HCM, 7th Report, Part 1, pp. 343, 351.

7 *Ibid.*, p. 376.

8 Chapman, *Great Villiers*, p. 269.

9 Burghclere, *Buckingham*, p. 164.

10 CSP, Domestic, vol. 23, 1 January–
    31 December 1682, p. 82.

11 Chapman, *Great Villiers*, p. 270, 271.

12 *Ibid.*, p. 271.

13 *A Short Discourse upon the Reasonableness
    of Men's having a Religion, or Worship of
    God*, 1685.

14 *The Duke of Buckingham His Grace's
    Letter, to the Unknown Author of a
    Paper, Entitled, A Short Answer to His*

*Grace the Duke of Buckingham's Paper
Concerning Religion, Toleration, and
Liberty of Conscience*, 1685.

15 Burghclere, *Buckingham*, p. 390.

16 For details of death, see Ellis,
    Correspondence, vol. 1, p. 276, Duke of
    Hamilton to Dr Sprat, 17 April 1687;
    HMC, 6th Report, Part 1, p. 467;
    Burghclere, *Buckingham*, pp. 393–400.

17 Chapman, *Great Villiers*, pp. 280, 281.

18 *Ibid.*, p. 283.

19 Burghclere, *Buckingham*, pp. 398,
    399, quoting from a letter of the
    Duke of Buckingham to Dr Barrow,
    Quarterly Review, pp. 109, 110.

20 Aphra Behn, *To the Memory of the
    Illustrious Prince George Duke of
    Buckingham*, 1687.

Epilogue

1 Bryant, *King Charles II*, p. 164;
   Hutton, pp. 449, 453.

2 Hutton, p. 134.

3 *Ibid.*, p. 448.

4 Burnet, *History of My Own Time*, vol. 1,
   p. 182.

5 HMC, 6th Report, Part 1, p. 368.

6 Dryden from *Absalom and Achitophel*;
   Butler from his *Character of a Duke of
   Bucks*.

7 Chapman, *Great Villiers*, p. 185;
   Parker, *Nell Gwyn*, p. 116.

BIBLIOGRAPHY

Albert, E., *A History of English Literature*, Surrey, Nelson, 1984

Ashley, M., *Charles II*, Hertfordshire, Panther Books, 1973

Bagwell, R., *Ireland under the Stuarts and during the Interregnum*, vol. III, London, Holland Press, 1963

Bryant, A., *King Charles II*, London, Longman, Green & Co., 1931

Burghclere, W., *George Villiers, 2nd Duke of Buckingham 1628–1687: A Study in the History of the Restoration*, London, John Murray, 1903

—— *The Life of James, First Duke of Ormonde, 1610–1688*, 2 vols, London, John Murray, 1912

Burnet, G., *History of My Own Time*, 2 vols, Oxford, 1897, 1900

Carte, T., *The Life of James Duke of Ormonde*, 6 vols, Oxford University Press, 1851

Chapman, H.W., *Great Villiers, A Study of George Villiers Second Duke of Buckingham 1628–1687*, London, Secker & Warburg, 1949

Coote, S., *Royal Survivor. A Life of Charles II*, London, Hodder & Stoughton, 1999

Davies, G., *The Restoration of Charles II 1658–1660*, Oxford, Oxford University Press, 1955

Davies, N., *Europe, A History*, Oxford, Oxford University Press, 1996

—— *The Isles, A History*, London, Macmillan, 1999

Duffy, M., *The Passionate Shepherdess: The Life of Aphra Behn 1640–1689*, London, Phoenix Press, 2000

Fraser, A., *King Charles II*, London, Arrow Books, 1998

Gardiner, S.R., *A History of England Under the Duke of Buckingham and Charles I, 1624–1628*, 2 vols, London, Longman, Green & Co., 1857

Greaves, R.L., *God's Other Children. Protestant Nonconformists and the Emergence of Denominational Churches in Ireland, 1660–1700*, Stanford, Stanford University Press, 1997

—— *Deliver Us from Evil. The Radical Underground in Britain, 1660–1663*, New York/Oxford, Oxford University Press, 1986

—— *Enemies Under his Feet. Radicals and Nonconformists in Britain, 1664–1677*, Stanford, Stanford University Press, 1990

Greene, G, *Lord Rochester's Monkey*, New York, Viking, 1974

Gregg, P., *King Charles I*, London, J.M. Dent & Sons, 1981

Hanrahan, D., *Colonel Blood: The Man Who Stole the Crown Jewels*, Stroud, Sutton, 2003

Hopkins, G., *Constant Delights: Rakes, Rogues and Scandal in Restoration England*, London, Robson, 2002

Hutton, R., *Charles the Second, King of England, Scotland, and Ireland*, Oxford, Clarendon Press, 1989

Kenyon, J., *The Popish Plot*, London, Phoenix Press, 2000

Lockyer, R., *Buckingham: The Life and Political Career of George Villiers, First Duke of Buckingham 1592–1628*, London and New York, Longman, 1981

Lonsdale, R., *Dryden to Johnson*, London, Sphere Books, 1987

Lord, G. de F. (ed.), *Andrew Marvell Complete Poetry*, London, Dent, 1984

Love, H. (ed.), *The Penguin Book of Restoration Verse*, London, Penguin Books, 1997

Marshall, A., *The Age of Faction: Court Politics, 1660–1702*, Manchester, Manchester University Press, 1999

—— *Intelligence and Espionage in the Reign of Charles II, 1660–1685*, Cambridge, Cambridge University Press, 1994

—— 'Colonel Thomas Blood and the Restoration Political Scene', *Historical Journal* 32/3 (1989), 561–82

Mizener, A., *George Villiers, 2nd Duke of Buckingham: His Life and a Canon of his Works*, PhD thesis, Princeton University, 1934

Murray, N., *Andrew Marvell: World Enough and Time*, London, Abacus, 2000

Morrill, J., *Stuart Britain: A Very Short Introduction*, Oxford, Oxford University Press, 2000

Norrington, R. (commentary), *My Dearest Minette. The Letters between Charles II and his Sister Henrietta, Duchesse d'Orléans*, London and Chester Springs, Peter Owen, 1996

O'Neill, J.H., *George Villiers, Second Duke of Buckingham*, Boston, Twayne Publishers, 1984

Parker, D., *Nell Gwyn*, Stroud, Sutton, 2001

Petherick, M., *Restoration Rogues*, London, Hollis & Carter, 1951

Phipps, C. (ed.), *Buckingham: Public and Private Man. The Prose, Poems and Commonplace Book of George Villiers, Second Duke of Buckingham (1628–1687)*, New York and London, Garland, 1985

Pinto, Vivian de Sola, *Enthusiast in Wit: A Portrait of John Wilmot Earl of Rochester 1647–1680*, London, Routledge & Kegan Paul, 1962

Scouten, A.H. and Hume, R.D. (eds), *The Country Gentleman: A 'Lost' Play and Its Background*, Philadelphia, University of Pennsylvania Press, 1976

Seaward, P., *The Restoration*, Hampshire and London, Macmillan Education, 1991

Sobel, D., *Longitude*, London, Fourth Estate, 1998

Swatland, A., *The House of Lords in the Reign of Charles II*, Cambridge Studies in Modern British History, Cambridge, Cambridge University Press, 2002

Wilson, D., *All the King's Women*, London, Hutchinson, 2003

Wilson, J.H., *A Rake and His Times: George Villiers, 2nd Duke of Buckingham*, London, Frederick Muller, 1954

Yardley, B., *The Political Career of George Villiers, 2nd Duke of Buckingham (1628–87)*, PhD thesis, University of Oxford, 1989

INDEX

Note: (*Cm*) = mistress of Charles II